Sir Denis Forman was born in 1917 at Craigielands in Dumfries, and was educated at Loretto and at Pembroke College, Cambridge. His memoirs describe the germination of two of his main interests: entertaining an audience, and music. The first led him – after service in World War Two during which time he was wounded at Cassino – into films and television, culminating (when he was Chairman and Managing Director of Granada Television) in *Coronation Street* and *Jewel in the Crown*. The second gave rise to his only book before this one, *Mozart's Piano Concertos*, and to his directorship of the Royal Opera House, Covent Garden.

Son of Adam

Denis Forman

Futura

A *Futura* Book

First published in Great Britain in 1990 by
André Deutsch Limited
This edition published by Futura Publications in 1992.

A CIP catalogue record for this book is available
from the British Library.

ISBN 0 7088 4990 3

Phototypeset by Intype Ltd, London
Printed in Great Britain by
The Guernsey Press Co Ltd,
Guernsey, Channel Islands

Futura Publications
A Division of
Little, Brown and Company (UK) Limited
165 Great Dover Street
London SE1 4YA

Contents

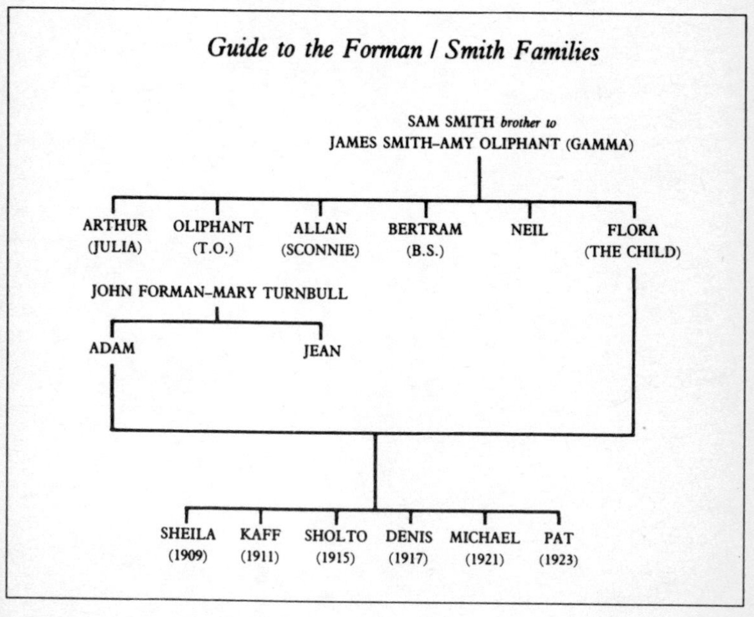
Guide to the Forman / Smith Families
SAM SMITH brother to
JAMES SMITH–AMY OLIPHANT (GAMMA)
ARTHUR (JULIA)
OLIPHANT (T.O.)
ALLAN (SCONNIE)
BERTRAM (B.S.)
NEIL
FLORA (THE CHILD)
JOHN FORMAN–MARY TURNBULL
ADAM
JEAN
SHEILA (1909)
KAFF (1911)
SHOLTO (1915)
DENIS (1917)
MICHAEL (1921)
PAT (1923)

1

A Very Pretty Place

My first memory is one of humiliation. It is a vivid memory and complete and it concerns the episode of the hatchery pond. This pond was really no more than a dam on the Kellobank burn. It had been landscaped into the environs of the walled garden with a fountain on one side and on the other the arbour – a sort of red sandstone apse built into an artificial mound covered in dog violets. Together these formed an elegant composition which my father was busy destroying by cutting down the huge rhododendrons on each side of the encircling walk. Already the hatchery itself was naked and staring out of the bank. At the moment of the hatchery episode my father had turned his attention to some smaller and rather rare specimens which my grandfather had planted some thirty years earlier. The pond was almost empty with only a trickle of water escaping through the outlet. My brother Sholto leapt from the concrete shoulder of the outlet grid across the stream and landed safely on the sticks and mud on the other side. 'Don't try it,' he shouted over his shoulder. 'It's much too far for you.'

I mounted the outlet block and looked across. It was indeed a formidable leap, yet it never occurred to me that there was any question of not jumping. Sholto had done it and he had said I couldn't do it. This amounted to an absolute imperative. So I jumped, landed in soft watery mud, and stuck fast. I struggled until I felt my heart would burst, but only sank deeper into the slime. Shame and mortification flooded over me, but there was nothing for it but to give in. 'I'm stuck,' I shouted. 'I'M STUCK.'

Sholto and my father came running to the scene, the former with a disagreeable smirk on his face. I was hauled out, leaving one boot behind which my father fished out with a stick, and was carried over to the huge bonfire which he had sited on the ghost of a grassed-over bed near the fountain, thereby no doubt baking the precious daffodil bulbs beneath. He put me on the grass near the fire, took off the remaining boot and socks and weighed into me. Silly thing to do. Showing off. Always trying to do things that were impossible. Too young to be left on my own. Would have to stay in the nursery. Silly thing to do. During this homily Sholto kept saying 'I told him not to, I told him not to, I told him not to.'

All this time I sat silent. If I had only gone a little further to the left, I thought, the ground might have been harder. I might have thrown myself flat. I might have walked round and gone backwards to the brink and planted two deep footprints in the mud and then shown them triumphantly to Sholto.

Later as we walked up the steep south drive back to Craigielands House, my father and Sholto in front, myself behind, each carrying his appointed rhododendron-cutting tools, I began to cry, silently and bitterly. Must never happen again. He said it was impossible. Nothing is impossible. Nothing, absolutely nothing is impossible.

Craigielands House – the Big Hoose as it was to everyone who lived outside it – stood against the backdrop of a high wooded escarpment stretching for half a mile on either side. The bank of giant trees which rose almost vertically behind it was fronted by a green reef of rhododendrons. Along the foot of the wood ran the Back Road. On it, to the north, were the stables block, only a hundred yards away, then the kennels, the laundry and, some distance further, the sawmill and the Back Village. To the south the Back Road dipped to the rosary, the ice-house and the walled garden, sited – as ever in Scotland – at a safe distance from the Big Hoose to spare the gentry the smell of the kailyard.

Behind the house and the wood, up on high and out of sight, lay Craigielands Farm; in front and below, the part with the two drives, north and south, sprouting from the front porch like a pair of horns, cutting a semicircle with absolute precision through the great park trees scattered apparently so artlessly across the slopes. Beyond the park, the lake; beyond the lake another belt of trees; beyond that the Dumfries road, straight as a die from North Lodge to South Lodge; and beyond that again, on the floor of the valley, the old Caledonian Railway where goods trains made their music throughout the night.

Viewed from the other side of the valley, some two miles away, the house stood out like a white ship in a dark sea – all else, the lake, the Back Village, gardens, stables – all were concealed by trees and the eye was directed to the shining, four-square Palladian front with its tall piano nobile, and its central Doric porch – an odd intrusion, one might have thought, into the Scottish countryside, but seeming very much at home squatting there in its dove-grey granite, its outlines picked out by white-painted sandstone cornices. A Union Jack of generous size floated over the central lantern.

But the chief glory of Craigielands was not the inward but the outward view. Standing as it did upon a plinth above the tree-tops of the park, it offered an unbroken one-hundred-and-eighty degree panorama of the Moffat hills, in the distance White Coombe, Hartfell, Bodesbeck twelve miles away up the Moffat water, then Crofthead and Loch Fell much nearer, and finally Poldean, standing square-to directly across the valley. Since the house faced east, the hills were silhouetted against the rising sun, side-lit at noon, and as sunset approached so every nook and corrie was frontally lit from the west, the light lingering on the upper parts of the amphitheatre long after the shadows of the wood had moved across the park almost as fast as a man could walk and the whole valley lay in a blue haze. Later still the upper rim would still shine on above the rest of the world, just as today the sun's last rays catch an aeroplane high above the earth.

This was the Craigielands I loved, and loved with a passion I have formed for no other place since. I knew that my grandfather, James Smith, must have loved Craigielands too, because he had chosen it from amongst all the properties in South-West Scotland, even though the house was too small to hold his family and he had been forced to enlarge it. He had stocked the lake with trout, brought in tanks on a train from Loch Leven, and built the hatchery to populate the river Annan and over a dozen hill burns. He had designed and planted the newer coverts for the pheasant shooting. He had planted the second generation of trees in the park, made paths in the wood, placed seats at the good viewpoints. He had started the curling club and built the curling rinks, enlarged the stables and built modern cottages for the tenants. He had worked over Craigielands and perfected it as a sculptor would bring to life a rough piece of rock. He left no legacy in written form, for unlike other members of his family he wrote no books and left few letters. Instead he bequeathed us Craigielands, which had more influence upon two successive generations and was more powerful in shaping our lives than any books he might have written or any collection of fine art, and was certainly more wholesome in its effect upon the way we grew up than a legacy of money.

Fifteen years after his death, once a quarter on a visit as regular as that of Mr Brydon the barber or Miss Anderson the seamstress, the three elderly McLaren cousins would come to tea just as they had done when he was alive. Cousin Agnes, the oldest and by far the largest, would gossip endlessly about local affairs whilst at the same time consuming innumerable scones; Jessie, the youngest, sat mainly silent, her lips formed into an O of a diameter varying to suit the degree of surprise, approbation or disapproval required by the tenor of the conversation. The third, Jack, would take his tea on the hoof, roaming the room to inspect the paintings – some of which he had painted himself, for he was an accomplished water-colourist – and looking out of the three great drawing-room windows at the grounds and the hills beyond. As time went by expectation mounted among us children, and he never failed us. When the moment came he would turn from the window, cock his head on one side, half close one eye and in his high-pitched parrot-like voice deliver his line. 'Very pretty place,' he would say, and then again, a little more *piano*, 'Very pretty place.'

Indeed it was a very pretty place, everyone agreed on that, from Maggie Hutchinson who kept the village shop and who had written a poem on the beauty of Craigielands woods, to the famous Professor Blackie from Edinburgh. It was James Smith who had made it so.

He had come to it from New Brighton on the Wirral, which was in those days almost in the country, where he had a comfortable family house called Dalmorton. He moved his household from one establishment to the other at set times of the year, leaving a skeleton staff behind to maintain the abandoned base. In some ways the domestic economy of both houses was like that of any liberal Victorian household of the day, but in others it reflected the strong individuality of my grandmother, universally known as Gamma, and the shrewdly applied benevolence of James himself.

Inside as well as outside Craigielands was laid out on the Palladian model, and almost a half of the piano nobile was taken up by the central hall, two storeys high, lit by a lantern and with large glass windows round its circumference. The drawing room, dining room and library led off the hall, and at the back there were the two master bedroom suites occupied by Gamma to the south and by my father and mother to the north. This was the accommodation for the ruling class: above and below lived the subordinate societies.

Upstairs there was the nursery, with a complement of the head nurse, Nan, one or two undernurses, from four to six children and two dogs. At first the nursery catered for you comprehensively, bar an hour or two a day spent downstairs. Then lessons began to intrude and at about nine or ten a good part of the day was spent in the schoolroom or, in the case of the boys, accompanying my father on an expedition to whatever eccentric form of field works he might have in hand at the time. But even when schoolroom persons hived off from the group and had schoolroom tea with tutors, or with Gamma reading aloud over the bread and jam, they still remained a part of the nursery community, the girls as they grew up tending to become surrogate undernurses. The lines of power in the nursery were clear. The undernurses were the charge-hands; the head nurse was the manager responsible to my mother. The children collectively regarded my elder sister Sheila as the shop steward. In cases of truly frightful behaviour a meeting of adults might include my father and Gamma, but this was rare, and the nursery, like the farm and servants' hall, really ran itself within its own unwritten constitution.

Below stairs there was the servants' hall, consisting of eight women of graduated status, a highly organised social group, but nevertheless subject to many subtle internal forces. The servants were close to us. We called each other by our christian names (except that the cook was always 'Mrs Henderson'). They were our friends and our enemies, sometimes our intimates. Even Gamma called them Alice, Agnes, Sarah (but never by an abbreviated name. Nettie was Henrietta, and Jessie Jessica. I can't recall, however, whether she stretched things so far as to call Lena Magdalena). They called her Ma'am, referred to my father and mother as Mr and Mrs Forman, to the uncles as Mr Arthur or Mr Allan, to their wives as Mrs Arthur or Mrs Allan and to the children by a variety of titles depending upon age. When I was about eight the servants when talking to a grown-up would refer to the four brothers as Mister Sholto, Master Denis, Michael and Wee Pat.

Outdoors there was the farm, a working social unit of its own. There the head man was Tom Quigley, raw-faced, shy but assertive when the occasion demanded. Under him there were two horse-keepers, five agricultural workers and a boy, sometimes two. Apart from my father, who had regular and often uncomfortable meetings with Tom Quigley in his office, the rest of the grown-ups had little traffic with the farm. The children had more, but showed greater interest in the animals than in the humans. The names of the horses (Prince, Polly, Dick, Ned, Major) and the milking cows (Tibby, Betty, Dorothy and Kit) were more familiar than those of the workers.

Finally there was the less remote social group of the outdoor servants and estate workers. In reality they were hardly a group at all, for they went about their businesses in ones and twos and each had a direct link to one member of the family: the gamekeeper, the two electricians, the carpenter and the gardeners to my father; Tom Rheilly and his son Jim, the chauffeur, to Gamma; but also they were friends and confidants to all of us.

At first I did not understand the invisible barriers between the cultures. One afternoon when I was sent down to the drawing room in my best smocked dress I said I wanted to play with Sissie. Sissie

Sharp was a bird of passage, a between-maid who for some months helped the undernurses and the downstairs maids by carrying loads of coal, trays of food and cans of water up and down stairs. I had been playing with her earlier that day in the kitchen. She fondled me a lot, which I liked, and she smelled nice – besides I needed help in my plans to move the big bricks around and neither my mother nor Gamma were co-operating. 'I want Sissie,' I said. It was explained that Sissie did not come into the drawing room. 'Yes she does, with the coals,' I said. 'I want Sissie.' I was told again that Sissie was not possible, but kept shouting 'I want Sissie' until my mother became impatient and gave me a little slap. At this I bolted for the door and was half-way down the back stairs before she had got out of the drawing room. I ran into the kitchen and jumped into Sissie's lap and sat there as good as gold, sucking my thumb. This was an awkward one for my mother. She did not fancy an unseemly brawl with her son in front of the kitchen staff. An undernurse was despatched from the nursery to get me out and return me to the drawing room, but each time she made a pass at me I started yelling and screaming and clung to Sissie's neck. The undernurse went away and came back in a few minutes with Nan, who took in the situation at a glance. 'Let Sissie carry him up to bed,' she said, and when we got there Sissie sat on the bed and Nan sat down too. She told the undernurse to go down to the drawing room and tell them that she had put me to bed. Then Nan and Sissie changed places, then Sissie left and Nan held my hand until I went to sleep. But it was several years before I mastered the niceties of the protocol that governed the relationship between the ruling members of the family, the nursery staff, the servants' hall and the estate workers.

The several Craigielands social cultures were together the formative influence on my early life. To begin with it was the nursery that made up almost the whole of life: my parents and Gamma were there, but a long way off, and the strains and stresses lying ahead did not yet cast so much as a shadow.

2

Everybody Friends

It has to be said that I was not a great success in the nursery. It was mainly the undernurses that were the trouble. They could not manage me and this made them desperate. It was no good pointing out how good the other children were (untrue) and how bad I was (true), pleading got them nowhere and heavy verbal abuse was off limits within earshot of anyone who might tell my parents. So there were only two options – a report to a higher authority or a clip over the ear. Of all the undernurses (there were usually two at a time and the turnover was rapid), Isabella Ogg – Bell to us – a sturdy client from the slums of Edinburgh, grey-faced and breathing halitosis as a dragon breathes fire, had the shortest fuse and the most feared left jab. The routine was always the same. 'Wull ye tak a tellin,' she would bawl at a recalcitrant child, and when child showed no desire to take a telling, she would seize it by the ear and yell again, 'If ye'll no tak a tellin, take *that*,' giving it a sharp blow on the other ear with her free hand. But some of the undernurses were sweet girls and there were at least two who could be reduced to tears. This was awful, much worse than being beaten about the head by Bell.

There were some, however, who won through. Kathy Grieve, the gamekeeper's daughter, had easily the longest and most successful reign. Cheerful and immensely stout and strong, she got through a day that would have daunted a commando, lighting the nursery fire at six-thirty and getting it to roar by applying the lid of an old coal scuttle (the blower), carrying trays crowded with food and huge buckets of coal up two long flights of stairs, ploughing her way through a nursery with from four to six vigorous children under her feet, conducting walks in the rain, feeding the nursery dogs, often saving them from torture, scrubbing the floor, dominating the bathroom at bedtime – she was a paragon of the undernurse trade.

Above the fray was the head nurse, darling Nan, who knew just when to intervene and when to leave the warring factions to fight it out, whether it was boys against girls, single combat or a united mutiny against an undernurse. At times when the nursery was in turmoil with widespread punching, hair-pulling and spitting, Nan would appear round the nursery door and taking each combatant by the shoulder in turn would say to him in soothing tones, 'Now, now, everybody friends'. She was something of a saint, more of a Martha than a Mary, practical, always sympathetic and a ready place of resort in distress.

I remember one occasion when the undernurses had despatched a detail of four little boys down to the drawing room dressed in hideously uncomfortable sailor suits. I saw Nan's watchful head over the bannisters. She beckoned to me to come back, and when I got to the top of the stairs she kissed me and said, 'They are terribly tight in the crotch, aren't they? Let's go and take them off.'

Before going to sleep each night I went through the rather bizarre procedure of placing in order of precedence those around me who I would least like to die. Nan was always first, my mother second. The rest of the field fluctuated according to the state of personal relations, although Andrew Grieve the gamekeeper and Davy Sloan the carpenter usually rated higher than my father. My grandmother could be very high or off the list altogether. It depended how the day had gone.

It would be wrong to imply there was no respite in the war against the undernurses. Most of the time we rubbed along well enough and sometimes when I had hurt my knee or said something nice about one of them they would kiss and cuddle me, a procedure which left me unaffected when carried out by the plainer ones, but when by the one or two who were pretty left me hot, red in the face and a little confused.

One had to be vigilant in a cuddling session because the upper part of an undernurse's starched apron was as sharp as a razor and could inflict a nasty wound. Under the white starch they wore grey cotton uniforms which began to give at the seams as the calorie-rich Craigielands food did its work. Their status in relation to the housemaids was an open question. The housemaids wore white caps with black bows, and undernurses went bareheaded, but this distinction was taken by each side as a sign of superiority. Nan wore a white cotton dress under her apron, the bosom of which was much softer than the undernurses' and bulged out from her person so as to accommodate always a handkerchief and usually a clinical thermometer, some safety pins, hairpins and a piece of ribbon.

Nursery routine was invariable. It was compulsory to stay in bed until seven-thirty, then some very perfunctory washing of teeth and face, get dressed or be dressed by eight, breakfast of Force or Shredded Wheat, sausages, bacon or fried eggs, toast, butter and marmalade. Neither jam nor bread was allowed at breakfast; a spread of Bovril was permitted only for cousins who claimed it to be their staple diet at home.

After breakfast, 'do your jobs'. Here no mercy was shown and the two lavatories and the several pots were all manned until success was registered.

Once, sitting in the Green Room by myself, I was unable to perform but desperate for action. I tore some of the asbestos coating off the central heating pipes (which were newly installed and no doubt asbestos was one of my father's experiments), rubbed it between my palms, dropped it into the pot and shouted out the accepted signal 'Fini'. The undernurse (it was Annie Burns) came to inspect my performance and called in Nan. They were perplexed. 'It's very yellow,' said one. 'And very flaky,' said the other: they considered the doctor but thought better of it. For several days nature took its course and all was well, but when I was stuck again and tried the same trick Nan noticed that I had shunted my pot from one side of the room to the other, saw the ravaged pipes, put two and two together and said, 'You know I shall have to tell your mother'. But she was laughing so much I knew no ill would come of it. This episode greatly encouraged me in evil and deceptive practices which, I quickly realised, if properly handled could be turned to one's advantage.

After pots, a little self-regulated play until nine-thirty when we were all packed off to Prayers in my mother's room. She was to be found propped up in bed on a wedge of pillows, and we perched all about her, each one who could read rehearsing in turn a verse from the statutory chapter of the Bible followed by a general slide on to the knees on the floor for the prayers said by my father, ending with Our Father in unison.

Then more enterprise play in the nursery or lessons for those old enough, until eleven-thirty when, wet or fine, the walk took place. Here the programmes often divided, the larger ones going with one undernurse and the younger and those still pram-bound with another. Often Sholto and I would go with my father to assist him in cutting down trees or digging ditches.

So to lunch and after that – rest, one hour flat on the back, books allowed but no talking. The rest hours must be accounted the longest of my life, for at least until I began to enjoy reading I was temperamentally unsuited to lying still. Indeed two of my most notable crimes were born of pure frustration and committed during the rest period.

The first was to tug at a loose end of wallpaper in the Green Room which obligingly came away in my hand. I pulled off strip after strip until a third of the wall was bare. This was immediately reported and my father smacked me. For some reason I do not remember the intensity of the punishment, but I do remember his saying as we both reappeared in the drawing room, 'I have just been showing Denis what he did to his bedroom wall.' I disagreed with that: he didn't show me anything, he just hit me. I also recall that I claimed I was trying to make a map of the lake. A lie, of course, engendered by the fact that the devastated area seen after the event did have some resemblance to the shape of the lake. It was better than saying nothing.

The second adventure was much more daring and much more dangerous. Round the top storey of the house, just below the level of the windows, there ran a lead gutter perhaps eighteen inches wide. Bored to distraction by enforced rest, I piled up furniture high enough to reach the window fastening. I unfastened it, opened the window and crawled out along the lead guttering. There was no motivation for this foolhardy act, only the conviction that to do something was better than doing nothing. Some forty feet below my sister Sheila was passing by: she looked up, saw me, and was duly appalled. With characteristic presence of mind she shouted, 'I've got a special sweet for you in the nursery. If you go back in I will give it you.' I then discovered a thing that many ledge-crawlers must have found out before me – you cannot turn around. I therefore backed towards the window – a good ten feet away – and as I did so was aware that the room inside was filling up. When I got within reach I felt my father's strong hand seize my waistband and whisk me back inside. There I saw sisters, brothers, nurses and my father all reacting to shock by laughing, crying, kissing me. It was terrific, and although subsequently lectured and told how near to death I had been, there was no punishment. But Davy Sloan had rabbit wire nailed across the apertures of the two windows within the hour.

Subsequently when visitors came to tea I heard these two examples of bad behaviour recounted with relish, and I began to realise that bad rates more attention than good. Shortly after this time, too, I saw on our Kodak projector, along with Charlie Chaplin two-reelers, a short called *Pecks Bad Boy in Church*. In this instance the bad boy let ants loose in church so that they crawled up the legs of all his elderly relations, and higher. It was an interesting idea, but I had no ants. The general conclusion, however, did not escape me, namely that the bad boy is a sort of hero to those who dare not be so bad as he. I thought there might be a career in it and from that time on was to cultivate my bad boy persona with some success. It gave me a cachet with the grown ups and enhanced my status in the nursery. The little ones were fed on the belief that I was so bad I might do anything and hence they treated me with circumspection and were all the quicker to fall in with my wishes in the matter of giving up favourite toys and the like. Even my seniors treated me with caution, as they treated the nursery dog that occasionally snapped. The one that never snapped had a much harder life.

The dreaded rest period over, the afternoon walk took place, this time weather permitting. The second walk was short, for we had to return at three-thirty when we were subjected to another hideous ritual; getting dressed for the drawing room. For the boys there were sailor suits or the kilt, also tussore suits (smocked and adorned with pearly buttons in styles cut from catalogues by my mother and run up by the visiting seamstress, Miss Anderson); we never, as I recall, appeared downstairs in trousers and jacket. Each set of suits was handed down (after a little attention from Miss Anderson) from elder to younger brother. Sailor suits were loathed and despised except for the lanyard and whistles, which in those days were an essential article of sailor costume furniture. Because lanyards and whistles were in such demand for teasing the dogs and other essential purposes, we were often one short and the ensuing argument usually ended in a walk-over for the eldest and youngest and a ding-dong between the middle two. Kilts were worn with bodices, ready-made up to the age of perhaps nine or ten but every body eagerly looked forward to the day he would have his own strap kilt made for him by Mr McKinnon of McKimmie and Co on one of his periodic visits from George Street, Edinburgh. Strap kilts were not handed down. They were capable of being let down and expanded and were personal property.

The tussore suits, however, presented a confusing scene. The different styles were numbered from one to four, but it could well be that on a certain day there was no number three to fit one boy who had grown unduly fast and one of the number twos had gone for repair, and numbers one and four had both been worn already that week. It was my brother Michael, a serious and methodical boy, who at an early age mastered the matter of the tussores. He would run to Nan and say, 'If Pat and I wear number two Denis can have Sholto's old number three and Sholto can wear his new number three.' As in later life, his plans were always well thought out and usually adopted.

The girls had an even greater variety of frocks, skirts, blouses, sashes and ribbons but we did not pay much attention to them. They were dressed in the West Room by one undernurse, we four boys in the Night Nursery by the other undernurse, with Nan floating between the two. Once dressed, there was a cleanliness inspection, hands, faces and ears. Here there was an occasion for confrontation, for if one's general state was satisfactory but there was a single blob of jam or soot or whatever on the face, the undernurses tended to take out a greyish handkerchief, lick one corner, insert their index fingers behind the spittle and attack the offending spot. This I could not stand and I would fight, scream, kick and bite to avoid the threatened handkerchief. 'SPONGE,' I would yell, 'SPONGE. I don't want your spit on my face.' And sometimes I might add the punishable (but often true) insult, 'You smell, anyway.' Tears before going downstairs led to questions – we all sensed this and so we used our power unmercifully. I usually got the sponge.

We trooped down to the drawing room at four o'clock. If there were guests to tea we left at four-thirty. If not we stayed until five-thirty, the younger ones playing with the downstairs toys (huge wooden bricks kept beneath the window sills) and the older ones organising games, racing demon, carpet bowls (only my father preferred to play on a wooden floor without a carpet, which pretty well eliminated any element of skill), halma, draughts, in summer rounders or bicycling on the lawn, croquet (with no regard for or indeed knowledge of the rules), archery or other desultory pursuits vaguely related to some regular game, such as hitting a tennis ball about with a golf club or playing French cricket with a golf ball.

Nursery tea at five-thirty was probably the rowdiest moment of the day. Freshly released from downstairs and sensing the impending doom of bedtime, we made the most of it. The undernurses were all in terror lest we started pat-buttering. This exercise involved laying one knife flat on the table and putting another one at right angles across its handle with only a short piece of the upper knife's handle projecting. Then a small piece of bread or toast was laid on the blade of the upper knife with a pat of butter on top of it. A sharp blow on the handle of the upper knife would send the missile flying up to the ceiling. If the bread struck to the ceiling, that was success. If it fell back that was failure and the thing had to be eaten. When the four Craig girls, who were avid pat butterers, came to tea there was often frenzied activity when the undernurses were out of the room, with all manner of edibles whizzing through the air, leaving the nursery ceiling spattered with bits of buns, biscuits, scones and bread. The undernurses complained a good deal and Bell would lay about her. They had to sweep the mess off the ceiling with a broom, but the butter-marks remained and it was possible for several days after to draw someone aside, indicating a particular butter-splodge, and say, 'That was my currant scone.'

After tea the bathroom was still rowdy, but only for the boys. The girls had their baths separately and delicately at strange times. The boys bathed all together, although not more than three were allowed in the bath at any one time and two were preferred. After bathing, straight to bed and reading for half an hour. Sometimes my mother came up and read to us, sometimes it was an undernurse, but the day always ended with a thirty-second visit from my father and a recitation of 'Lighten Our Darkness', delivered strangely enough not on the knees but in a recumbent posture ready for sleep.

The social structure of the nursery changed rapidly as babies grew into toddlers and little girls into young ladies. When I was six, the epicentre of my nursery days, my eldest sister Sheila was fourteen and about to become a schoolgirl at Wycombe Abbey. The second, Kaff, was twelve and a schoolroom person. Sholto was eight, Michael two and Patrick a few months old and the charge of a separate baby nurse, Nurse Black, commonly known as Doggie, who entered into nursery life as a supernumerary but took no responsibility beyond the care of the baby. In holiday times – summer, Christmas and Easter – the nursery filled up with cousins. Two of these – Roslin whose age lay between that of Sholto and Kaff, and John, who similarly fitted in between Sholto and myself – became permanent members of the family when their mother, a widow, was killed in a car accident. But by that time John was at Loretto and Roslin was a schoolgirl at St Leonards.

Schoolroom persons were still anchored to the nursery. They

had breakfast there, then disappeared, came back for lunch and disappeared again; but later in the day they were usually around to lord it over us and occasionally to recruit us to play some game that required child fodder to make it work. They were superior in their attitude, especially in matters of knowledge. 'Didn't know *that*?' they would say. 'Didn't know how many miles to Dumfries? Good heavens', (good heavens was allowed because of the plural, but Good Lord was not and when I tried out Good Lords I was checked – very unreasonably, as I thought). 'Good heavens, I knew that when I was *six*.' But we admired the schoolrooms and especially Sheila, who was our leader, our chief, our organiser. She was always fair, always conscientious and she controlled us through an instinct for pack leadership. The laws of the pack lived happily alongside the system of discipline applied by parents and nurses. Sheila seldom found me unmanageable. In the end I would always do as she said, because I loved her. Kaff was quite a different matter, temperamental, rebellious, irresistibly funny as a mimic, given to gusts of affection for the favourite of the moment and equally prone to passing hatreds and to fits of black despair. After me, she was the naughtiest, and at times it was a close run thing between us. Roslin was less remarkable and more complaisant than either and these three made up the top team of our nursery life. They were different, they were older, they were girls, they had secrets we could not share.

The second team – Sholto, myself and later John – shared everything with each other. We were good friends on the whole and although Sholto and I went through all the irritations of a close relationship between two people of very different temperament, we nearly always stuck by each other in public; although he would occasionally take the side of the girls against me and I would persuade the little ones to turn against him. He was, however, quite genuinely a much better person than I, and always determined to see things done right. Thus he gave me many well deserved lectures (and still does) but when it came to the push he seldom reported me. I was a great trial to him, I fear, and often a great disappointment. John Smith, when he joined us, was a boon companion, a joker, a sportsman and not at all an *homme serieux*. He was an excellent fishing companion, but, aside from earnest discussion of field sports, his conversational powers were limited to usually successful attempts to twist whatever the subject might be into some ludicrously comical fantasy.

At the tail end of the family came Michael and Pat, always known, until they were very large, as the little ones. They were artful and crafty in looking after their own interests, as tail enders have to be. They were teased almost as much as the dogs but, on the other hand, as the youngest they had the lion's share of the affection from my mother and the nurses. On the whole they earned it, for they put on a very good show of innocence and charm. If I had stopped to think about it I would have found that I was fond of them too.

The dogs were a part of nursery society too and one had a close relationship with each one. Barrie, a wily Aberdeen, was the doyen of the nursery dogs and commanded the prime position in the nursery armchair. Others came and went: Kim, an Airedale, a boring dog, puffed up with vanity because of his good looks; Rory, a red setter, foolish and gullible; Larrie, a morose West Highland, bald in patches and smelling like a pig; Jock, a cairn with an independent air and a short temper. One of the great dog events of the nursery was the day that Jock fell out of the window. He was sunning himself on the window-ledge when the nursery door burst open (one had to get a grown up to open the nursery door because the knob was placed five feet above the ground, and a cluster of children was often dammed up outside it, rattling the old impotent knob which stood at the usual height). The sudden inrush startled him and in turning round he lost his balance and disappeared over the windowsill. A stampede to the flagstones three storeys below was met by Jock strolling across the lawn, looking quite unconcerned. Others said that he snapped more after the experience, but I didn't think so because he had always snapped at me quite a lot, especially when I teased him by sticking a small piece of toast butter-side down on top of his nose. He could see it and smell it but not reach it and after some frenzied contortions I used to egg on one of the other dogs to snatch it off him. This might lead to a scuffle, something one was always trying to promote and the undernurses striving to prevent.

Within this moving world of growing children and dogs self-protection was a paramount need. Attracting attention was another. Getting one's own way was a third. When I look at my own children and my grandchildren, my great nephews and nieces scattered over the land in twos, or in extreme cases threes, when I see their close relationship with their parents, the thought and care that goes into their upbringing, the hours spent in parental deliberation over each option open to each infant, I marvel at their good fortune. I reflect that on some days I saw my mother for perhaps an hour and a half and my father for less, that although they may have given me a passing thought from time to time, on the whole they considered that my upbringing was pre-ordained by God and the family system. I also wonder whether or not the children of today are fortunate in missing the hurly-burly of the sort of nursery life which undoubtedly gave me my grounding in the matter of self-preservation.

Downstairs in the basement there was a very different community, more orderly and more regular in its habits. One could always rely on a full assembly in the servants' hall four times a day: for breakfast at a quarter to eight, by which time the housemaids had dusted the reception rooms and lit the fires; for elevenses at ten-thirty, often with one or two extras in attendance, perhaps the chauffeur or the two washerwomen; for dinner at twelve thirty; and for tea with all manner of scones – girdle, pan, soda, treacle, potato to say nothing of rock cakes. Supper was a more fragmental meal, some eating before dinner was served upstairs, the kitchen staff and table maids waiting until the dinner remains came downstairs, tepid and unappetising.

At the head of the table in the servants' hall sat the housekeeper, Maria as she was called by Gamma, Marnie by everyone else. She was Nan's sister and thus shared the old Dalmorton connection with the Smith family, but the two had little else in common.

Marnie wore a wig – a poor mousy thing – and she was dressed in many layers of black bombazine. She was not fat, but all of her bulk, some of it natural, some made up with bustles and pads which may have had something to do with her ailments, was gathered round her hips. Her legs were layered in crêpe bandages visible under black cotton stockings when she raised her skirts; her face was of yellow-white parchment stretched across her nose, her eyelashes almost albino, her eyes watery. When she yawned her upper dentures swung slowly down across the opening of her mouth until they rested on her lower set, and although she held up her hand to conceal this gruesome event, she never got the line of sight right and one could still see above, below or round one side of her hand, the grinning row of yellowish teeth descending in a phantom bite. She wore steel-rimmed glasses insecurely hooked to her wig and she walked, owing to some serious malfunction of her legs, with a stick in either hand and with her trunk almost parallel to the ground. This was on the flat, for when she met the stairs she went on all fours, her legs straightening up behind and her elbows resting two risers ahead. In this position, her huge posterior towered up like a black hayrick wobbling unsteadily up or down the stairway. It could take her a full five minutes to achieve one flight, breathing heavily and when reaching the point of exhaustion emitting cooing noises like a wood pigeon. No one could pass her when in passage and frequently small orderly queues formed at the top and the bottom of the stairs, waiting for the way to clear.

It was not the sight of Marnie on the stairs, however, that was most worthy of remark, nor the sounds she made, but the smell. She had without doubt the richest smell of anyone on the Craigielands scene. This was freely released when her skirts were raised in her stair-mounting position and was wafted far and wide by the currents of air fanned outwards by the struggling motion of her upper legs as she strove to gain (or lose) each step. The smell itself had a basis of unwashed underparts (very powerful), on top of which there was a layer of embrocation, emanating from a white sticky fluid she rubbed on her legs at night. Next there were her armpits and finally, but only if you got close enough, her wig smell, something like dead mouse blended with nutmeg. I can remember Michael sitting at nursery tea, wrinkling his nose like a rabbit and saying, 'I can smell Marnie coming' when she was still a passage length and two flights of stairs away.

By day she sat in the housekeeper's room, a desolate dark place, full of cartons of tinned fruit and sacks of flour. By night she slept behind a screen in the same room except when Nan moved out of the night nursery to some other part of the upper floor to be with a new baby or an invalid. Then (horror of horrors) Marnie moved in, small and all, and took Nan's place in the big double bed where we were accustomed to slip in for a morning cuddle. Worse still, whereas Nan modestly dressed and undressed in the bathroom, Marnie apparently could not move until she had bandaged her legs and put her wig on. The bald head with only a few residual strands of hair was unspeakably shocking. The crêpe bandages she used were grubby and the veins in her legs a horrifying shade of navy blue. She would start at her toes, using two or three bandages on her way up, until she reached her crotch where, with a good deal of panting and cooing, she affixed a huge safety pin.

Marnie had evidently been a great support to Gamma in the early days at Dalmorton, but now we children could not really see what she was for. We disliked the way that tears rolled down on each side of her nose when she sang hymns on Sunday or when she spoke of some dead or even just absent member of the family. We found her sentimentality abhorrent and avoided her whenever we could. We were not sorry for her in her constant state of suffering from her disabilities, for children tend to accept permanent disability as a natural state. She still took orders from Gamma every morning and must have seen to their execution. She moved about the house as a combine harvester moves through narrow lanes, spreading her aroma fore and aft. Aside from eulogies of the dead, her conversation was limited, and tended to be confined to short telegraphic messages about forthcoming menus, such as 'fish for lunch'. In general we regarded her as pretty bad news and certainly as a very bad smell, but she was there, she was part of the scenery and we accepted her.

At the other end of the table sat the tall rangy figure of Mrs Henderson, the cook. Then as a rake, dressed in black cotton with a white apron and bib, her hair piled over her ears in two huge plaited earphones, she had something of the pantomime dame about her. She was a highly strung woman, quick to move and quick to anger. At times of great stress she became hysterical, throwing her apron over her head and making noises like a railway engine taking in water. It was impossible to tell whether she was laughing or crying, what was certain was that she was very upset. She was always dangerous. No one could swat a marauding hand on the edge of a pastryboard with greater dexterity and she was deadly accurate with a serving spoon or ladle and could inflict a stinging blow just above the ears. She was snappy with her inferiors and impatient of the teasing farm boys who brought down the milk and who would show her pictures of brassières in lingerie catalogues and ask her (she was straight up and down in front) which cup size and degree of support would suit her. This would drive her into a frenzy of shame, disgust and anger. She once seized a broom to chastise Jock Wilson but he ducked out before a blow was struck.

Despite the danger, it was impossible to leave Mrs Henderson alone. If you pulled a dead mouse attached to a thread across the kitchen floor she would shriek and jump up on a stool. If you told her that Marine wanted to see her immediately she would go and knock on the door of an empty housekeeper's room and stand there for five minutes. If you tickled the back of her legs with a feather and blamed the dog, she would turn on the dog, carefully placed but innocent, without fail. She was in fact infinitely gullible and never failed to take the bait. Despite this, she maintained the dignity of her office and ran a well-ordered kitchen. Everything was in its proper place, clean and regularly checked. The daily routine was observed to the minute, meals were on time and on baking days the griddles would be off the range and scraped in good time for the evening meal to move in.

The only real sadness about Mrs Henderson was that she simply couldn't cook at all. At best she could be called a cottage cook. Dinner in those days ran to five or six courses (soup, fish, entrée, game, savoury, sweet) and her natural range did not extend much beyond boiled mutton and cabbage, so she was working in unknown territory most of the time and the results were dreadful. Roasts were over-roasted, vegetables swam in water, soups all tasted of carrots, savouries of stale cheese, trout were thrown into boiling water to curl up like whiting on the instant and lose half their skin, partridges came to the table as dry as biscuits, jellies tasted of stale pond water and the milk and cream used in puddings were almost always off. Luckily for her no one seemed to notice that anything was wrong. To do her justice, her baking, like that of all rural Scotswomen, was excellent, as was her porridge.

Down each side of the table in the servants' hall sat the rank and file. Even in the lower reaches there was a rigid hierarchy, headed by Aggie Crosbie, the head tablemaid, good-natured, loquacious, an unfailing source of information about upstairs by reason of her constant eavesdropping at meals and her great familiarity with all the family, the nurses and the chauffeur. (Only Gamma and my father and mother managed to keep her at something of a distance.) She bubbled over with laughter at every tidbit of gossip and her curiosity was insatiable. Miss Kaff threw Miss Sheila's knickers out of the window and they stuck on a drain pipe (laughter); Mr Denis tied a tin can under the De Dion and had everyone working all over the car for two days until they found it (suppressed laughter because it was naughty as well as funny); Jimmy White had pains to his stomach in the night so bad he tore the sheets (hoarse whisper, popping eyes).

Aggie presided in the tablemaids' pantry just inside the front door, where she could monitor all comings and goings; and in the afternoon, because of her privileged position and owing to some alleged weakness in her knees, she was allowed to do her embroidery reclining on the dining room sofa, from which she could still keep a watchful eye on the front door. She was a heavy woman and after a time she left her mark on the sofa in the shape of a deep hollow at the east end. When Gamma noticed this it was blamed on one of the dogs who had very sensibly appropriated it as a natural resting place. When I heard of this injustice I was outraged and went straight to Gamma. It wasn't Rab that made that hole in the dining room sofa, I told her. It was Aggie. Aggie was very much a part of the confederation of children and servants and sometimes her co-operative spirit led her into trouble, as when from time to time we filled the salt cellars with Enos and when once a huge ashet was placed in front of Gamma who was not pleased when she lifted the cover to find a large live toad puffing out its stomach in the middle of an otherwise empty dish.

I have no doubt that Aggie was checked by Gamma for conspiring with us in these tricks, for she would emerge from her room red in the face and biting her lips. When upset she found comfort in writing long letters to George, to whom she was perpetually engaged to be married. George was one of the heating engineers who had installed the central heating in Craigielands some five or six years earlier. Much of her time on the dining room sofa was devoted to her trousseau, which, as the years rolled on, must have filled several bottom drawers. I recall in particular her working on an item which she called a modesty vest and wondering how much modesty any vest could provide given her huge undisciplined bust and consequently profound cleavage that seemed, when she laughed – which was very often – to run up to her Adam's apple.

After Aggie came Alice, second tablemaid and in slack times housemaid too, a neat, retiring woman who would back against the wall and dip her eyes whenever one of the quality went past. Then Lena, an over-plump lumpkin of a girl who always seemed to be acting in character and rather badly at that, as if she were in the chorus of a touring opera company. And finally Nettie, the daughter of the farmer of the second farm on the estate, prognathous, with a stammer approaching a state of lockjaw, neurotic, dangerous when teased, lunging out with the wild eye and straggling hair of a wild goat. She was occasionally to be found weeping uncontrollably behind the curtains in the housemaids' pantry.

The housemaids had a dreary routine, making beds, carrying cans of hot and cold water and emptying the pots under each bed into a slop pail until it was nearly two-thirds full and then pouring it down one of the lavatories with a crash that could be heard all over the house. Why was it, I wondered, that there was such immense security surrounding he act of passing water, yet the final disposal of the same water was more or less a public act? There were, of course, several persons' water mingled together so the flush could not be attributed to any one individual, but nevertheless there must be some collective shame in it being known that at some time the proprietor of the water did actually have to go through the act of passing it. After all, one knew from which of the bedrooms it came.

The housemaids had the most fun with the Daisy. The Daisy was a wooden box mounted on pram wheels with a large cast iron wheel on the front and a small hole at the back. One housemaid turned the wheel by means of a wooden handle and the other fixed flexible metal pipes and rods on to the hole. At the end of the last rod there was a sucking-shaped mouth and the whole contraption acted as a manually-driven vacuum cleaner. Inside it there was a sort of bellows which, when activated, made a noise like a dog retching, which we were forbidden to imitate.

Below stairs there was a long-lasting kitchenmaid, Nancy, big-boned and well-built with enormous well-formed breasts that appeared to keep their contours with no artificial aid. She was young, good natured and a bastion against the rages of Mrs Henderson from whom she also protected a succession of teenage girls from the village who as assistant kitchenmaids were the lowest form of life and one of whose jobs was to make the tea and prepare the meals for the servants' hall.

Latterly Nancy was walking out with a one-armed ploughman and it was a matter of mild interest that she began to grow larger rather quickly. This was nothing new in itself. When she had first arrived she had been a girl of modest proportions, but living at the centre of the food supply and having access to all scraps before they reached the dogs she developed into the huge Amazonian figure of her later years. Now the increase in her size was only somewhat more rapid than usual and was not thought to be remarkable until one night she woke my sister Sheila and said she had scarlet fever. Sheila diagnosed the problem correctly and hustled her off to her mother, where she almost immediately gave birth to a fine child. Within the household scarlet fever remained the accepted reason for her disappearance, but loafing around the servants' hall one day

I overheard one say to another that since he had only one arm she must have helped him put it in. This gave me cause for a great deal of thought and speculation.

The servants had practically no private life. Mrs Henderson had a room to herself furnished with an iron bedstead, cupboard and a trunk on top of which was a photograph of her son. His letters to her from Canada were the events of her life. One day when we were momentarily good friends, she called me into her room to look at some snaps he had sent her. I cannot remember the snaps but I can remember that she sniffed a lot and wiped her eyes with her skirt. This made me put my arms around her neck and give her a hug, which she returned with such violence that I was a little frightened. Next day, however, normal relations were resumed and we were at each other again.

The other maids lived in two dormitories, one in the basement and one in the attics, small rooms each containing three breathing, sweating, apple-eating young women. The odour of the maids' bedrooms was famous and provided a sort of basis for comparison with other smells. They read a few 'books', *Tit Bits* or women's magazines, seldom a real book although my grandmother made out a reading list for each one and there was a well-stocked bookshelf in the servants' hall. I often wondered how Lena, for instance, dealt with Gamma's enquiry as to how she was getting on with *The Mill on the Floss* or *The Pilgrim's Progress*. Marnie was a great reader and acted as Gamma's agent in directing the education of the maids, but I don't think it ever amounted to much. In fact I doubt whether Lena, Nettie and Nancy were able to read with any facility.

On a working day there was not much free time and what there was was spent sitting gossiping in the servants' hall, knitting, or writing letters, which was a private activity, in the bedroom. Except for Marnie no one from below stairs visited the nursery, but the servants' hall was a hospitable place. Nan had a place of honour at Marnie's right hand and there was always room for an undernurse off duty or the farm boy who brought down the late milk. But Mrs Henderson would soon put an end to a visit if there was too much loud laughter or any hint of undue familiarity.

Bedtime was early, nine or nine-thirty; reveille was early too, six o'clock for most, earlier for some. Sanitary arrangements were deplorable. In the basement there was one bath in a dark cavern under the pantry stairs, its enamel stained brown as if by nicotine, its taps rusting, and behind that a shaky lavatory with a broken seat and a rope which you pulled to flush it from some distant cistern. There were no windows, only a naked thirty watt lamp. It took courage to use the lavatory after dark because the back of the bathroom lay across one of the rats' main traffic routes and they were numerous. The upstairs maids had a more civilised loo, shared with the children, but none of them, upstairs or down, had access to a washbasin with running water. What they had was a bowl with an accompanying can of water in their room.

Days off were once a week, but there was nothing for the maids who did not live on the estate to do unless they walked to Beattock and took either the train or the bus to Moffat, where they would sit in a café for an hour or two, or visit friends. They were all advised not to walk in front of the windows when off duty, and if they were going to Beattock station or the garden they took the Back Road. Since they were provided with working uniforms, food and housing it was considered that they had little need for cash. I do not know what the higher ranks were paid, but Nancy had five shillings a week. (This should be seen against an agricultural wage of thirty shillings, which often had to support a man and his family, including, in some cases, rent.)

For the children the servants' hall was the most attractive centre of social life in Craigielands. The conversation was more personal, the laughter more ready, the sense of camaraderie infectious and there was no moralising (except an occasional speech form Marnie or some dreadful warning from Mrs Henderson, which soon passed) and no obligation to make polite conversation with visitors. Dress and behaviour were both relaxed and one was treated on one's merits. If you were funny you got a laugh, if shocking a short intake of breath, if too tiresome you were bawled out.

The servants' hall was my first audience, and I loved it. What my father called showing off and Sholto bumptiousness was in fact a deep desire to play to an audience, a desire which was only finally gratified by making television programmes for an audience of millions. But this was no more challenging than the audience of a dozen or so women who sat around the great beechwood table in the Craigielands basement, cups of dark Indian tea held in both hands, elbows on the table, eyes bright with anticipation, clucking with chatter and gossip. If one could first get the ear, then raise a giggle and build it up until the table was in a roar, that was success, that was glory.

In due course Nan did die, and I was duly devastated, but not so much as I might have been, partly because I was now a schoolroom person, partly because her absence during her terminal illness softened the shock of separation. Years before she had been an undernurse to my mother, known to her as Liz, and they remained intimate up to the day of her death. When my mother had her first baby, Liz came to look after it. She was walking out with a young man at that time and they had made their plans for a wedding. The man, however, disappeared, I was never told how or why. When my mother was trying to comfort her Liz said, 'Oh well, if I can't have children of my own I'll just have to look after yours.' Which she did, and greatly to our benefit.

3

The Late Mr Smith

The phrase 'the late Mr Smith' was still often heard twelve years after my grandfather's death, in the Craigielands of my day. His presence was still to be felt everywhere, through the life-size portrait which greeted you in the vestibule; through his salmon rod still lying in the rod rack, and his cartridge bag still in evidence on shooting days; through his name which still adorned the farm carts whose nameplates read:

James Smith
Craigielands Hill
No 1

– up to No 6 – all in exquisite copperplate.

His posthumous judgment was often called upon to support a case, to express approbation or displeasure. 'The late Mr Smith would never hae had them pit doon,' said Tom the coachman as red granite chips were laid on the north drive. (It was an idea my father had picked up from a visit to a hotel in Lanarkshire. Tom was certainly right.) 'The late Mr Smith could nae hae done better hissil,' the keeper said to a visiting gun who had felled seven out of eight towering pheasants at the greenhouse peg. 'The late Mr Smith wud hae liked that yin,' Jim Porteous the curling blacksmith shouted to me as I laid a good lead stone. The phrase warmed the air, people glowed a little at the mention of his name. All anecdotes about him were happy or funny. He was remembered as the benevolent deity who presided over Craigielands' golden age.

Not so his brother Sam. Memories of Sam triggered off one of two responses – laughter, because he was thought to be absurd in his self-importance and pomposity, and a groan of remembered boredom. 'Poor old Sam,' my father would say with his special Uncle Sam smile, 'Sam was the most awful bore.' 'Sam!' my mother would say. 'We used to run away and hide in case we got Conditional Immortality again.'

And yet the two stories I remembered best about Sam were greatly to his credit. He achieved the record catch on Craigielands lake, 94 trout in one day averaging 13 ounces. My Aunt Violet described the scene. 'It was a wild stormy day in March and Sam stood in his frock coat on the peninsula by the big oak tree, his beard streaming across the lake. He was hooking them so fast he sent Kerss [the first generation Craigielands keeper and ghillie] to get a second rod so that as soon as one trout was in the net he could immediately throw a cast with the other.' A very sensible plan, for at something like fifteen trout an hour, one every four minutes, he would have lost nearly half his fishing time without a second rod.

The other story was thought to be humorous. Sam lay on his death bed and James stood by his side to receive his final wishes and thoughts. 'James,' said Sam, 'have you seen the papers the day?' (the brothers retained a modified Lallans brogue throughout their lives). 'No, Sam,' said James, 'I came straight here to be with you.' 'James,' said Sam after a pause, 'I think we should buy long.' And with that piece of almost certainly correct terminal advice to his partner, he expired.

Much later in life I began to find out about Sam, mainly from his autobiography, *My Life's Work*, but also from correspondence, parliamentary reports and contemporary records. From these sources I discovered quite a different Sam, a scholar, philanthropist, social worker, Liberal MP, Privy Councillor, and a business man of immense vigour and imagination. His father, a dedicated farmer, nature lover, fisherman and curler, had brought up his family at Borgue in Galloway in the midst of the yellow blaze of the gorse and the emerald green of the sea grass of the Solway coast. There is no prettier spot in Scotland and both brothers throughout their lives shared a love of the country, Sam majoring on mountains,

James on field sports. By the time he was thirty, Sam had travelled the world to study the likely effects of the American civil war at first hand, to start a new cotton trade with India, to seek business opportunities all over Europe and to satisfy his own curiosity about those regions of the middle east which provide the background to the Old Testament. He had also set up with his brother James the immensely successful cotton broking firm of Smith Edwards and was about to build two large spinning mills in Staleybridge.

There is one great sadness. Sam himself is fully documented, James not at all. Even in the autobiography Sam's references to his brother are terse and incidental. 'My brother James joined me in Liverpool.' 'My brother James managed affairs so well in my absence that I took him into partnership,' and so on. Thus James becomes a sort of Myecroft Smith to Sam's Sherlock. He did not go to any university, was not a letter-writer nor a good public speaker, kept no diary and yet on the evidence of his life – and even more so of his death, for his funeral was even more fully attended than Sam's – he was just as well-known, and better liked than Sam, both by the business community in Liverpool and the neighbouring citizens of the Wirral.

One letter from the fifteen-year-old James written in his first year in Liverpool survives. It reflects his cheerful, businesslike approach towards matters in hand, in this case the receipt of a consignment of game from Roberton:

Egremont, November 17th, 1855.

My Dear Mama,

It would be fruitless for me to attempt to make up for so many kind letters, but I intend to write you a few lines to tell you about the safe arrival of the packages. When school came out today I first of all went down to Sam's office and was greatly surprised when I heard what an immense quantity of game and other things were coming. I first of all got a strong boy for 3d and took him to the Dock and paid the freight which amounted only to 11d. I opened the bag and took out the sack with the meat and the shoes and carried it myself and the remainder, which consisted of the Game, 5 hares, 4 rabbits and a pheasant I gave to the boy. After a very hard pull we got them down to Sam's office. I took out 2 hares there and left them with Sam for Mr Martin. We then took them down to the landing stage, but Lo and Behold! there was no Egremont boat, it being very foggy.

So I was obliged to go by Seacombe. I had to pay 1d there for them, then I got two little boys and divided the packages into three parts, took one part for myself and gave one to each of them. One of the hares got its head out of the poke and was an object of mirth to passers by. We got them all safe to Egremont and I gave the little boys 1d each. So I got them all home with the expense of 1s/6d from the time they left Kirkdbt. I have seen us having to pay a good deal more than that for freight alone. We intend giving Mr Nicholson a hare and the pheasant, and Mrs Anderson a hare and Miss Green maybe a rabbit or more. Sam is not home yet so I have not decided yet how to do but I think that will be the way we'll distribute them.

I daresay I almost frightened Miss Green when I came in with such an immense load, but it helped to calm her when I told her we were not going to use them all ourselves. I am very well pleased with my shoes, they will last me a long time now. Sam's drawers that I sent home are to be mended and sent back when you are sending anything again.

Please excuse this hastily written letter, receive my love and believe me dearest Mama
your loving son
James Smith

Meanwhile Sam was making rapid progress. In 1857, at the age of twenty-one, he became manager of the cotton salesroom, in 1859 he shrewdly decided to visit North America to determine for himself what effect the imminent war between North and South would have on the cotton trade, and in October 1860 he set up in business on his own account.

Within weeks the cotton industry was in turmoil. The outbreak of the American Civil War caused speculation on an unprecedented scale. Sam had a good understanding of how the trade from the Southern States was likely to be affected, but many brokers had not, and within two years, at the age of twenty-eight, he had surged ahead and was able to set up the firm Smith Edwards which within a decade became one of the best known names in broking and spinning. He visited India to see what could be done with the cotton trade there, and James managed the firm so well in his absence that he took him in as his partner.

So began twenty-five years of successful partnership between the brothers. They formed a part of the Scottish/Merseyside community comprised of young Scotsmen who had moved onward and upward as their businesses prospered. The lodging houses of their early years in Egremond and Liscard were soon left behind for commodious country houses on the Wirral.

In 1872 James married Amy Oliphant, whose father Thomas ran a seminary for young ladies in Edinburgh known as Oliphant's Academy. It occupied the last two houses on the south-east corner of Charlotte Square, that most lovely and enduring monument to the genius of the Adam brothers. Amy was first a pupil in the school, then an assistant teacher.

As a young married woman in Liverpool she must have found that her life offered her almost all she could desire: a successful and well-respected husband, a home the equal of any other Liverpool Scottish establishment, a growing family, a lively circle of friends interested in Liberal politics, literature and religion, and everlasting activity in the innumerable charities and church enterprises that she and James supported. No doubt she taught her own children, as later on she taught us, her grandchildren. And no doubt her influence pervaded the Dalmorton household, as it was later to pervade Craigielands. For if it was the memory of James Smith that animated the spirit of the several Craigielands societies of my time, it was the living presence of Gamma that made them run. She dominated the scene, exercising her command with unquestioned authority. Her mode of speech was quiet and deliberate, her voice was raised in conversation only when her natural sense of oratory demanded it, never in anger and never in hilarity. Her movements about the house gave the impression of controlled power, one could not see her feet at work under her long skirts and she seemed to glide rather than walk. I never ever saw her hurry, much less run. Her smile was ready, her laughter brief and spontaneous. Of medium height and with snow-white hair parted in the middle she wore elaborate gowns, beautiful shawls and all the accessories of the late Victorian fashion – huge bonnets, elegant hair combs, a black velvet choker, a tasteful array of pinchbeck jewellery and a reticule which dangled inside a slit in her upper skirt. Indoors she wore black slippers, very insubstantial, like ballet shoes. Outdoors she wore button boots and a muff in winter. The modes of the Edwardian period and the twenties passed her by. She did not possess a pair of Wellingtons, a jersey or sweater of any kind, nor one single skirt above ankle length.

She ruled her domain from a small room adjoining her bedroom suite called the writing room. All important business was conducted here. It was in the writing room she saw the housekeeper each day, wrote bundles of notes, some the 'messages' for Jim Rheilly the chauffeur to execute in Moffat, others instructions to the washer-woman, a note of sympathy about her sick child to Mrs Sharp at the North Lodge, a weekly schedule of what was required of the housekeeper or instructions as to how the game was to be parcelled up and despatched. It was there that each Friday she made up the wage packets herself and handed them personally to the household staff with a word of admonition or praise. Most weekdays she would conduct lessons there for perhaps two hours in the morning. Punishments, which she administered with great art, were announced there, and if my parents wanted to borrow yet another thousand pounds from an uncle to send the next growing child to school, the discussions would most likely be held in the writing room.

As small children we respected Gamma as we respected no one else in the world, and feared her a little, not as we feared our father, who would bark out orders or criticise us often in a most hurtful way, but rather as a backbencher in his own party might have feared Mr Gladstone, who was one of Gamma's heroes. Her authority was absolute and we accepted it as if it were one of the laws of nature. She was friendly to the children, and told good stories, and also acted out an unending saga of one Mr Dunderhead, an exceptionally foolish man who was very accident prone. She had limited tactile communication, handling children firmly but without sentimentality, as a vet handles small mammals. She smelt of camphor and lavender and she washed each morning in an ewer of cold water using Coal Tar soap. She brushed her hair daily for a long time sitting before a mirror. One day I rushed in suddenly and in the mirror I saw her naked breasts. They were the first I had seen and I found the sight of them at the same time exciting and disturbing.

As we grew older we began to recognise the power of her intellect and respond to her love of learning. My father and mother also taught us, but he in a schoolmasterly learn-by-rote manner (he never really dropped the housemaster's mantle he had worn at Loretto) and she in a wild and eccentric fashion which depended upon the mood of the moment and had little relationship to any graduated steps in learning (she would often be making toffee on the spirit lamp at the same time as teaching sight-reading at the piano). But Gamma was a scholar. Her main subject was scripture. She had studied Hebrew in early life and also enough Greek to allow her to read the New Testament in its earliest form. She had absorbed all the data then available about the comparative study of archeology and history and could relate Egyptian, Minoan and Anatolian cultures to the books in the Old Testament in a way I did not encounter again until much later in life. She was well versed in the standard interpretation of Scottish, English and European history, regarding facts, dates and kings and queens as the backbone of all historical study. The other subjects she taught were English, geography, arithmetic and French. She was a good teacher, but a hard taskmistress. Sloppy work received a serious rebuke, and lack of effort was punished.

Her love of teaching and her high standards dated back to her own schooldays: her father's school was a serious one. Indeed, Thomas Oliphant had a reputation as a man of great learning, though his few surviving letters suggest – as does this note to his son-in-law James Smith – that he could wear his learning lightly:

> I can now, accompanied by Sandy, take pretty long walks every day and, though I no longer possess "the elastic foot that mounts the stile with ease" I am still able to scale a stone dyke when it would bar my progress – no contemptible feat for one who, if spared, will complete his 70th year the day after tomorrow.

The reputation of his school suffered a setback, however, when one of his sons, an assisant master, ran off to France with one of the young ladies. The episode was seldom referred to in the family, and then only in hushed tones. My mother alone thought it funny rather than shameful and would pull a special face for the Oliphant black sheep who, for some reason I never could fathom, she always referred to as What-You-Put-Your-Name-To-Jack. Although Edinburgh was no longer the city of Sidney Smith and the *Edinburgh Review*, which for a decade and more had made it the literary capital of Great Britain, the cultural life of the young Oliphants as they lived amongst the classical symmetry of the recently completed New Town must have been lively and invigorating.

Gamma's girlhood was thoroughly Christian, both in her family life and her intellectual development. To the grandchildren she spoke little of her mother, a great deal about her father and incidentally about her sisters – never about What-You-Put-Your-Name-To-Jack. I listened avidly to Gamma's reminiscences, for she had the knack when telling a story of making the words stick. 'My sister Agnes,' she said, 'was a big-framed woman and she wakened me every morning by the sound of splashing water. I saw her head against the frame of the window bobbing up and down as she dashed cold water in her eyes, which were red-rimmed and weak.' My own eyes were red-rimmed and I tried dashing cold water on them for a week or two but soon gave it up. It didn't seem to do any good and perhaps I was not big-framed enough, or of the wrong sex.

Gamma's voice took on a golden tone when she described her visits to her great-aunt Melville Christison (whose daughter, also Melville, was destined to marry our great-uncle Sam Smith) at the Biggar Manse. She was allowed to help her great-aunt with the housekeeping, counting the eggs as they came in from the farm, checking the dry stores, stirring the puddings, turning the scones on the griddles. Two of her most famous stories amongst her grandchildren recounted adventures on shopping expeditions with her aunt to Biggar. One, the Sugar Story, concerned a stone of caster sugar in a bag with a hole in it which laid a powdery trail behind the dogcart all the way from the grocer's to the Manse back door, by which time there was none left. The other, the Salt Story, had to do with confusion at the general store between common salt and some foreign chemical substance. It was a long and complicated tale and finished with Aunt Melville licking her finger, poking it into a pot on the kitchen table and saying, 'Salt! Salt! This is no salt. This is saltpetre.' (It turned out to be bicarbonate of soda.)

Another lasting memory was that of her summer holidays spent with the family in that part of the Clyde estuary where the Highlands and Lowlands meet. Tighnabruich was one favoured location, the island of Arran another. When in later life she spoke of those summer days her eyes took on a more distant focus, just as they did when she was telling us those parts of the story of Jesus which moved her most. Her Highland holidays were to form the background for her two novels, *Claire* and *Vida*, and for many 'tales' which she and her sister Annie would tell to us.

There is no evidence of how she met James Smith. The most likely assumption is that she went to stay with Annie, who had married a Liverpool Scot by the name of Lindsay. The Liverpool Scots were a numerous and closely-knit group and once an understanding was reached between James Smith and Amy Oliphant there would have been opportunities enough for him to court her in the distant and respectful fashion of the day.

Ten years after they were married James Smith bought Craigielands. He could leave the office of Smith Edwards in Bold Street and four-fifteen on a Friday, catch the 'corridor' north, slip off at Beattock at a quarter past seven, jump into the dogcart and be sitting down to dinner with his family around him and the sun setting on the Moffat hills by a quarter to eight. As life went on the weekends grew longer, the shooting and fishing days more frequent and towards the end of his life perhaps as much as six months in the year were spent in what was then quaintly described on our writing paper as North Britain.

James was the opposite of a social climber: his friends were mainly good-humoured sporting men, drawn from his wide business acquaintance in Liverpool and contrasting also with Gamma's circle. She too was indifferent to 'society' – but avidly sought out her intellectual equals to discuss the religious, philosophical and literary topics of the day. I have often wondered what happened after dinner in the Craigielands of those days. Certainly the sexes would not have segregated except for the conventional withdrawal after dinner (as a boy I established that with only one lavatory on the ground floor, the minimum time to complete the natural functions after dinner for twenty-two was about twenty minutes). I assume that after James drew off one or two of his friends on the excuse of a game of billiards and would sit in the smoking room discussing the problems of driving grouse round a hill in a high wind, whilst upstairs Gamma and Professor Blackie were at it hammer and tongs over Ruskin's *Stones of Venice* or Carlyle's *History of the French Revolution*.

James' freedom to enjoy Craigielands was, however, soon to be circumscribed by a profound change in his brother Sam's career. In 1882, the year Craigielands was bought, Sam was approached to stand as Liberal parliamentary candidate for one of the Liverpool seats in a by-election. At first he rejected the offer on the grounds of ill-health. But deputations called upon him, his friends were persuasive, and eventually he capitulated. 'I owe it to my brother

James,' wrote Sam, 'that but for his loyal support, and the load of business he took off my shoulders, I should not have been able to accept.'

Sam's political career was not an unqualified success. He introduced some private member's bills to improve the lot of the poor, in particular poor children, and became a Privy Councillor and a friend of Mr Gladstone, succeeding him as the Member for Flint, where Gladstone had his country seat at Hawarden Castle. It is clear, however, that he became a figure of fun to the less serious backbenchers in his party. What with his wispy beard, Scots accent and falsetto voice it was hard for them to treat him with the dignity his mission demanded. A parliamentary report in *Punch* on May 22nd 1901 catches the spirit:

> House of Commons, Thursday Night. – Nineteen years has Mr Sam Smith dwelt in the wilderness in the House of Commons, and its ways are still dark to him. Just now, called upon by the SPEAKER, he rose to put a question concerning the welfare of the London barmaid. Why should Members burst into roar of cheers, turning to a shout of laughter as he meekly surveyed the scene? Difficult for him to understand why in any circumstances grown-up men should laugh. The present lapse into temporary insanity was quite inexplicable. 'Twas ever thus. Whatever be the subject he takes in hand – the purlieus of the theatres, the back of the stage at the music-halls, the iniquity of certain plays, Piccadilly Circus after midnight – no sooner is his plaintive voice heard asking a question or driving home a moral than ribald Members opposite, others below the Gangway on his own side, break forth into a cheer of suspicious vigour.

Gamma had little interest in the goings-on in the House of Commons. It is difficult to know what view she took of the politician Sam. As James' brother, lifelong partner and closest friend he must have discussed politics with her frequently, but her political interest was more philosophical, his compassionate and partisan. Similarly in literature Sam was a voracious reader in the fields of science and religion and a formidable classical scholar, Gamma's tastes were more purely literary.

Reading for her centred around the nineteenth-century novel. The core of her literary taste was Scott: she knew the Waverley Novels almost as well as if she had written them herself. Then Thackeray, Dickens, George Eliot, Meredith and – later and with some suspicion – Conrad. In later life any serious new novel was absorbed and evaluated in letters, usually to her son Thomas Oliphant (known as T.O.), and also in family discussion around the dinner table. At the lighter end of the spectrum she was sometimes persuaded to read a thriller – *Trent's Last Case* or *The Murder of Roger Ackroyd* – or a bestseller – Edna Furber's *Showboat*. But she found the characters in such trivial works either disreputable or uninteresting and would revert with some relief to *The Heart of Midlothian* or *Bleak House*.

Her territory in poetry was equally well marked. A few of the cavalier poets were known to her, as were the better known poems of Gray and Pope, but she came into her own with the Lake poets, in particular Wordsworth, and at the heart and centre of all she thought best in poetry stood Tennyson. I never heard Chaucer mentioned, nor Dunbar, nor Henryson, nor any of our national poets save Burns and Sir Walter. She also had a penchant for the versifiers of the day – Hood, Campbell and Fletcher. She knew 'John Gilpin' and 'Marmion' by heart but apart from the Seven Ages of Man and Portia's speech on mercy, scarcely a line of Shakespeare, who was regarded less as a poet than as a great national institution related to the theatre.

It was this diet of prose and poetry which nourished her style of writing fiction – but alas, it must be admitted that it is almost unreadable today. Her two novels, *Vida* and *Claire*, centre upon the fortunes of young girls in the throes of growing up. Although certainly not autobiographical they rely greatly upon recollections of her own adolescence and might have conveyed the rather touching innocence of Victorian girlhood had it not been that Sir Walter and William Makepeace sat so heavily on her shoulder. Both books are crowded with sonsy Scottish characters who speak in the broadest vernacular – as in the Waverley novels. The upper-class characters have a preoccupation with proper behaviour and good feeling which reflects the 'good' elements in Thackeray's society without catching the richness of character and strength of plot that lie below the surface. For today's readers they must be amongst the most boring novels of the late Victorian era.

Nor is her poetry much more rewarding. She was, however, a versifier extraordinary, her doggerel was always workmanlike and usually effective, as in this electioneering squib written in support of the Liberal Free Trade candidate in a Liverpool by-election.

How shall we bind the Empire?
By running down our trade
By piling up statistics
Of industries decayed;
By lowering British credit
In every foreign state –
That's how we bind the Empire,
And make her commerce great!

Forth goes the invitation
To bind the Empire so;
It lies before the nation –
How will the verdict go?
Who knows? But here's my finding
Whatever yours may be –
If this be Empire-binding,
Let's leave the Empire free!

Nearer home, she wrote innumerable simple family rhymes and poems of which the following is perhaps the shortest:

'Shall we go and visit Venice?'
Said a little boy called Denis
'Yes and see that fine Rialto'

Said another boy called Sholto
'Better not forget your cycles'
(that was just a joke of Michael's)

Occasionally she would attempt a jeu d'ésprit for recitation at Sunday tea. The following is about our local village which boasted, at the head of the High Street, a particularly ugly statue of a ram representing the chief local industry; also the South of Scotland Tennis Championship, a golf course and a mineral well:

A sandstone sheep that some men scoff at
A statue there's a drinking trough at
A park the tournaments come off at
A moor that people go to golf at
A well they come to drink and cough at
By all these signs you may know Moffat.

It was when she took to serious verse that her good sense seemed to desert her and it is painful to read her poems today because they in no way reflect the wit and warmth of the person I knew. Indeed it could be said that Gamma's published prose and poetry fairly reflect all that we today find most daunting in Victorian literature.

Not so her private journals and correspondence. Her letters to her two more literate sons, T.O. and Allan, adopt an easy conversational style (later to be developed into something of an art form by my mother), which was unfortunately deployed upon subjects such as Welsh Disestablishment, the Irish question and the nature of the Trinity, all of which may have been of interest then but today have lost any glamour they once had.

Perhaps she was at her best in that peculiarly Scottish literary form, recording a death. One of the few surviving documents written by James is a full and touching account of his father's death. This may have been Gamma's model in chronicling all deaths in her close family, the two most deeply felt by her being those of her infant daughter Louise and of James himself, the latter written in simple unadorned style, as follows:

October 23–26th 1909. It was on the 26th of October, Tuesday morning, at half-past six, that my dear husband died.

He had gone to London the Thursday before, after having seen Neil and May [this youngest son and daughter-in-law] sail on the 'Orcoma' for Buenos Aires. He returned on Friday, the 22nd, about five o'clock, and told me he had not felt well in the morning, and had not attended his Bank meeting, but had taken the twelve train home. He said he had been taken ill in the train, adding, 'For a moment or two I hardly knew where I was, but I pulled myself together, got my bag, and came home.' He went to bed. When Dr Floyd came, he told me – after speaking of the attack in the train – that he had not felt quite well for the last few months and got easily tired walking. The doctor said the present attack was due to over-strain on the heart, remarking, 'Well, Mr Smith, I suppose you would like to get back to your usual activities as soon as possible?' He said, 'I should like to do a bit yet.' His breathing was a little troublesome and he did not sleep much that night, and asked me if I thought he could have sulphonal, but I feared to give it.

Next day, Saturday, he was much the same. We tried reading aloud a new book of Arnold Bennett's, but I saw it was tiring him. Then he suggested Scott – 'How about "Anne of Geierstein", Oliphant's edition.' I went up for it, and read him a little, but I saw he found that tiring too, and stopped. We chatted often through the day.

We passed on to talk of the children, and he spoke of how they were all settled now to our satisfaction speaking several times of 'his wee lass', as he called the baby [my sister Sheila], and mentioning 'our son-in-law, who's devoted to us.' [Adam Forman, my father].

He asked me to pay the gardeners, and write to Allan, [third son] asking if he could be at Craigielands for the Cover shooting on November 13th, as he himself would not likely be well enough to go.

Speaking of Arthur, [the oldest son] who was not well, and

consulting Dr Moneham, and referring also evidently, to Oliphant [second son], he said wistfully, 'Poor children, I wish I saw them strong!'

Service, Oliphant's man, began from Saturday to help in the nursing. It was a great relief to me not to have to call a stranger. My husband liked having him, and as the end drew near, depended upon him more and more. He was most kind and untiring, as well as skilful.

My husband was interested in hearing of one or two friends having called to ask for him and express sympathy, saying, 'Yes, there are a few people who would help us, I think, if they knew how.'

He did not suffer pain, only discomfort at times in breathing, and I felt hopeful of his recovery, but I think he began to think otherwise, though he always spoke brightly to me, and was interested in any little thing that turned up. He had not much rest on Saturday night, and was glad when he saw the dawn, saying, 'It's not the days I mind, it's the nights.' On Sunday morning, he asked if I would drive over to church with Mr Hunt and his daughter who were staying with us. He had no concern, apparently, or nervousness, about himself, but sometimes said to me, 'Poor lass, you're getting no rest.' Mr Hunt on his return from church, kindly sent him a little note, telling him how much he had enjoyed Mr Goold's service, and this pleased my husband.

He was now obliged to sit up in bed on account of his breathing, and began to have heart attacks, which looked distressing, but caused him no pain, only made him unconscious for the time. Coming out of one, he would say, 'You are giving me brandy – have I had one of these things again?'

During the day he said to me, 'Now it's Sunday, and I want to have a little reading and prayer.' We did not read, but I knelt beside him, and he prayed, just in his usual way, giving thanks for God's goodness to us, and for guidance in the past, and asking that we might be guided in the future, and that God would bless our children. I feared he was trying his breathing too much, and begged him to stop; then I added a few words, as our custom was, and kissed him, and he seemed satisfied.

When Service said something about his getting out again soon, he answered, 'Well – it may be,' adding, 'We are in good hands.' Then a moment after, 'I have had a happy life – singularly so.' Then looking at me, he said brightly, 'And now, you see the third generation has arrived, to call us blessed!' [My elder sister Sheila].

Another time, he said, 'It is all for the best, Let one more attest, I have lived, seen God's hand through a life-time, And all's for the best Service,' adding, 'God moves in mysterious ways His wonders to perform.'

When I was alone with him, on his coming out of a heart attack, he said, 'if we have one or two more turns like this, you'll have to be thinking where you're to lay the old man.' Then 'I think it'll have to be at Liscard, beside the wee girl – not up north.' He spoke so entirely in his usual way, quietly and contentedly, that I hardly took it in earnest, and only told him, smiling, that there would be plenty of time to think of all that. He said nothing further to me, but I found afterwards he had repeated his wish to Service, saying, 'I have mentioned this to Mrs Smith, but no one else.'

On Sunday afternoon, he asked if I had written the children about his illness.

That evening Dr Glynn came along with Dr Floyd. Their report was favourable, and we were all relieved and hopeful. But the improvement did not last.

I had intended to be with him through the night as before. But about twelve, when Service came in to raise him in bed, he said to me, 'It would be far better for you to go off and get some sleep, and Service and I will make a night of it – like the Corsican Brothers!'

He had no rest. In the morning, before I returned to him, he said, 'It's been a bad night, Service – no sleep either for you or me. I did not expect to be here now.' Then he directed him to take his keys, and go down to the safe, and bring up his will, saying, 'I feel I must complete my life now.' After reading the will, he asked, 'Now, do you think you can pull me through today? I have a little matter to arrange with Arthur today, so you must keep me going.'

Afterwards, when I was with him, he asked me for a block and pencil, and wrote two pages firmly and clearly (a codicil to his will) which he asked me to give to Arthur. Later in the day, when Arthur and the lawyer's clerk were expected, he said, 'You'll let me see the boy?' I said, 'Well – not for long.' He said, 'I want to shake hands with him.' When they came, the doctor gave him some strong stimulant, and after signing the papers, he was able for a little chat with Arthur (who had been away for ten days). Arthur spoke cheerfully to him about his own health, which pleased him.

When I said something about Maria, her goodness and thoughtfulness, he said, 'Yes – she knows what it means when two doctors come, day after day.' (We had had Dr Glynn again.)

He said to me, 'I had thought of distributing some more money among the children, but it won't matter now. If I get well, I can still do it. And if not, they'll have their money so much sooner than they expected!' Then he said, 'The only rascal we've to dread now is Lloyd-George – *he'll* be dipping his hand into our pockets!'

During the afternoon, he said, 'I wonder if there's anything in the paper today,' and later he pointed out to us a beautiful sunset cloud. Between the heart attacks, which were now very frequent, he looked exactly himself, as the late afternoon sun streamed over him, sitting up in bed; and I shall never forget the picture he made then, with all his usual bright colour, the blue eyes and white hair, and the gentle, ready smile when anything was suggested for his comfort.

He several times asked Service how Oliphant was, and said, 'Poor boy!' and 'I hope my illness doesn't upset him. I know you'll do your best for him, Service. God bless him!' About six, another man came to help nursing through the night. While they were both out of the room, I said to my husband, 'Service knows this man, it seems, but he evidently considers himself a cut above him, and gives him his orders.' 'Ah, well!' he said. 'We can't *all* be owners of house property!' referring to the story of the Prince of Wales and Poole the tailor. (Service had told us he owned a house at Ripon.)

About eleven, at the doctor's suggestion, he was moved into an armchair by the fire.

I had gone a little later to lie down. When he was told I was sleeping, he said, 'Thank God!'

Then he added some loving words about me, and said, 'Ours has been a very happy life.'

Further on in the night, when they were applying oxygen, etc, he said, 'You're battling with death, Service.' Service said, 'Oh no, Mr Smith, I never say Die.' 'Aha,' he said, 'you're trying to snatch me back. But you know, a man's life here is threescore years and ten. And I have been fifty years in business in Liverpool.'

After that, he began to tell of his early home in Scotland, how his father had been a farmer, and had small means, and how he had come as a boy to Liverpool, etc.

He also told Service that he thought he was the strongest of his family, and said, 'I used to tell my family there were so many "crocks" amongst them that I felt obliged to take care of myself.'

Towards morning he spoke of Neil and May, who were at sea, hoping they would arrive safely and adding that 'he was sure they would lead a happy, useful life together in the noble work they had taken up.' (Neil had been ordained into the Church of England.)

In this way he talked at intervals, telling Service once that he felt very weak, but had no pain. He asked a cup of tea which was given him, and he drank it and said it was good. Then the collapse came quite suddenly. He only said 'Service! Oh, Service!' and caught his arm, then he became unconscious.

> They called me, and I found him sitting, with peaceful, white face, and closed eyes, quietly breathing out his life. I went for Arthur, and a few minutes after we returned, he passed gently away. The calm and serenity that were all his own through life did not fail him to the last.

By the time I came into her ken, ten years later, James was no more than a memory, her family grown up and her role was almost exclusively that of the chief executive of Craigielands. Beyond the servants' hall lay an outer ring of domestic activity which she ordered and controlled.

There was, for example, the visit of Mr Brydon the barber who came from Moffat on his bicycle every three weeks or so to cut the hair of all the Craigielands males. Mr Brydon took all his tools from his Gladstone bag and placed them on the broad marble flange of the bath. He set a chair and a dustsheet with meticulous precision and he was deeply anxious to please. He knew it was impolite to exhale bay rum over his clients and so tried desperately to breath only through his nose, but this was more than he could easily manage and his sleek rectangular face would go redder and redder until an explosion was imminent, when he would turn away into a corner and blow like a porpoise until the oxygen supply was restored.

There was also Mr McKinnon of McKimmie and Co, Tailors and Outfitters to Loretto School, who would arrive from Edinburgh with a suitcase full of kilts and tweeds ready for fitting. Mr McKinnon kept his mouth full of pins and panted, 'Ay Ay Ay Ay' whilst he probed and encircled one's most private parts with a tape measure. As he went about his work he gave a running commentary mixed in with the panting, something as follows, 'Chest Chest Chest Ay Ay Ay thirty-one thirty-one Ay Ay Ay – and the rest' – this was some sort of joke we never understood). 'Waist Waist Waist Waist Ay Ay Ay Ay twenty-four twenty-four Ay Ay Ay Ay – and the rest – Ay Ay Ay Ay.' The most dreaded moment was when he panted his way towards Inside Leg. Meanwhile the pins in his mouth undulated like a snake but he never took them out and seldom used one, preferring to employ a piece of triangular chalk, which was yet another hazard if applied anywhere near Inside Leg.

The third regular visitor on Gamma's schedule was Miss Anderson the seamstress, who wore silk blouses and horn-rimmed glasses before they were much known in North Britain. She moved from one sewing machine, a treadle Singer, to another, a table Singer, and there was always a great pile of garments and pieces in disarray on every piece of furniture in the room. In the midst of this chaos Miss Anderson remained in good order and perfectly genteel at all times, crooking her little finger a good half inch higher than the nearest contender (Aunt Jessie) when she drank her tea. But as with Marnie, the outstanding thing about Miss Anderson was her smell. It was something to do with the paraffin-like mixture in a bottle which she used for dry cleaning but it was also a deep dark body smell and when the two were mixed the result was something quite out of the ordinary: it was generally thought that a combination of exhaust fumes, the inside of a spaniel's ear and a dead rat came about as near as any to a definition of Miss Anderson's smell. One day Kaff and I were loafing about on the upstairs landing and she said, 'What are you going to do?' 'Nothing,' said I. 'Then let's go and smell Miss Anderson,' said Kaff, which we did.

There was one brief period of the year when Gamma's dominance over the Forman family was relaxed, and this was during the summer holidays which were taken on the East Coast, usually at North Berwick, sometimes at St Abbs. A cortege of five or six cars laden with Formans, their nurses and servants, bed linen and sometimes cutlery and food, would set off into the swirling August mists up the Devil's Beef Tub or over by Birkhill and St Mary's Lock. Every half hour or so the column would stop to wipe clear the windscreens of hired Daimlers, for unlike the Craigielands cars they were not kitted out with gadgets such as mechanical windscreen wipers. Some of the males might creep behind a dyke to pee and there could be a distribution of rations to the hungry (Rich Tea biscuits and apples). My father led the convoy in the Star, or later a Talbot. Jim took the rear position so that if any Daimler became indisposed he could run up to the front and report to his leader. I suppose the average speed was some twenty-five miles an hour, so the eighty-mile journey would be completed in something between four and five hours.

The strange thing was that Gamma wasn't with us. She stayed behind at Craigielands and for one reason or another this affected everyone's spirits for the better, especially those of my parents, who carried on as if they were kids let out of school. My mother bubbled with jokes and laughter – at least until her travelling headache came on; and I myself shared the general sense of exhilaration. I had a rule that every year as soon as I saw the distant sea I sang to myself alternately verses of 'The Road to the Isles' and the Prize Song from *Meistersinger* until we arrived at our boarding house.

One year we all had chicken pox at North Berwick and for some reason of quarantine I was sent home with Kaff a day or two before the main body. We travelled with Jim and an undernurse, and as soon as we pulled up at the Craigielands front door I rushed around like a mad thing. Coming home after two weeks away was every bit as exciting as going on holiday. Had the men scythed the long grass round the house? Had they finished whitewashing the stable? Had the new boat arrived? Having satisfied myself on all major outdoor points, I went into the house and found the door of Gamma's wing and of her bedroom wide open, for it was a hot day. I rushed in to find Gamma lying on her back on the bed in her underclothes, her hands folded on her breast and her mouth open. I reeled back in shock. My God, she's dead, I thought, and in her underclothes too. The horror of the scene was not so great that I did not take in the full details of the subterranean engineering that controlled her corsetry (complete with whalebones), the canvas mechanisms surrounding her bust and the wealth of tapes and strings that lay around her waist, for everything had been loosened and she was in total deshabille. Suspenders for her white silk stocking sprang out just below her hips and they were black as black and looked odd amongst the pinks and whites that covered the rest of her body. I stood gaping at her. Was she really dead? I knew about mirrors and breath and was on my way to the dressing table to pick up her hand mirror when I heard the faintest snore. I turned round sharply and rattled a table, at which she started up and blinked at me. We stared at each other for what seemed a long time. Her hair was down over her shoulders like an old tramp. 'Go out now dear,' she said, 'and I will come and see you shortly.' She lisped, for she had no teeth. I had never twigged that Gamma had false teeth, but there they were in a tumbler of water on her bedside table. Good Lord! I left the room with my mind reeling and ran to tell Kaff that I had seen Gamma stripped down to her basics. The shock of that encounter never quite left me and from that day whenever Gamma touched me or came close to me I shrank away from her. I was always aware of the whalebones and the black elastic suspenders beneath her elegant gown and when she laughed I imagined her teeth might disappear from her mouth and continue their independent life in the tumbler of water.

In the early days she represented absolute power. My father could bark out commands which were obeyed, but his right to authority was suspect and soon to be challenged. My mother used persuasion as her means of getting her way with her children, not always successfully. But Gamma was different. Gamma's word was law and demanded instant compliance, and her power extended right to the extremities of Craigielands affairs. I remember that one day two men arrived to cut down one of the great park trees, as instructed by my father. My mother was on the gravel sweep in front of the house and was horrified as she saw the axes and the cross-cut saws. She rushed to the office and a few minutes later my father walked down and told the men to suspend action – he was having second thoughts. Of course the men, who had seen my mother, knew exactly what was going on and Davy Johnstone, as he leant against the tree bole, said sagely, 'It'll no be what Mr Forman says and it'll no be what Mrs Forman says; it'll be what Mrs Smith says.' And he was almost certainly right.

Gamma's exercise of authority could be much more direct. We had seen Jim the chauffeur go white and stand twisting his cap when Gamma checked him for dallying in Moffat too long; we had seen housemaids burst into tears during an encounter in a corridor, throw their aprons over their heads and run sobbing down the kitchen stairs; we had seen visiting bishops silenced and humbled by a sharp critique of their failure to understand the true mission of God's representatives on earth; we had seen her during lunch tell Uncle Artie, the head of the family and chairman of Smith Edwards, to move his car from in front of the dining room windows because it obscured her view of the lake; we had seen my father go scarlet and drop his eyes when she challenged the truth of one of his wilder statements.

I liked to see other grown-ups put in their place by Gamma. It did them good, I thought, to be taken down a peg or two, especially my father. But as the years passed I realised that Gamma was beginning to direct her attention particularly towards me, because I was thought to be on the whole a pretty bad boy and in need of correction. This I did not like so much. I could see no way of challenging her authority and no chance of making any impression upon her inflexible will, so I bided my time. But now she never appeared in my top ten.

4

To Learn You Something

Beyond the nursery and the servants' hall there lay a wider world which offered both pain and pleasure. The greatest penance of the week was Church. Every Sunday morning at eleven o'clock two cars – the Star with my father in his Sunday tweeds at the wheel and the Charon chauffeured by Jim Rheilly – would draw up by the front steps. At ten minutes past eleven the party embarked, the children clamouring to go in the back of the Star where they could fly a dingo (a handkerchief tied to a piece of string) out of the quarter-windows, Gamma making a stately progress to the back of the Charon. As we neared Moffat all dingoes were hauled aboard, ties were straightened and there might be some last minute spit washing.

At twenty minutes past eleven we de-bussed to the horrid noise of the bell of St Mary's United Free Church (Continuing) – a title only just long enough to identify one of the smaller sects formed by the continual process of fragmentation from the old Free Church.

I hated the bell: it had no identifiable pitch but projected a splodge of sound rather like a mezzo soprano thunder sheet. Inside the church we sat in the gallery, nearer to the bell than ever. If I covered my ears with my hands I was checked (disrespectful). If I sat at the end of the pew I could surreptitiously poke a handkerchief into the one ear that grown ups couldn't see. But this only halved the torture. When at half past eleven, the bell stopped, it was as if a dentist had hung up his drill. But not for long. The organist would embark upon the adagio from the New World Symphony on a mass-produced Carnegie organ that had not been tuned since its installation half a century earlier. The choir (eight stout matrons, Mr Hetherington the chemist, Father Barr from the Treasure Grotto and the one-armed postman) would strike up the opening paraphrase and from then on the service was punctuated from time to time by renderings of Scottish psalms or paraphrases set to tunes of painful banality. Those who know the Scottish repertory only through Kilmarnock, the Old Hundredth and Crimond have no idea of the dirge-like nature of its lower depths.

The church was hideous and smelled of pitchpine and gas. What to do? One could plot and scheme future enterprises but that soon palled. One could count how many women's breasts were visible. One could recite the Lord's Prayer backwards.

The extempore prayers droned on and on – 'we pray for the armed services, for our administrators and legislators, we pray for the royal family'. So back to counting the organ pipes, and to fantasies that grew ever more violent. Suppose enough gas leaked out of one of those hideous brackets and the whole church blew up. The windows would go first and the people sitting near them might be blown out too. The rest would be dead or stunned. What would Jesus do about that? Probably very little. Probably nothing. Then there was the desperate thought of putting a machine gun like the ones I had seen in the armoury at Edinburgh Castle in the pulpit and shooting down the congregation, starting with the organist and the choir. One would have to get rid of the minister first and this would be done by elevating him by wires under his armpits, worked by a capstan on the roof. When the congregation had been dealt with the machine gun would be turned upwards and fire a burst between his legs. His blood would drip on the bible lying open on the velvet cushion on the front of the pulpit.

Back to reality. Kicking the hassocks was taboo, so was playing trains with the holy books on the pew shelf. To ensure discipline children were sandwiched between grown-ups – if they were outnumbered and two children sat together there was certain to be pinching, shoving and other forms of mayhem. Bad behaviour in church was usually quelled by a piercing look from the nearest parent, accompanied by the hissing of one's name and an admonitory gesture. If this failed, the look was repeated and a sharp blow was delivered below the level of the pew top to any available hand or leg. The third and ultimate sanction was for my father to rise slowly and quietly and lead the offender downstairs to the vestry where he had to stand until the congregation came out and saw him in all his shame. After this had happened to me twice I took counter measures and went round the side of the church and tried to dig up a particularly disagreeable laurel with a broken plank. I failed – but got my Sunday kilt jacket dirty and suffered the subsequent chastisement cheerfully. I had busted their ultimate sanction. Now what could they do if I misbehaved? As so often happens in life there never was another expulsion and so I never found out.

Second only to Church the most dreaded event of the week was dancing class. As soon as lunch was over we were hustled into sailor suits, kilts or tussores, which felt strange so early in the day, led down to the Charon and deposited with an undernurse at the Masonic Hall, a hollow cube of granite without and pitchpine within, with small high windows. It was always cold, everyone had goose pimples, and the smell of Moffat gas was overpowering. At three o'clock precisely Miss Haseldean made her entrance from the dressing room, meticulously turned out in the high fashion of the year before with white gloves up to the elbows and a deathly white face. ('You could bake a scone with the flour off that wumman's face,' said Bell.) On entering she struck the floor three times with her heel and clapped her hands. 'AT!' she cried, and again 'AT!' None of us know what AT meant but we knew that at that point we had to stand up and bow or curtsey to Miss Haseldean. 'TAKE PARTNERS FOR THE OPENING GALLOP,' she cried. Sheepishly the boys and girls took each other's hands. There were always some too shy to make a move until Miss Haseldean got in amongst them and pressed two unwilling bodies together. No one spoke a word. The girls looked straight ahead with unfocussed eyes, the boys looked at each other and winked or smiled bravely. 'AT!' shouted Miss Haseldean. 'AT! THREE FOUR,' and the lady at the piano pounded into the gallop of the day. After the gallop, 'KEEP YOUR PARTNERS,' yelled Miss Haseldean. 'FIRST THE TWO-STEP. NOW REMEMBER' – and she would demonstrate the two-step first by herself, to the full stretch of her narrow tube skirt, and then with some luckless boy as her partner.

The breaks between dances were short, the girls huddled on one side, the boys on the other, with often some outsider sitting by himself, sometimes in tears. The very small children ran back to their nannies, but this was contemptible. The girls were not an attractive lot, mostly gangling and skinny and smelling of camphor. But there were two beauties, sisters, Sylvia and Betty: Sylvia a blonde with ringlets down to her shoulders, Betty dark with hair cut in the current style of Louise Brooks. They both moved beautifully and although they did not yet have breasts it was clear that they were not far away. The boys at the top end of the pecking order made a beeline for these two at the first clap of Miss Haseldean's hands. No one was allowed to book in advance and no couple could dance together more than twice. It was a magical afternoon if one achieved the double, two with Betty and two with Sylvia. When they danced, whilst looking demurely straight into your eyes, they jammed their pelvises against your crotch, which even at the age of six caused an agreeable sensation. From dancing with these two I also learnt my first lesson about women's backs. Moira Hope Robertson was bony, Jenny Blacklock like dough, but both Betty and Sylvia had backs which were both pliant and firm and which could answer a gentle squeeze with a muscular tremor that made one breathe rather quickly and squeeze again.

Just before half time Miss Haseldean broke sweat. By now the hall had warmed up and she had been at it non-stop for nearly an hour. First one saw her brow begin to glisten, then little rivulets began to run down each side of her nose which she dabbed with a hopelessly ineffectual little white handkerchief. Then the dam burst. Her neck, her arms, her gloves were dripping with sweat which she began to sprinkle around like a watering can.

After half time Miss Haseldean reappeared in a fresh costume, fresh flour on her face and no sign of sweat. Now it was our turn, for the shorter second half was made up of reels and country dances and the hall was now like a tropical greenhouse. The climax of the dancing class was not so much one of movement, although by now everyone was going at it hammer and tongs and the boys were beginning to get rough, but one of smell. To the basic blend of gas and pitchpine overlaid by Miss Haseldean's perfume (something like the essence of chocolate creams) there was now added the camphor-smell of the girls' best dresses, the residue of a good deal of fairly uninhibited farting, Miss Haseldean's sweat, which was sweet and sickly, the body odour from the pianist which increased in strength as the dark patch under her armpits spread downwards to her waist, and finally a blend of all the several different sweats from some twenty or thirty young bodies. One could hardly even distinguish the smell of one's own sweat (always pleasant) in the midst of this rich mixture.

Parties were dreaded almost as much as dancing class. They usually fell into three phases, the first of intense shyness and total inertia whilst sergeant-majorish grown-ups press-ganged the children to play pass the parcel or musical chairs – games for which our nursery had a profound contempt. The only way to shine was to refuse to play at all or else to bugger up the game in some spectacular way such as throwing the parcel out of the window or withdrawing a musical chair just as a heavily built adult was about to sit down on it. But such feats were rare, and belonged more to the fantasies and mythology of the nursery than to real life.

Phase two was tea. The nature of the sandwich was a matter of great importance. Michael, the greediest member of our nursery, would disappear on arrival and come back with news: 'Eggs, cucumber and lettuce,' he would say. That was a good menu. At the bottom of our list were Bovril, dates and bananas. Ham and chicken were the top, jam acceptable but as common as dirt, and all party jams tasted the same.

The third phase of a children's party was when the boys got rough. It took three or more boys together to reach this exalted state and it usually started as a breakaway from some action game, such as blind man's buff. A squad of boys would start racing up and down corridors, perhaps beating a gong or chasing a dog. If the frenzy were intense enough the boys would get into a trance-like state and become impervious to grown-up interference. They would beat the starched bosoms of their nannies with clenched fists shouting, 'GO AWAY, GO AWAY, GO AWAY,' also totally disregarding the orders of the mothers, and if captured would wriggle and twist like an eel in a trap.

Getting rough led to one of the most mortifying moments of my life. It was an all-age party and I was perhaps eight and Sheila sixteen. She was sitting demurely on the bottom step of a staircase talking in a grown-up way to a young man with the early signs of a moustache and a posh English accent. She had an ice-cream on her lap. I was in the midst of a gang of boys who had got rough. I stopped opposite her with a whoop, seized her by the legs and pulled her down the last step to the ground. Her skirt was above her waist, I could see the top of her stockings, her suspender belt and her knickers, her ice-cream fell on her chest and she bumped her head on the last stair. At once I knew I had done something dreadful. I bit my tongue and raced out of the front door to a damp and gloomy lawn where I walked about in misery until my name was called and we went home.

I sat opposite Sheila on the folding seat in the Charon. I tried to seek out her hand and hold it, but she pushed me away. Then I began to cry, then – much worse – I realised that she was crying, a thing I had never seen before. I knew it wasn't the bump, not the spoilt dress, she might have laughed about both of them. It was because boys and men had seen her suspender belt and her bare thighs just where they went into her knickers. She was ashamed. I had made her ashamed.

When we got home Sheila went straight to my mother and I was sent for. She had heard the full story from Sheila and was white with rage. 'Denis,' she said, 'hold your hand out.' She hit my hand perhaps a dozen times with a ruler. It didn't hurt in the least, but it was the most terrible punishment of my childhood. As soon as it was over I threw myself upon Sheila, kissing and hugging her, and gradually she relented, gave me a little cuddle and led me to the night nursery sobbing uncontrollably.

We seldom gave parties at Craigielands except at Halloween and Christmas for the tenants' children. Both were uncomfortable events. The boys wore damp-smelling tweed jackets and shorts, the girls the cheapest frocks from Patterson's in Moffat. On arrival they moved into the hall and stood in a huddle, speechless and petrified. For the Halloween party in the centre of the hall there was a shallow tin bath with apples floating in it. My mother shook hands with each child – 'How are you, Sam? No, it's Fergus, isn't it?' 'Willie, Ma'am' the visitor would say. Gamma sat in a distant armchair surveying the scene. My mother would then sit down at the Steinway. 'When I play a chord,' she said, 'the first three boys will duck for apples. Sam, Willie and Johnnie, you be the first three.' The children looked at each other in perplexity. There was no one called Sam. Nevertheless when she struck the first chord three boys advanced to the tin bath and put their heads down. 'Now,' my mother cried, 'keep on ducking until you get an apple or until the music stops.' And she would swing off into one of her own compositions, sometimes becoming so absorbed as to forget that she was part of a game and would play on until the wretched boys nearly drowned.

I hated this scene. I knew all the children quite well. We threw stones at each other or had met at rat hunts or at harvest time. Now they had become puppets, wiping their noses and saying Yes Ma'am. Soon we nursery lot were allowed to mingle and we all showed off abominably. We had practised getting apples out of the bath under our chins. We could crack nuts faster, eat apples off strings better and roll turnips more accurately than the tenants' children. Sometimes the class barricades were dented by a small fight between one of ours and one of theirs. I remember once beckoning to Willie Boa to join me under the table where I had a store of stolen sandwiches and we spent some time in happy collusion, just as we would on the farm. But for the rest the ghastly routine worked its way to the finish, Sir Roger de Coverly, with no one able to dance it properly, and on to the farewell handshake with the gift of a poke of sweeties and a warm garment.

I met the same children in a different relationship at the two great fixed events of the year, the Beattock Show and the Dog Trials.

Beattock village is no more than a strip of semi-detached butt and ben cottages on each side of the main Glasgow road, built to house the Caledonian Railway workers at Beattock station, the base from which a fleet of tank engines pushed the heavier trains over Beattock summit. The west side of the village belonged to us, the east side to Beattock House. Our side had the village shop, the village hall, the smithy and its emergent garage. Their side had nothing. Our side shone white with lime wash, the steps 'redd up' with soft red chalky stone; their side was plain granite and scruffy. Our side had a rich variety of personalities and surnames; the other side was clannish and once when a stranger there asked for a Mr Moffat he got the reply, 'Moffat? There's naebody of that name on this side. We're all Johnstones and Jardines here.' Which was approximately true.

The Beattock Show was held on a field between the village and the railway. Every fortnight through the winter and spring the all male committee had met in the village hall under the chairmanship of my father, deciding the range of classes for scone-baking and chrysanthemum growing, appointing judges and devising a programme of events. The gate was all important and bitter arguments raged over the rival drawing power of horse racing and a brass band. For two years it was horse racing, but the jockeys tended to get drunk and one year one fell off and was kicked in the head.

I was right on the rails when this happened, and not yet familiar with drunkenness I had seen men sitting or lying outside the Black Bull in Moffat on a Saturday afternoon and I had heard other men speaking in loud angry voices, but we were hurried away from such scenes and it was therefore with absolute horror that I watched the jockey fall, his eyes glazed, foam on his lips and a string of strange words coming from his mouth. He got on to his knees as a second horse flew by and caught him just on the cheekbone with its off hind leg. The jockey of the second horse looked back to see how he was, and he too fell off. But the first one was a shocking sight. Blood streamed from the gash on his face, he put both his hands up to contain it and danced around in tiny circles screaming. Then he started to vomit. Some people ran out and laid him on a rug and all around I heard tongues clucking and realised that they were not sorry for him because he was drunk. But I was sorry for him and too shocked to move until the ambulance came and took him away.

On show day I had a special role. I sold programmes. This started when I was a very small boy and went on until I was the head programme seller, responsible for counting the money and handing it over in £5 bags to Mr Lock and Andrew Grieve at the gate. The other programme sellers were all village children and there was tremendous rivalry. When the day was wet and the gate low each arrival was surrounded by a pack of children thrusting bedraggled programmes under his nose. When the day was fine and it was a good gate it was all we could do to keep up with demand. But wet or fine the moment of truth came when each programme seller crawled under the brailing of the Industrial tent and in the aroma of trodden grass and newly baked scones, made his account to the head programme seller. Underneath the trestles the two would crouch, counting the unsold programmes against the takings. If there was a discrepancy the matter was taken to Mr Bulman, the schoolmaster and treasurer of the show. By this time he too had difficulty in adding up, and it was not until long afterwards that I realised that he was regularly drunk by four o'clock on a show day. The result was that it was difficult indeed for a head programme seller to reach a satisfactory final account. Sometimes the total of £50 or so was out by as much as half a crown. I thought I knew where the dishonesty lay but kept quiet because the suspects were bigger than I.

As the day wore on the pressure on the programme sellers grew less. By three-thirty there was no need for more than two on shift at the same time. By five o'clock programmes were given away free. Liberated from toil and with their wages of two shillings to spend, the team relaxed with ice-cream cornets and a group inspection of the animal tent. We felt part of the management and swaggered a bit, straightening the prize tickets, putting water in the animals' bowls, jumping up on the trestles to knock a nail in. Andy Smith tried to change the prize cards on the long-eared rabbits' cages to give his father first instead of third, but he was spotted and reported to his father who strapped him that night with his leather belt, which was a full six inches wide.

Children again played a leading part in preparing for the Dog Trials, held on a bleak hillside and in those days attended only by enthusiasts. A single rope held up by stobs marked the spectators' standing ground. This plus a strip of canvas to conceal the gentlemen's urinal (there was none for the women – goodness knows how they managed) was all that there was on the ground. But the children were in demand for all sorts of jobs early in the day, buchting (penning) the sheep at the head of the course, carrying tea-urns up the hill, marking the shedding ring and later in the day once again selling programmes. The Dog Trials were boring to watch and the boys spent most of the time fighting. Sholto and I fought the two Calder brothers, Jim Calder against Sholto, Donald Calder against myself. The method of fighting was always the same. No blows were struck but the combatants wrestled, pushed and pulled until one or other was spreadeagled on the ground, his opponent sitting on his chest and pinning his arms down decisively. The Calders always won. This was noted by everyone present and the men on the farm would be sure to refer to it. 'Donald Calder,' Jock Wilson would say with a grin. 'He's the one to learn you something.' This was humiliating and since we didn't enjoy the fighting at all it is difficult to understand why we did it.

The Show, the Dog Trials and the school playground were the places where I encountered the village children en masse. I was afraid of their mockery, always trying to avoid the Little Lord Fauntleroy image by being dirty and as rough as they were. The ultimate embarrassment was when we were dressed in tussores for dancing class. If the Charon stopped in the village one could be seen in all one's shame. This once happened when all the children were streaming back from school, and it was a long stop. On the other hand, they were a good audience and if one could catch their eye with some bold gesture or make them laugh, there was some glory in it. I formed loose friendships with one or two of the boys and had romantic thoughts about at least one of the girls, but nothing much came of either.

On the whole I learnt more about the outside world when I was alone. From the age of four or five we were allowed to wander about on our own provided that we stayed within bounds. These were gradually expanded as one grew older, from the rectangle of roads surrounding the house to a larger enclave bounded by the white gate, the three sisters (three oak trees grown, it was said, from the same acorn), the laundry and finally anywhere within the two lodge gates and the farm.

In making a sortie from the nursery on one's own there was seldom any plan or aim, and indeed no expectation beyond the hope that something would crop up. One might not get past the cold press in the basement if it were being filled with ice, nor the chute at the top of the back door steps if the carts were discharging coal down it with a crash like thunder and black clouds of coal dust, but usually one reached the garage or the stables without too much distraction. Here there was certain to be activity. My father enjoyed experimenting with the internal combustion engine and one might well find the front end of the Star completely dismantled, the cylinder head, the nuts, bolts and smaller parts on a grease-stained green canvas. Jim's overalls would be covered in grease too, and he might be engaged in a boring repetitious job like filing down a casting, in which case he would talk endlessly, or he might have reached a moment of crisis, straining his muscles, holding his breath and going red from the neck up. If talkative, Jim's main topic would be family gossip, jocular and a little cheeky. He grinned all the time he spoke and often broke into his laugh which was famous and imitated widely in the nursery. Did I know that Annie Burns got a letter every Thursday with the same handwriting on it? Must be a fella. Did she talk about him? Aggie Crosbie's George had crushed a finger in a monkey wrench and it had to be amputated, that meant cut off! (Forearm gesture as if with a surgeon's knife whipping off his own finger.) How long would it bleed? A fortnight, easy. Did Miss Sheila know where she had lost her hat? He knew (tremendous laugh). No, he wouldn't tell me. He would only tell Miss Sheila. It would get her into trouble if my father knew (another laugh and a sidelong look calculated to excite maximum curiosity). No he wouldn't tell me. (Enormous laugh.)

The garage abutted the old harness room, which one climbed into through a low window. There was not much tack left but Tom Rheilly, Jim's father, would sit polishing a bit or putting dubbin on a bridle. He was the shape of an old jockey, with crinkled cheeks, and always a quid of tobacco in one of them. He didn't talk freely like Jim but would answer questions carefully and precisely. He had driven my father and mother to their wedding in the carriage? Yes, with the two greys Sam and Simon. What did he do during the service? Steadied the greys on the church gravel where he could see Miss Flora through the window. Was it raining? It was, and windy too. And so on.

The workshop was part of the same complex but here conversation was less easy, partly because of the Petter oil engine driving numerous pulleys and belts, partly because the workers were absorbed in what they were doing and gave monosyllabic answers to questions. But there was almost inexhaustible interest in watching their hands at work and trying to decide what it was they were making. The workshop smelled of wood shavings, engine oil and putty.

A little further on was the laundry, in action on only two days a week. One was always made welcome by the washerwomen Mrs Brown and Mrs Little, but again they were so active working the huge mangles, pulling out the mighty warming frames on each side of the central furnace or waltzing and pirouetting through the steam holding the corners of huge linen sheets that they had little time for chat. It was a spectacular act but one soon tired of it, partly because the laundry smell of soap, hot metal and damp cloth soon became offensive.

The sawmill was the workshop on a grand scale. Outside there were the dams, the sluices and the heavy black water turning the eighteen-foot waterwheel like a spinning top. Inside the scream of the saw as it met the tree bole on the bench, the anguished descending scale as the saw slowed down and the wheel almost stopped, the acceleration as the tree was backed off, and then the whole cycle over again and again. But it was dangerous work and the men were preoccupied.

Many years ago Bob Wilson's uncle had his hand cut off. Davy Johnstone had his leg broken when a spruce bole slipped between the trolley and the saw bench. The only time for a little conversation was at lunch (a can of cold tea and a 'piece') at ten o'clock, but they were tired and tended to joke and tease in response to serious questions.

Down the other drive lay the garden with its team of three who worked separately. Croall, the head gardener, was always ready to pass the time of day but he was patronising and a bore from Cumberland, and did not produce much enjoyment. Jimmy White, the one-armed second gardener, would never stop what he was doing. He had to work twice as fast as anyone else, I thought, to make up for having only one arm. He would carry a bucket or a basket on his hook and we wondered how heavy it would have to be before it pulled it off. His son, also Jimmy, was handsome and dashing and rode a motor bike. He had no time for little boys, so the garden was socially a poor place; but it was full of interest for the explorer on his own with the many micro-climates of the greenhouses, piles of rich-smelling leaf mould, fruit in season, a puzzling sundial, all dominated by the huge high walls that enclosed the Scotch acre of vegetables and wall fruit.

Wandering alone one learned most, for on walks with an under-nurse and other children you still carried the culture of the nursery along with you. Sometimes there were events. The undernurses might fall into conversation with a young man and if one listened closely one could pick up quite a lot. Once we passed a car smash with groups of people standing around, one of them lying on the ground, but we were hurried past and were told that the man was just resting, which was patently untrue. Michael claimed he had seen blood. One day Bell, Sholto and I were on a mission to take some game to Mr Finlayson, a pheasant and a duck. This placed Mr Finlayson, the minister of the local Beattock church, low in the scale of my grandmother's regard. He would have received two brace of pheasants if she had approved of his theology and his style of life. But neither was satisfactory and it was his ministry that had driven the Smith family to worship in Moffat rather than in their own parish church of Kirkpatrick Juxta, Beattock. He was a pitiable soul. On opening the manse door he appeared unshaven, smelling of whisky, wearing a dressing gown over his dog collar even in the afternoon.

To reach the manse we had to cross a bridge over a burn and pass the school playground. The burn was in spate, the playground was full and I was carrying the game. As we crossed the bridge a glorious impulse seized me and I threw the duck and the pheasant into the middle of the torrent. Bell immediately gave chase and was joined by a dozen or more schoolchildren who raced down each bank whooping and yelling and trying to get the birds back to land. I stood on the bridge like a great impresario and watched the scene with satisfaction. In the end a stout boy waded in up to his knees and fished them out. They were presented to Mr Finlayson with an apology. I expected punishment but received none. Indeed the story was told in the nursery with undisguised relish. As for Mr Finlayson, he eventually committed suicide by wandering out one dark night on to the railway line. We hoped it had been the Night Scot that killed him, for there would have been some glory in that, but it turned out to be only a local goods train.

There were ports of call on some walks, such as the village shop, kept by Maggie Hutchinson and her sister Mearn. Maggie had a hunch back, whiskers and red carbuncles on her nose and was tireless in her praise for the Smith family, Craigielands and all associated with it. 'What beautiful eyes you've got, Mr Denis,' she would say, gazing into them soulfully, her head shaking from side to side. 'Beautiful eyes,' Mearn would repeat. 'What a lovely address your mother gave at the Institute last week,' said Maggie. 'Lovely address,' said Mearn. 'Here's a wee poke of sweeties for ye,' said Maggie. 'Poke of sweeties,' said Mearn.

We always got a poke of sweeties. They were the cheapest – turnips, huge boiled sweets that made the cheek distend, or jelly babies, tasting of soap or of liquorice which were disliked by one and all and given to the dog.

I hated Maggie Hutchinson. I hated her shop and in particular I hated her fat sister Mearn. But she was an institution revered by grown ups, trotted out before visitors and called 'the salt of the earth' and 'a great character', and her sickening flattery was repeated – certainly as a joke, but with pleasure nonetheless.

Along with walks there were outings. Sometimes an undernurse and two or three children would go on an errand in the pony trap which could go well beyond walking range, perhaps as far as Miss Anderson the seamstress to take her a piece of material, or perhaps a note to neighbours at Auchencastle or Marchbank Wood. There was competition to hold the reins and to handle the brake and here Tom was totally in command, deciding also who should get out to walk up hills, who could run behind on the level and when and for how long we could stop. The undernurse faded into insignificance. She hardly exchanged a syllable with him and turned her face away every time he sent a jet of black tobacco juice flying over Tibby's crupper.

More prized were outings with Gamma in the landaulette. Our own carriage horses had been disposed of some years earlier so he hired this vehicle from Moffat twice a week in fine weather to give her the carriage exercise to which she had been accustomed all her life. She only took one child with her at a time and saw the outing as an opportunity for interesting and improving conversation. When I was her companion we sat side by side on the slippery leather seat with a huge carriage rug, mackintosh on one side and tweed on the other, placed across our knees. I could not see much unless I stood up, which I was allowed to do on the Dumfries road but not on the drives or the country roads. Gamma would talk about people she had known, giving examples of exceptional kindness or unselfishness. Sometimes she would tell of people who behaved badly, being rude or thoughtless, and this was more interesting unless one realised that one of the examples was rather close to what had happened in the nursery earlier that week. There was one event, however, that claimed all of one's attention, and that was when the horse stopped to piss.

One of the most favoured circuits took us over the Red Brae, a steep ascent up a rough road made up of red clay and stones. When the horse reached a short plateau about half-way up he would stop, stretch out his hind legs, groan a couple of times and give vent to a foaming cascade of piss that made a little watercourse down the hill behind us. It was a noisy, smelly and highly spectacular event and only I seemed to be aware of it. The driver sat impassive. Gamma continued her conversation as if nothing was happening. Apparently only the horse and I knew what was going on. When it came to defecation the horse didn't stop, but trotted in with the steaming brown lumps falling onto the big black strap that ran round his buttocks. Again this spectacle was riveting to me but completely ignored by my two companions. I wondered why people had to shut themselves away to perform their natural functions. If they did it on the lawn other people could pretend not to see them just as if they were horses. After all, they didn't do so much. From that time on I treasured the occasions when adults went blind in the face of dogs lifting their legs, or copulating, animals in fields relieving themselves, bullocks practising for the real thing or even our swans when they showed a desire to raise a family.

Communal outings were less frequent and usually took the form of picnics. The house party of up to twenty people would pile into cars and drive a dozen miles or so to one of the picnic spots favoured by my mother. She was an enthusiast for picnics; nearly all the other adults disliked them. It was often windy, sometimes wet and always cold. The food was excruciating, huge slabs of bread with ham or cheese between them, cold pieces of congealed mutton, dry crummy cakes, ginger pop and apples. Someone would try to erect a wind break. Someone else would try to light a fire. A child would fall into a stream. Another child would be sick. As the shivering adults cowered on rugs with mackintoshes over their heads you could hear my mother's clear soprano ringing out, 'It doesn't matter what the weather is like, there's nothing like a picnic, is there?' From picnics I learned that grown ups frequently have to pretend to be enjoying themselves when they aren't.

The most precious outings were birthday treats, which we were allowed, within reason, to choose ourselves. One year I chose to ride round the lake with Tom and to have a picnic lunch with him on the seat on the far side facing the house. This was approved and Tom put on his coaching boots and his brown derby in honour of the occasion. We mounted at the front door and rode down the south drive, Tom on Tibby and myself on the little Shetland, Biddy, and looked back to see a crowded nursery window watching us go. We rode slowly round the lake until we got to the seat. Tom let me open his gold repeater watch. It was worth ten pounds he said. He unscrewed one of his back teeth and let me hold it, black with chewing tobacco as it was. Then we ate our lunch, a bacon sandwich and oatcakes and honey, and then slowly we rode back up the north drive to an envious reception committee on the front steps. The whole treat cannot have lasted much more than an hour, but it was an hour of the purest happiness.

We got another glimpse of the outside world on the weekly trip to Moffat for shopping. This was when we were dragged around by adults into strange-smelling shops to try on shoes or new underwear. Sometimes we had to undress in front of fizzing gas stoves to try things on and the assistants used to turn discreetly away whilst undernurses pulled tapes and undid buttons. It was a disagreeable and undignified business. Then one would hang about waiting, sometimes in a shop, sometimes in the Charon. We would look out for the Moffat prize figures who scored 10 for whoever spotted them: the White Wolf, a six-foot-six baker's assistant, white from head to toe and carrying a bowl of dough on his head; Mr Gunn Budge, the provost and owner of the shoe shop, with his waxed moustache (Minnows when they grew their whiskers were called Gunn Budges); Dr Park, known as Resurrection Willie from his habit of telling patients that but for his arrival at that moment they would have been dead; the one-armed postman; Sergeant Gillespie, the senior policeman of whom we were a little afraid; and Father Barr, a diminutive bald-headed Glaswegian who kept the Gift Emporium. Those who scored five included Tony the ice-cream man; any elder of our church; and a woman without a hat. There was a lot of cheating, and in the end each sighting had to be witnessed before it was accepted as valid.

Once on the way back from Moffat Tom crashed the Charon into a hedge. He had never really taken to the motor car, and used to talk to it while he fumbled with the gears as he would to a horse. 'Geddup Wuman,' he would say as he released the brake and, 'Steady now steady,' as he slowed down. But no exhortation could avert the inevitable crash. It came as he was about to enter the north drive and met an oncoming car. He was not sure whether he should pass it on his left or on his right, so he took the safer course of steering into the hedge. No one was hurt but Tom gave up driving from that day. I was not in the car but up at the house when I saw the Moffat party coming up the north drive on foot. Kaff pulled me aside and said, 'Sheila and I have been scratching our cheeks all the way up the drive so as not to look white and frighten Mother and Dad.' She was always one to heighten the drama.

A visit to Edinburgh offered the furthest and deepest penetration into the outside world. In two hours by train you were transported into this foreign place, where people pushed you and didn't say Good Morning. The air was harsher, there were houses everywhere, everything looked different and smelled different. The mere fact of wearing your best clothes all day put you into a strange mood. Nearly every reason for going to Edinburgh was a bad one: dentists, doctors, visiting aunts, hanging about in shops while my father bought fruit or fishing tackle. Once I was on a trip to Edinburgh with Nan, she and I alone, and after the dentist we had a jolly tea at McVitties and went on to the Caledonian Hotel – the Cally to us – to play cards until it was train time. For some reason now forgotten Nan made a mistake about the train time and when we got to the ticket gate our train had gone. 'Stand there like a stone until I come back,' said Nan, giving me over to the ticket collector. She dashed off and came back with her most worried face. There was no train until nine thirty that night and it had a bad connection; we would not get to Beattock until one o'clock in the morning. So we sat in the Cally for hours, then took the train to Carstairs where we sat in a waiting room for hours. Nan was very loving and worried and I remember her saying to my mother afterwards, 'Every time he said "I wish I was home" it went straight to my heart.' As for me I made the most of it and boasted about the whole episode most dreadfully. My most preposterous lie was to tell the rest of the nursery that I came home so late that it was the morning and I could hear the birds singing.

Such were my excursions beyond the limits of the nursery into the outside world. Soon to be just as influential was the way in which the outside world came in to me. One day I saw the Matchetts – a father-and-son team of electrical engineers who would turn their hands to anything – and my father messing about with wires from the big oak tree to a pole on top of the house. When we went down after tea we were taken down to the office where there was a big cabinet like a coffin filled with light bulbs, wires and electrical gadgets. On a table there was a small black box with holes in it. Solemnly we were all given earphones and the jack plugs were stuck into the holes. I heard a small crackly voice in my ear reading *Treasure Island* and then other voices talking to children (not, I thought, to me), and every now and then they said in a sing-song sort of way HELLO TWINS. It was 2 LO. It was the beginning of the wireless. It was the British Broadcasting Company's signal coming from Daventry to Beattock through the air. From now on my father was to spend half his life (with the Matchetts) fiddling and experimenting with this new thing and my mother was to take her duties as a listener very, very seriously.

But perhaps it was not 2 LO that was to become the most important voice from the outside world. When I was only three or four that voice could only just be heard on the nursery Victrola but was louder and stronger on the machine downstairs. In the nursery I heard the El Capitaine March, Gems from *Martha* and the incidental music from *Monsieur Beaucaire*. Downstairs I heard Calve, Patti and Melba like singing gnats, with an accompanying noise that I later learnt to be the distant sound of an acoustically recorded orchestra. At that age, although I listened more than anyone else. I did not know that within the next few years that instrument, the gramophone, was going to be my tutor, my most beloved companion and my guide along the high road to all music.

5

Such a Decent Chap

From the early eighteenth century each first-born Forman son of our line was called Adam, and with equal regularity each one became a minister in the Church of Scotland. There was Adam Forman of Carmunnock, Adam Forman of Kirkintilloch, and Adam Forman of Innerwick. In 1843 the Innerwick Adam came out at the Disruption. Perhaps he could not persuade his flock to follow his example or perhaps he heard an irresistible call from the other side of the Forth, at any rate he moved to Leven in the Kingdom of Fife, and set up a Free church, known to this day as the Forman church. It has a window bearing his name in heavy gothic lettering amidst a wealth of puce and orange stained glass. Alas, continuity was broken when his eldest son, the next Adam Forman, was drowned bathing in the river Leven while still a youth. His brother, John, as a second son and lacking the name Adam, evidently did not care to risk a career in the service of God who although known to be against the Establishment might think that this was too great a break with convention. So after a sojourn at the Royal High School in Edinburgh and at Glasgow University he settled down amongst the Liverpool Scots as a marine engineer.

Having invented a steam capstan of some significance he married a dull woman, Mary Taylor, who subsequently became known to me as Grannie Forman. Socially she was a clear cut above her husband, spoke in a cultivated English voice and was tall, plain and grumpy. They had two children, Adam and Jean. John contracted tuberculosis and it was thought his condition was aggravated by the Liverpool climate, so the family sailed for the Canaries before the children were of school age. For the next ten years John Forman was gainfully employed in building the mole for the harbour of Las Palmas. He never came back to England.

It was in Las Palmas that Adam, my father, spent his childhood. There seems to have been little rapport between him and the other members of his family. He never spoke of his father at all and it is clear that the mother and daughter already formed a compatible and conventional pair whom Adam regarded as the enemy. Indeed his pony Potro seems to have been first in his affections, an then one Hilde Ross, the wife of a distant relation, who had travelled out to Canary to tutor him. Adam spent his days roaming the island, riding bareback on his pony, and had no schooling to supplement his tutoring until in the late summer of 1890 he departed for Loretto. For the next five years Loretto and Craigielands were to be his two homes.

Loretto, in Musselburgh just outside Edinburgh, was then under the spell of itsfirst great headmaster, Hely Hutchison Almond, known to all as the Head: an educational theorist of an unusual kind, an eccentric in the grand manner, a hero and at the same time an object of good-natured ridicule to his pupils. By the end of the century he was certainly the most famous schoolmaster in Scotland.

His main preoccupation was to re-examine all conventions and when necessary to defy them, especially those associated with what he called 'Mrs Grundy', and to run his school as a community 'visibly living according to the dictates of right reason.' 'Right reason' reflected, of course, his own view of what was right. His biographer defines the main objects of his system as building Character and Physique, cultivating Intelligence, learning Manners and gaining Information. This rather uncomfortable piece of shorthand did truthfully reflect his scale of educational values, so long as it is understood what each of his five labels signify.

His ideal of Character was something between that of Arnold of Rugby and the concept of Scouting to be promoted in the next century by Baden Powell. Indeed in later life many Lorettonians found themselves much at home as scoutmasters – some, including my father, moving into the upper reaches of Scouting as District Commissioners, Silver Wolves and the like. The Head's character requirements were that a boy by manly, truthful, pure and a sportsman. The last is a word that became central to the Loretto ethic. 'A good sportsman cannot but be a good man' was one of the Head's tenets. A 'sportsman', apparently, not only played rugby football or cricket or fished for salmon with total commitment, but he was also generous in defeat or disappointment. Thus when he lost a twenty-pound salmon or was bowled at cricket he must smile bravely as if nothing had happened, although his competitive spirit (an essential element of the sportsman) must have been badly bruised. A sportsman always put the team first. 'No matter how good a batsman or a bowler a boy may be,' said the Head, 'there is no place for him in Loretto cricket eleven if he slacks in the field.' But the Loretto sportsman had extended characteristics, such as great daring. When Blondel attempted to cross Niagara on a tightrope he was a sportsman. When a ridiculous anecdote was told about the first Lord Leverhulme who, when informed he was almost broke and only had £10,000 of credit left was said to have replied, 'Spend it on Advertising', two uncles and my father, all Lorettonians, chorused in unison, 'What a sportsman'.

Manliness was much the same as Baden Powell's Gordonstoun's and Outward Bound's manliness, but was carried by the Head into several unexpected areas of life, such as poetry and – most surprisingly – music. 'Manly' music was typified by the choruses in Handel's *Messiah*. But not all. 'Surely he hath borne' was melancholy and 'He trusted in God' the Head called the mocking chorus: neither was permitted in Chapel. Mendelssohn was sentimental. Diatonic music was good, chromatic passages (Spohr) were abominable. He once booked two seats in the back row for a performance of Tannhäuser to which he took my father. He sat enraptured during the choruses but as the chorus left the stage he left the auditorium and paced about in the foyer. 'O Star of Eve' was not manly.

Truthfulness carried its simple connotation, and Purity must have meant freedom from sexual fantasies, avoiding masturbation and not getting into bed with other boys, since there were few other opportunities for impurity available. Purity of thought, a concept that was frequently on the lips of Lorettonians, apparently meant something rather more than this, but it is not easy to grasp exactly what.

These were the elements that together made the Head put the greatest store on Character. Gaisford, when Provost of Eton, once said to a parent, 'Madam, I am here to teach your son Greek, not morals.' The Head thought this was 'the most abominable and immoral thing ever said'.

In pioneering the importance of developing character the Head had fellow spirits, but in his belief that a healthy physique was of prime importance he was at that time a lone voice, and appeared at his most cranky. In the 1860s English public schools still wore the traditional garb of academia, the masters gowns, the boys Eton jackets or – lower in the social scale – subfusc suits with stiff collars. It was thought dangerously unhealthy not to wear a cap or hat outdoors. The Head wore a white flannel shirt, open at the neck, a pair of white flannel trousers and carried a Harris tweed jacket over his arm. He wore no hat and no overcoat and was generally thought to be a little mad.

The boys did not immediately attain this state of grace in dress. For the first decade of his reign they wore red and white horizontally striped stockings, knickerbockers, lavender waistcoats, tweed jackets and a glengarry, that most ludicrous of all Scottish headgear. The glengarry was the first to go. Waistcoats went in 1868. At the same time a rule was introduced that if the temperature in any classroom reached 60 degrees fahrenheit coats must be discarded. In 1872 anatomical boots were introduced, square boxlike structures designed to give the toes 'natural space'. At the same time flannel was adopted for all clothing next to the skin and the school uniform became a symphony in flannel, white shirt and shorts and a scarlet flannel jacket.

Open necks and no constriction of the lungs became a central tenet of the Head's creed. He would not allow a Cadet Corps in the school because of the high choker collars and the constrictions of a tight military jacket. When soldiers fainted at a Trooping of the Colour he would write to *The Times* pointing to the Army's total disregard for the principles of healthy dress. To Loretto dress he attributed great virtues: 'What induces vigour with us,' he wrote, 'is that everyone wears a flannel shirt open at the neck and no starch. High-collared boys would naturally want to lounge about and gossip at intervals' (the Loretto word for breaks between periods of school work). 'Our boys are always doing something with a ball at such times.' He sometimes took his passion for hygiene to extremes. 'If a child of mine were to become a Roman Catholic,' he said, 'I should be sorry. If he became a Mohammedan I should endeavour to reason with him; if he wore tight boots and unhealthy clothing I should disown him.'

The Head's concern for the physical welfare of his boys went far beyond the matter of dress. Cold tubs before breakfast, followed by a brisk run in all weathers, kept the circulation going. 'Grubbing' between meals was forbidden. 'What I consider to be the greats blot on our public schools today is what I will briefly call the "grubbing system". Food sent from home should be consumed at meals or in the case of fruit directly after them. Between meals there should be no eating whatsoever. The stomach needs to rest. "Grubbing" in boys is very apt to pass to tippling in men. "Grubbing" is as bad for boys as smoking is for men, yet schoolmasters seem to regard the former as not evil at all and take an absurdly overstrained attitude about the other. I can tell the extent to which grubbing flourishes at a school by the complexion of the boys. Grubbing is debasing both to intellect and character. High thinking is not consistent with luxury and self indulgence.' So much for 'grubbing'.

The remaining three of the Head's educational objectives – Intelligence, Manners, Information – were not so remarkable, nor so strongly pressed as the first two. 'Intelligence' must have meant the training of the intelligence, for even then intelligence was known to be a natural endowment rather than something that could be taught. In teaching the boys manners he was singularly successful, particularly in the matter of gallantry and courtesy towards women (still called 'the fair sex'). The old story of the woman entering a room with a Wykamist, a Harrovian and an Etonian in it would have gone quite differently had they been Lorettonians. In the original the Etonian said, 'Would you like to sit down?' The Wykamist offered her a chair and the Harrovian sat down on it. Three Lorettonians in these circumstances would each have seized a chair and caused considerable physical and social confusion by begging the lady to sit on theirs. Such a scene I have witnessed more than once. All Lorettonians were desperate to show good manners but they often lacked the social perception to do it gracefully.

One must take the Head's objective of Information to cover the whole matter of academic study, which many people then thought, as some still do, to be the chief purpose of a school. He soon realised that a systematic course of teaching in the classroom was not for him. He was impatient, discursive and inclined to make the boys run around the classroom when he got bored. But he would read right through the *Iliad* or the *Odyssey* with two or three chosen pupils on a Highland fishing holiday. He would spend two hours in his study explaining a principle of trigonometry to one boy. He would address a class with great enthusiasm on the subject of the stars. He abominated the examination system, saying, 'Scripture and History when taught for examination are an utterly different thing from the same subjects taught to elevate and widen the thoughts.' He had a low opinion of English literature. 'What is the use of talking to you,' he said to one scholar, 'when you would rather be Tennyson than the Duke of Wellington and I would rather be W. G. Grace than Tennyson?' At another time he said that he considered Lord Shaftesbury to have been a greater Englishman than Shakespeare. And so it was that at Loretto, 'work' took a low place in the scale of priorities.

The Head was probably at his best addressing the school assemblies (or Doubles as they were called) on subjects ranging from the importance of flannel next to the skin to the policies of Gladstone, the innate selfishness of the game of golf, the virtues of Handel as opposed to Mendelssohn, the performance of the school rugby team or the disastrous effect upon character of eating biscuits between meals. Second to these extempore addresses came his sermons, which he worked out with care and delivered more than once. In these he extolled the virtues of manliness, but also of humility and gentleness, virtues not prominent in the record of his life.

The undoubted success of the Head, who ruled over Loretto for over forty years, can be explained by only one thing. He treated boys as equals, he understood their sensibilities and saw life from their point of view. One of his golden rules was never to wound the amour-propre of a boy. He hated sarcasm and saw it as 'the fatal blemish' in a schoolmaster. 'Your boy is one to whom any sort of lecturing or preaching can do nothing but harm,' he wrote to a parent. 'The way to influence him is to get on good terms with him and to give him what boys call "a good time". Boys will often then do anything one wishes without pressure.' 'The Head's confidence was easy to win,' wrote Sidney Lamart, one of the Craigielands set, 'and once won it was a thing to retain, to treasure.' He showed his confidence by placing the leadership of the school almost entirely in the hands of the prefects, who had beneath them a hierarchy of heads of Rooms, who were given total authority in their own sphere at a very early age.

The boys laughed at his more extravagant ventures but only amongst themselves. To the world outside they were fiercely loyal. Some stories, however, leaked out and one was the story of Loretto time. Mr Napier, the drawing master, lived in Edinburgh and to make the time of his classes fit with the arrival and departure of his trains, the starting time had to be put a quarter of an hour earlier. This meant that all classes had to be put a quarter of an hour earlier. Rather than face such disruption the Head simply changed the clocks by fifteen minutes to Loretto time. Long after Mr Napier had left Loretto time continued – it was not synchronised with Greenwich until some ten years later. New rules, even absurdities such as this, were seldom introduced by dictat. Each major change in the regime was first proposed by the Head in Double, then debated by the whole school, discussed between the Head and his prefects and then either introduced or not depending upon what was thought to be the consensus.

Gradually the good sense of the Head's views on dress and hygiene became accepted. Numbers – fourteen when the Head bought the school in 1862 – went up to over a hundred. He was invited to become headmaster of other Scottish schools. A public school in New Zealand was set up on Loretto principles. No doubt through the bush telegraph of the Liverpool Scots, James and Gamma heard reports of this remarkable man. They went to Musselburgh to visit him and were impressed. Their two eldest sons were entered for the school, and in due course the rest followed.

James Arthur Smith (known for some reason which remains mysterious to me as Julia), the eldest of the five brothers, went to Loretto in 1886. Thomas Oliphant (T.O.) the same year. Allan Ramsay (Sconnie, another inexplicable nick-name) arrived there in 1889, Bertram (BS) in 1890 and Neil in 1892. My father Adam Forman went to Loretto in 1890 at the mid point in the succession of Smith brothers. Of these six boys three were Head of School, all played in the first fifteen, three got blues at Oxford or Cambridge for rugby football, one captained Oxford and Scotland. In 1909 my father became chaplain and housemaster at Loretto. A year earlier Sconnie had returned to be headmaster. Thus in the forty years between 1886 and 1926 there were only eight full years in which one or more of the Craigielands set was not present at Loretto either as a boy or as a master. To a greater or lesser degree they all adopted the Lorettonian creed.

Well, not quite all. The two elder Smith boys, Julia and T.O., passed through Loretto comparatively unscathed, both getting first class degrees at Oxford. They were perhaps closet Lorettonians rather than Lorettonian activists. They wore waistcoats and ties by preference, read *The Times* and showed a considerable interest in the outside world. Julia drank whisky and in my time at Craigielands overtly grubbed between meals. But beneath their superficial failings their moral tone was Lorettonian, they used the good words – 'sportsman' and 'gentleman' for men, 'a ripper' (for women) and their apparently worldly attitude rested upon a sound substructure of Lorettonianism. Sconnie Smith was more openly a Lorrettonian in all he did and Adam Forman was an activist, a leading disciple of the Head and all he stood for. Bertram followed Adam's example but in a more relaxed manner and Neil, the tail-end Charlie, tagged along in the Loretto manner but was more inclined towards holiness than perhaps a good Lorettonian should have been.

Adam's father died in 1892 and thereafter his mother and sister returned to Liverpool. But he spent most of his school holidays at Craigielands where he and Bertram were to unleash Lorettonianism in full force upon the Craigielands set. Until then the customary round of placid country house pastimes had included tennis, croquet, amateur theatricals, boating, shooting, fishing, picnicking and occasional dances. The wagonette would go over to Craigieburn where Uncle Sam and guests spent the summer. 'Tennis all day,' notes one Craigielands team member, 'and we beat.' Theatricals ranged from a synoptic version of *Lohengrin* performed by T.O. with a stuffed heron as the swan and with my mother at the piano, to wild sketches in the Doric written by Bertram, and performed in the village hall, always including a part for a drunk which he played himself. These may have been slightly unconventional activities but nothing to what was to come.

Lorettonians were notoriously more at home in all-male society and in the Craigielands 'family' they outnumbered the females by six to one, the one being the youngest of all, Flora Smith, my mother. Friends who came to stay were also mostly male and Lorettonians and from this floating group of family and visiting Lorettonians a central core was formed, the Palship.

The Palship consisted of five members. B.S., Adam, Neil and two other Lorettonians, Angus Lindsay (Beelzie), a cousin, and Edvard Melville, a friend. The Palship first came together in order to navigate the Lowland rivers in punts: it was in March 1896 that four of the five embarked on the river Annan in one heavy ungainly craft, designed to carry a crew of three, the Triumvir.

After six days and nights they abandoned ship at Dormont, some ten miles short of their goal, the Solway at Annan. By August of the same year a fleet of five punts plus one luggage punt had been designed and built, and the Palship proper set sail again on the Annan. After five days of successful navigation they reached their final camp (Camp of Triumph) in Annan.

This was followed by trips down the Tweed (seventy-five miles in twenty-six hours on the water), the Nith, the Annan again (twice), the Esk, many land tours by caravan and finally the War Tour of the Annan which ended at Millhouse Brig (Camp of the Ultimatum) on Wednesday August 5th 1914 with the receipt of a telegram: 'Great Britain has declared war on Germany.' My father was twenty years old and Head Boy of Loretto when the Palship made its first trip. On its last he was a married man of thirty-eight with two children.

Punting down the rapid Border torrents was a different matter indeed from the slow and stately style of punting at Oxford and Cambridge. The punts were six foot long and about half as wide, built for strength. Luggage punts with tents and kitchen gear aboard were in two and in flood water there was a sense of high adventure in shooting rapids, dropping over weirs and navigating the fast rocky channels.

At night the Palship drew their punts on to dry land and set them in the form of a laager. From this rose a tent which was designed and redesigned on each trip. It contained a cooking annexe and and waste disposal system. After the evening meal the Pals would smoke and drink toddy and 'yarn' into the small hours, each pal lying on his own punt until yarning gave way to sleep. They rose late, ate brunch at noon, struck camp and embarked in the early afternoon. When the water was low and shallows lay ahead they would commandeer farm carts and the strange caravan of cart-borne punts would move on to deeper water by road. They were known to the local inhabitants and to the press as The Voyagers and aroused much interest. The log reports three hundred people on the bridge at Berwick to welcome them. From time to time they indulged in a touch of theatricality: they vied with each other in the extravagance of their scarecrow dress: each punt had its 'colours', a camp flag was hoisted and struck each day and they enjoyed playing up to the stream of gawping visitors.

This sort of ragamuffin venture, although in the best traditions of Loretto, appeared to horrify many of the more conventional citizens. One Sunday after church Gamma took a provincial German lady guest to visit the Pals in camp. On the return trip she remarked,

'It is *extraordinary*. On a Sunday morning in Germany the young men at play put on their good clothes and parade. Here the young men dress dirty and sit in boats like bargees.' At least this is the way the story was always told.

It was a sense of comradeship and shared adventure, common enough in the armies of the world, that mainly held the Palship together: but there was another binding agent in the knowledge that they were being very Lorettonian. Punting came to be seen as a test of manhood and sportsmanship which admitted the five into a brotherhood outside and above the rest of society. Within its fraternity the doctrine was simple and based on love: love of each other and love of the Palship's ideals, which were beyond the comprehension of common mortals (and never properly defined by any of the Pals themselves). The spirit of the Palship generated powerful emotions. Thus my father, in his farewell speech to the Palship on the eve of three years' exile to San Francisco, said:

> This is the last ceremony the glorious Palship will celebrate together for the next few years. Let it be a right merry one. True the outside world will not lament the "breaking up" of the Palship but that is because they do not know the great Spirit of Palship which binds us together. It is inexplicable to them because the scope of words is too small to hold it. Words after all are only finite and how would you have the infinite described by the finite? No, it only belongs to those who feel it – it is only our Souls that can know it because they too are infinite. Therefore it would be absurd to limit our Palship to words – it is enough for us to know that it is an infinite reality.

Today one can hear reverberations of a quasi-masonic order in the Palship. An oath of secrecy was there on some of the diaries and in the expedition logs each Pal was given a title. B.S. was always known as the GPM (Grand Punt Master). He was their leader and driving force. Adam, the second in command, was known as the Chief Engineer, Beelzie was chief Cook, Neil Luggage Master and Edvard something now forgotten. The spirit of the Palship was invoked in difficult times: when Beelzie had four teeth removed, Adam wrote in his Liverpool log – 'Beel had a fairly bad time. 4 big uns out last Tuesday. Walked home, however, and attended office next day. His punting spirit rose bravely above his troubles, and to all outward appearances he was in supreme form.'

From his diaries it is clear that to Adam the Palship lay at the centre of his life. The Pals wrote lengthy letters ('flips') to each other, full of 'therapeutics', passages of high emotion. The punting logs to which all Pals contributed contained, as well as a daily account of each voyage, poems (an ode to the chosen river before embarkation was obligatory), invocations to the spirits of the Palship, 'gags' (rather appalling jokes) and Purple Biscuit writing, in which fantasy was given a free rein. The logs had a sacred position in the order of the Palship and later would be read aloud whenever one or more gathered together of an evening. The mature B.S., writing in 1914 in an 'Afterword' to an edited edition of the punting logs, described the spirit of Palship as follows:

> I have left out many pages, some dozens of pages, of Therapeutics as we so loved to call them with our passion for divorcing a word wherever possible from its true meaning. They are in every log, (before the Grand Tour) and they run through the record of almost every day. They are often fumblingly expressed and they read queerly nowadays. Perhaps they are a little brazen and sentimental. But the interesting point is that they are *there* . . . that they speak on nearly every page of our burning loyalty to one another, our belief in our power to stand together against the world, our faith in Punting as the Greatest Thing on Earth. During the last four years of the last century if you had asked any member of the Immortal Five what was the thing above all others that he would most like to do, what was his greatest joy on earth, he could only have replied Punting.

But the Pals could not consort together all the time. when not in punts they had to mingle with Craigieland society, and there were women in it. Although their value as mothers and nurses had long passed away, Pals had to be polite to them – and if they were 'jolly', or better still 'ripping', it was not impossible to find pleasure in their company. There was one exceptional female, almost as good as a boy: my mother Flora. She was the youngest of the Smith family, pretty, sprightly and talented, and at school at St Leonards, of all the Scottish girls' schools the nearest to Loretto. She was the link between the Pals and their kind and young women of her own age – her cousin Mabel Oliphant and several school friends.

This group of perhaps ten to fifteen young people formed a closed society which centred on Craigielands and which stayed closely in touch until matrimony picked them off one by one. They showed a remarkable indifference to the affairs of the real world. When absent from Craigielands they kept in touch with each other through 'flips', which were passed from hand to hand, and whenever possible they would speed like homing pigeons back to their real or surrogate home – Craigielands Beattock.

There was a whiff of William Morris about the way they thought and in the way the women dressed, and of the pre-Raphaelites in their told-to-the-children approach to religion. But it is doubtful if they had first-hand experience, or indeed any knowledge, of either movement. Their interest in the visual arts was almost non-existent. They were, however, constantly discussing music which started for them with Bach (mathematical) and then leapt to Beethoven (a ripper), Schubert (tuneful), Schumann (deep), Brahms (great) and above all Wagner. They were all keen Wagnerites and spent a great deal of time trying to find out what Wagner was. Since there was no gramophone or radio and none of them, except B.S., had been to Bayreuth this was pretty difficult. Even a piano score of *Tristan* did not help much. B.S. did his best by writing little notebooks (and a bigger one on the Ring) spelling out the leitmotifs and hinting at the deeper significance of Wagner's use of the Neapolitan sixth. Although no musical scholar and entirely self-taught, he was musically literate and knowledgeable and was clearly the Guru of Craigielands music. My mother sang Schubert, Schumann and some operatic arias, nearly all of the set strummed on the piano, T.O.

composed and Neil played the flute. If it was not strictly speaking a musical household, it was certainly a household that listened to and talked about music. In later years their concert-going record was prodigious.

In literature they were un-Lorettonian in their conventionality. Homer, Virgil, Milton, Shakespeare, were the traditional poets. Burns was good – *and* Scottish. They had no knowledge of French, German or Italian literature because they could not speak French, German or Italian. The Russians were unknown. The best of the most recent poets were the Lake poets and the greatest poet of all was Tennyson. Sir Walter Scott was the best novelist – *and* Scottish. Thackeray was good but a little dull. Meredith and Eliot were modern and difficult. Jane Austen? Nothing known. *Alice in Wonderland* was a work of genius and Dumas in translation was a rattling good read. As to philosophy and science, so far as they were concerned Darwin did not exist except as a topic for a Sunday lunch debate, nor were their minds in any way disturbed by the arrival on the scene of Freud and Marx.

The Craigielands set, although they displayed the Loretto spirit of rebellion in matters of dress and social behaviour, accepted without question the conventional views of their elders on politics and religion. They were in fact an inward looking group of nice young people who were isolated equally from the upper crust of Scottish society and from the world of work and money. Isolated too from the working-class people who served them in the house, garden and estate, in their intercourse with whom they mistook a mutual bonhomie for friendship. They saw no one but their own kind, they evolved their own special vocabulary, and in short they remained a group of cheerful and vigorous children within the Craigielands cocoon until at last they had to meet the realities of life. For some, amongst them my father and mother, that moment never arrived.

In the summer of 1894, when my father was eighteen and my mother was fourteen, they went off together to the Mill Dam, high in the woods above the back village. Sitting in the fork of an oak tree above the water they agreed they should become engaged to be married. When this news was made known, probably some two years later, Flora's father was not pleased. He liked Adam but thought the idea of an engagement at so early an age between two such innocents belonged to the world of fantasy.

So the engagement was left as a private pledge between the two of them and on leaving Loretto at the age of just over twenty my father joined Balfour Williamson, a firm of general importers and exporters in Liverpool. His uncle Robert, a Scotsman on the make, was a director of the company and no doubt responsible for Adam's introduction. The firm allowed only three weeks' holiday in a year, which was not ungenerous, but for my father a drastic reduction in the time available for staying at Craigielands and for punting.

Robert Forman found his nephew feckless, full of eccentric notions and lacking in a sense of his familial duties and also in that essential to any self-respecting Scotsman – a desire to make money. Since he had taken control of the family's affairs when his brother John died, he felt responsible for his nephew. It was he who had arranged the evacuation of his sister-in-law and niece from Las Palmas to Aigburth on the west and cheaper side of the Mersey, where they were installed in a small stone-built house, Carlinda, which became the family home. There Mary Forman lived, badly off, and appropriately distanced from the Lindsays and the Robert Formans in their more stylish and commodious homes on the Wirral.

Luckily for my father two more of the Pals, B.S. and Beelzie, also worked in central Liverpool in the Smith family cotton firm, Smith Edwards, which was headed by Sam (now Liberal MP for Flint) and James (The Guv of Craigielands). The Balfour Williamson office was only two blocks away. From August 1898 to April 1899 my father kept a log, on the lines of the punting logs, and from it we can get a vivid picture of his life at that time. The Liverpool log begins in August 1898 when my mother was still at St Leonards and the two remaining Pals, Neil and Edward, were at Loretto.

In the Liverpool offices work began at eight thirty, sometimes eight o'clock, and finished at six, sometimes later. The Pals stuck closely together, often lunching at the Croc, the office restaurant, and playing rugger on Saturdays. (It was always touch and go whether they could 'bilk' the office in time to avoid the financial disaster of having to take a hansom.) They assiduously attended concerts in Liverpool and Manchester, went for long walks on Sundays, yarned about the next or last reunion of the Palship and the next or last punting trip.

The most popular venue for a yarn was the Club. This was one room, or possibly two, in Carlinda which had become a sanctuary exclusively for the Palship. On the walls there were maps of the punters' rivers, Annan, Nith and Tweed. Other trophies of the Palship adorned the room, including the ceremonial oar that each Pal was given at the end of a successful trip. The oars were in punting colours – green and white – and a legend in gold letters recorded the main feature of the voyage. My father's mother and sister Jean inhabited the rest of the house and were known as the Pigs. It is impossible at this distance to gauge how much affection, if any, and how much contempt this title carried. Certainly Adam and his mother harboured a mutual dislike that lost little over the years. She strove to live respectably by the conventions of the day, Adam scorned them. She was proper, he was outrageous. He also had a tendency to slip into a mode of pious self-pity whilst at the same time behaving to her, as she would think (had she known the word), like an absolute shit.

'I'm like Siegfried in the second act,' he wrote in the log – 'longing for the love of a mother. I have a mother, true – but not love. It is a horrible fact – there is a deep gulf between duty and love, the former I perform, the latter I cannot feel, although I have tried hard. It is a big want.'

There are, however, episodes in the Log which cast rather a different light on Adam's attitude. 'But better than all this,' he wrote one day, 'I have just fixed the Mater to go North on Friday – "Peace perfect peace" etc. We hardly hoped for it so soon but it is pleasant when you fall in with a bit of luck unexpectedly.' And two days later: 'Following episode is true. Mater refused to go North so I took a return ticket to Edinburgh, ordered a cab for the morning and told her to Go. Result, she caught the 10.05 a.m.

North this morning from Exchange – Peace perfect peace etc.' But not for long: 'Hear there is a distinct danger of the Mater coming home tomorrow. Sent her a wire yesterday to stay away – and hope for the best.'

He and one of the Pals would frequently play a Sunday morning trick on both Pigs: 'Mater got safely away to church and GPM and I walked about 10 miles having previously ordered dinner at 1.45 instead of 1.30 and put the clock back a quarter of an hour so we had comfortable appetite for a meal at 2.' But this practice was not to go on undetected: 'As usual I put the clock half an hour back last night but unfortunately the Mater discovered this by means of her own little clock and delivered herself of a long oration about clocks being delicate things etc etc and hoped I would not do it again. At this Sunday brekker crisis a brilliant idea struck me – and put *her* clock back too! – So before Beel and I started on our Sunday walk we put *both* clocks a quarter of an hour slow, ordered dinner at 1.45 and as usual had it at 2 p.m.'

But he did not have it all his own way. Sometimes his mother confronted him: 'Sunday 30 October. I was accused at dinner today of not taking up my home duties by the Mater (also she says Bob) but I failed to elicit any description of this species – and had to be satisfied with a most irritating vagueness. Church cropped up, however, and I gave my view as follows – that if A asks B to go to church in order that B may keep A company A shows very little respect for his religion and none for B's principles. I confess this sort of thing worries me badly.' But perhaps not quite enough to suit Uncle Bob who was forced to weigh in from time to time: 'August 13 – Bob gave me a fearful cursing – conceited, heartless and going to the dogs. There may be some truth in what he says but I would be more inclined to believe it if a Pal told me so.'

And in due course one of the Pals did tell him so: 'Sunday 18 Dec. Beel slanged me heartily and with a certain amount of reason for my general treatment of the Mater.' Beel's slanging was hardly surprising because on the return from the last Richter concert in Manchester Adam and Beel had evidently had a contretemps: 'I was not in the best of tempers especially as the Mater and Jean missed the 10.15. However I adjourned to the Croc and had a spanking lemon squash which set me up. Beel wouldn't come and I left him and Pigs standing in the middle of Bold Street, latter cackling badly.'

His seniors at Balfour Williamson were no more to my father's taste. He was a junior gentleman shipping clerk and soon began to have doubts as to whether he was in the right job. 'Bob and I don't hit it off a bit . . . the show's getting serious and I can't stand this sort of rot much longer. Unless matters clear up a bit I shall chuck Messrs Balfour Williamson and Co and set off on my own hook.' These doubts were intensified when Bob proposed to put an end to my father's habit of taking his holiday a week at a time (in order to allow three punting trips a year) and to make him take three consecutive weeks at a time of the firm's choosing. This led to the following outburst: 'So our holidays are to be planned by their Most Gracious Majesties the Right Royal partners of B. W. and Co, rulers of all things above and below for ever and ever. Oh ye pickled onions! Oh ye omnipotent lobsters, ye little snails and popinjays – what next and which is the nearest way out? Oh Guthrie [a director of B.W.] you spiritual teetotaler [sic]. Oh Bob you chewer of shilling Havanas. Oh B.W. you skintillating [sic] mass of grabbery, how long shall your bellies be filled with Tinned Apricots and Lemon Cling Peaches, how long shalt thou pot the wily salmon? Put not your faith in Potted Salmon nor in Canned Fruit, nor even in dried Fruit but rather try if ye may not touch the spirit of love and truth – the spirit of the True Sportsman. Think ye not that I am happier with my Punting Pals, with our great spirit of love, than ye are with all your thousands?'

But there was a snag. The Pigs were badly off and in business – 'biz' – he earned at least a little money. If he were to become a schoolmaster he would actually have to spend money. He wrote a long letter to his friend the Head saying that in spite of the Pigs and Bob he thought he was wrong in not being a schoolmaster. The Head offered a contribution of £50, and if the fishing were good £100. B. S. was in favour of schoolmastering and finally Adam had a good talk with Bob. 'We got on much better than before but he is still strongly against the show (ie schoolmastering or doctoring) but talked in a gentlemanly manner and threw a new light upon biz – and on doctors. We have quite a mutual understanding. He thought I could get on in biz if I stuck to it and that I would be chucking a probability for an uncertainty. This *does* hit me I confess not so far as I am concerned, but the Pigs. His next best argument was that granted a man has the spirit in him he will be useful wherever he is.' My father concluded that he should await developments; which came some considerable time later in the form of a flip from the Head advocating Biz. 'He may be right after all, but I'm going to have it out with Bob some day soon before I decide finally.' It seems a little peculiar that the Head changes sides with such speed. Perhaps he had received a flip from Uncle Bob or even James Smith, for there are grounds for speculating collusion between the two in arranging the next move in my father's career.

We do not know how soon James Smith and Gamma had become aware of the understanding between my father and my mother. Certainly they knew of it by this time and they still thought my mother (or 'the Child' as she was universally known) far too young at seventeen for any serious thought of an engagement. Adam Forman was a very good chap but completely untried in the matter of earning a living. But although Flora's parents disapproved, they were strangely lax in enforcing a separation.

The Liverpool Log has a private note on the front. It is only to be read by the Pals and Flora 'on condition that she skips the places marked with crosses.' (There are no places marked with crosses.) Almost immediately (August 1898) Adam is on holiday at Craigielands where he 'yarns with the Child in a hay loft.' There are declarations of love: 'Child – whatever people may say and however much they may jeer at sentiment – I love you.' The daily entry often ends 'Goodnight Pals, Goodnight Child'. On a later visit to Craigielands in September, 'Only a few commonplaces with the Child – our yarn got bushed owing to maternal complications.' On his return to Liverpool he seems to have been chastened, for he ruminates, 'We are far keener on each other than we ought to be.' Again in the same week he writes, 'Thank heavens there's the penny post [he had just received a bundle of flips from the Pals] – but to you Child it is forbidden – yes forbidden, and I must obey.' So either James or Gamma had put their foot down. No letters.

In December an entry in the log reads, 'I heard from the Mater that Bob wants to put me into the Valparaiso department but Balfour is against it.' Early in January, when the Child was staying at Dalmorton, 'I spoke – I spoke on the Sandhills. Spoke what? Well it might bore you Pals so I will pass on merely saying that I was very very happy.' And ten days later 'the Child has established a precedent by feeding here on Tuesday night with Neil.'

About a month later the blow fell. He was to be posted to San Francisco for eight years. At this point the log fades away, the only reference to his exile being the cryptic 'Was booked for S.F. last Monday in 6 weeks.' There is no mention of a final showdown with Bob, nor of doctoring nor of schoolmastering, nor is there any outburst nor any signs of protest. Could it be that Bob and James had seen him separately or together and told him that if he served well in San Francisco for eight years he and the Child could be married?

There is one final gloomy entry in the Log. My father had flu at Craigielands and was stranded. 'So I'm here alone. Heaven knows how I love this place. It is one of the saddest of my farewells. Do you remember GPM when our Palship was in its youth? Do you remember the trips down here from school? Do you remember watching the sunrise from the farm (I think the 5 were there)? I shall never forget that. Those hills – I can see them with my eyes shut. Everything, every tree, every hill and stream, seems sacred as it was then, fresh, green and bright. I love you Craigielands – and to leave you for 8 years. Here all punting began and ended. Nine years ago, just before I went to school, I visited you with my Pigs. B.S. took me in hand and little did I think then what an important part you were to play in my life. I shall love you, love you always and perhaps come back in 8 years to kiss you again. Farewell. And then to crown all – Child *you* live here.'

And in his farewell speech to the Palship he said: 'On the subject of the Child, you all know the "status quo" and on this score it gives me the utmost satisfaction to leave you all here with her.'

The next we hear of my father is from one Harry O'Rorke, who worked in the San Francisco Missions to Seamen. On May 15th 1989 he wrote to his family – 'There has come from Liverpool a fine healthy young man, Adam Forman. He is going to live with Mr Karney and help us here two nights a week.' Mr Karney and Adam were to become lifelong friends as a result of their working together in San Francisco. The mission there had a role far beyond tea and sympathy. The clippers returning from San Francisco round the Horn to Europe found it desperately difficult to recruit crews for the dangerous journey home, thus the ship owners organised gangs to dope and shanghai any unwary seamen on shore leave. Karney and my father quite often had to use physical methods to save their charges from the gang, although no doubt prayer was also of assistance. In later life Karney came to stay at Craigielands. He became my godfather, and his son Peter a sort of honorary guardian to me during my early teens.

On New Year's Day 1900 B.S. met my father in San Francisco and returned with a letter from him to the Pals. After an excessive display of therapeutics and a great deal about the nature of the Palship, my father announced:

1. That I have decided to come home, go either to Oxford or Cambridge, and be ordained.
2. That I am writing to mine uncle to say so.
3. That it is my duty to stick to biz until my family are provided for.
4. That if I am ordained the call will be perfectly clear. God makes no mistakes – if I am wanted he will arrange things accordingly – and until I am wanted I shall work here.

It appears that God did want him, but not immediately. I have no precise date for my father's return from San Francisco but he played rugby for Cambridge in 1904, 1905 and 1906 and was ordained in 1907, and therefore it would seem that he spent at least another three years in San Francisco.

Whilst still at Cambridge in April 1906 my father became formally engaged to the Child. Two years later they were married. He was thirty-two, my mother twenty-eight. It was fourteen years since they had come to their arrangement in the oak tree above the Mill Dam.

My father's first appointment was as a curate at Bishop Auckland, where because of his high lifestyle (which included a gig drawn by an American trotter) he was known as the millionaire parson. He did not stay long since he objected to wearing a dog collar on the grounds that it was un-Lorettonian and refused to serve Communion if 'only three or less old ladies turned up'. If the congregation wanted a Communion service they had to do better than that. The Bishop had a few words with him and he departed to become Chaplain at Loretto, where his brother-in-law Sconnie (Allan) was soon to be headmaster.

After he had spent three years schoolmastering at Loretto and two years as Gamma's estate manager at Craigielands, World War I broke out. My father at thirty-eight did not have any idea of joining the combatants. Instead he organised the collection and despatch of sphagnum moss for field dressings. This was his moment of glory: his organising powers were considerable and soon, with a battalion of Women's Army Corps workers at his back, he was organising sphagnum moss for the whole of Scotland. From far and wide lorries drove up to Craigielands laden with dripping sacks of moss which was spread to dry on frames on the tennis courts. Then, after a number of simple industrial processes carried out on machines invented by my father, the moss was shredded, packed and despatched. It was said to be twenty times more absorbent than cotton wool and to have saved many lives. For his efforts with sphagnum moss my father was awarded the CBE. Nothing he ever did in his life before or after was so practical or successful.

My father was still immersed in sphagnum moss when I was born in October 1917. I do not remember the operations themselves but numerous relics of the sphagnum moss age survived as a vivid reminder of wartime life at Craigielands. All manner of sphagnum detritus was piled into the Moss Room, a large loft where the final processes had taken place. There were wooden monorails and wide flat sleepers and two wheeled wooden trolley-like giant scooters upon which the army of women had pushed sodden sacks of moss from the water-logged swamps to the lorry at the road head. There were jute sacks in their thousands, looms, frames, Heath Robinson machines of all kinds, heavy clothing for the army women as they fought their way through the Scottish winter, and in one corner, like grain in a Pharoah's tomb, a dusty pile of sphagnum moss itself. One day when Davy Sloan was short of seasoned wood for a rough job he went into the Moss Room and broke everything up. What he could use he kept, what he could not, he burnt. I came upon him when half way through this act of vandalism. I was deeply upset and pleaded with him to stop only to be told that my father had sanctioned this orgy of destruction. But Davy was a kind soul and he spared one of the giant wooden scooters as a concession to my distress. It may well be there in the stable lofts at Craigielands to this day. In retrospect I was unhappy because in my subconscious mind the Moss Room was a monument to something noble and good that my father had done.

I believe that I genuinely wanted to love and respect my father. All around me there were people who appeared to do so but to me he always remained a figure of fun and a source of aggravation. I remember many years later, when I was Head Boy of Loretto – a position that seemed to me to call for outstanding qualities of character and leadership – wondering how it could be that my father, of all people, had once held the same office. I put the question to The Lam, Sidney Lamert, then Chairman of De La Rue, and a long-time member of the Craigielands set. He thought for a long time and I could see that he was pretty well gravelled by my question. 'Well,' he said after a long pause, 'well, you see, he was such a decent chap.'

And indeed he was a decent chap, nearly everyone else thought so: the family, his friends, all of Loretto, the curlers, the church people at the presbytery and the shopkeepers in Edinburgh and

Moffat. Decades later porters at the Caledonian Hotel in Edinburgh would ask, 'And how's your father? Keeping well? A great gentleman.' But was he such a great gentleman? He was hail-fellow-well-met; he was eccentric and would talk to anyone about anything; he was a character, and to generations of boy scouts, right up until he died a week before his one hundred and first birthday, he was an inspiration and almost a saint. Sometimes I felt ashamed of not liking him better, but then a moment's reflection would steady me up. The simplicity of his faith, his unquestioning belief in the rightness of everything he did, were beyond question, but was he not fooling most of the people for most of the time and himself for all of the time? Perhaps my judgment was sharpened because during my boyhood he saw me as a rival who could diminish the amount of attention paid to him, and to some degree he punished me for this. It is an interesting fact that of the four Forman brothers two take the same view of my father as I do and one, Sholto, who was the closest to him and in whom he always placed great trust, had, and still has, an affectionate and high regard for his good qualities which to his mind greatly outweigh the follies and eccentricities which I have so fully described.

There was a coda to the story of the marriage proposal in the oak tree overhanging the Mill Dam. My mother told me that she and my father had carved on the same oak tree the names of six children, two of them two years apart, then after four years another two, and again after four years two more. I know that some of the names were wrong (my father wanted to call the girls the names of trees, such as Ash and Birch) and I do not know how the spread and split of the sexes corresponded to what was to come, but in real life the pattern of births corresponded exactly to what was said to have been carved on the oak tree on that day. When my mother told me this story I immediately ran up to the Mill Dam to seek documentary evidence, but there was none to be found. Indeed both parents seemed a little vague as to which tree it had been. And when I asked her whether one of the names she had carved was Denis, she gave an evasive reply. Nevertheless, I believe the story to be essentially true.

6

What's Right and What's Wrong

So it was when I became a sentient human being and moved on to the Craigielands stage I found myself playing a part in Act II of the ongoing saga of the Craigielands set. The permanent residents were now my father and mother, Gamma, Nan, the undernurses, six children, Marnie and the servants' hall, numbering perhaps twenty souls.

My Smith uncles visited frequently, those that were married and had children taking up much more space than when they were single young men. Gamma's sister Annie, Grannie Forman and my father's sister Aunt Jean were other regulars. Beelzie had a sheep farm five miles away and came to lunch on Sundays. There were two absentees: B.S. had died of consumption, leaving vivid memories and a widow who lived close by, and T.O. had become a recluse in Eastbourne.

But this was only the beginning of it. Cousins, distant relations, connections (Scots for relations by marriage), friends and holy men of all sorts, especially missionaries, abounded as putative guests, and Gamma was hard put to it to find a time when the Pink Room or the Oak Room could be freed for spring cleaning, which sometimes did not occur until August. When we children attended Sunday tea there was usually a dozen or more people round the table.

The house guests did not trouble us much except those that had children. These were apt to overcrowd the nursery and introduce strange nannies and dogs into a region that was already crowded enough. Some of the grown ups patronised us, which we disliked, others tried to charm us, and this we disliked even more, but there were a few, a blessed few, who treated us as young adults.

Amidst all this coming and going the troika that ran Craigielands remained stable and constant. There was my mother, who was the supremo of all smaller children, my father who ran the estate and all things outdoors and Gamma who ran the household as a whole, including, it can be said, both of my parents.

My father was a very clean man. When the house was full he would use an outside lavatory two hundred yards away in the woods. My elder brother and I were expected to accompany him there to perform our functions in turn. When he emerged he would stand in the doorway, for there was little light inside, grope in the pockets of his capacious Norfolk jacket and produce a handful of cotton wool, detach a morsel about the size of a pea and carefully lodge this inside his foreskin. This operation must have been designed to prevent the last drops of urine from soiling his trousers in the summer when he wore no underpants, or his combinations in the winter.

Children are susceptible to smell and our family – as you will have gathered by now – had particularly sharp noses. We often described friends and neighbours by odour rather than by appearance ('she's liquorice allsorts and camphor – lavender and rotten apples – maid's drawers') yet never ever did any of us detect a whiff of body odour from my father even when he had sweated profusely by reason of cutting down a tree or running about with a rugby football. Similarly his breath was always neutral and never was a fart detected.

His spotless record of cleanliness was all the more odd because he never took a hot bath, believing as he did that it destroyed the thin film of body oils that lubricated and kept wholesome the surface of the skin. Instead, each morning he would run three hundred yards down to the loch with two or three shivering boys at his heels, cast off his towelling and plunge into the water stark naked. He swam six strokes in a circle and emerged blowing through his nose and sluicing the water off his arms and legs, displaying as he did so three bright red patches of pubic hair which shone out with singular brilliance. Once back in the house, panting heavily (for the return trip was so steep that it was tough going to keep running to the end), he would shave with a mug of hot water, a cut-throat razor and sphagnum moss shaving soap. His close association with sphagnum moss during the war years had left him with an exaggerated notion of its merits. He claimed it to be both antiseptic and therapeutic and he had caused to be manufactured, God knows where and how, not only sphagnum moss shaving soap but sphagnum moss toilet soap and sphagnum moss ointment. My grandmother, however, did not allow sphagnum products in the downstairs bathroom and my mother prohibited their use in the nursery, so my father made slow progress through the vast stacks of tins and cartons which stood in a press alongside boxes of air gun pellets and cine films.

When the ice was too thick on the loch (cat ice or a thin surface film were disregarded, but ice an eighth of an inch thick could inflict nasty wounds) my father and his followers resorted to cold baths. From his bathroom emerged the same snorts and the same sounds of slapping water off wet limbs and we deduced he was deploying the loch routine without the swimming. It was a matter of debate amongst us whether he made his entry into the bath face downwards in a constricted dive or in the more conventional arse-first manner.

There was evidence, too, of ancillary washing. This usually took place before dinner in the bathroom, audible but never visible. When the house was full he would resort to a huge ewer in the bedroom, filled (naturally) with cold water which left tell-tale splash marks on the carpet.

I was once lucky enough, when we were staying in the Cally, to witness his washing procedure through a door left open. He stood with a towel around his hips and splashed cold water into his armpits and over his chest, rubbing it in with sphagnum soap. He rinsed, and then dropped the towel and stood on it with legs apart and knees bent in the posture of a jockey with no horse beneath him. He then repeated the washing performance, giving special attention to his crotch. This was a memorable sight.

His bathing and his ablutions were not designed for the benefit of others, that he might look clean and have no smell, they were to satisfy an internal imperative – the need to brace oneself up, to keep up to the mark, to maintain standards. Rigorous personal cleanliness was an item in the code of moral and physical discipline, no more, no less.

Nevertheless, he did look an exceptionally clean man. His balding head shone in the lamplight, no doubt lubricated by natural oils, for he never used any form of dressing for his hair, not even a sphagnum shampoo. His cheeks and chin were always impeccably smooth (he shaved twice a day except on Sundays and other occasional days when we did not change for dinner). His heavily freckled hands with strong and well kept nails looked as if they had just been steeped (as did his feet when visible) in sea-water and sand, and his whole person breathed the faint scent of sphagnum moss, a blend of iodine and clover honey.

The first I saw of my father each day was when he visited the nursery, redolent of sphagnum moss, just as we were finishing breakfast. He rubbed his beautifully shaved cheek against mine as he made his way around the table and growled at each child. How this habit of using dog language penetrated our family I do not know but it became an almost universal practice to whimper like a spaniel if displeased, to howl out loud if hurt, and to hold out a hand drooping from a limp wrist simulating a sore paw when seeking sympathy. Growling could be friendly or antagonistic. Sniffing in loud whiffs was a sign of friendship. Of all who growled (and there was a lot of growling in the nursery) my father growled the loudest. Some years later when Michael and Patrick were schoolboys he took them out to the Braid Hills Hotel for lunch before which he led the way to the gentleman's lavatory, selected the central urinal and began to relieve himself. Patrick had lingered outside, diverted by a penny-in-the-slot machine. As Michael slipped in on the right hand side of my father a very small man slipped in on the other. Patrick remained outside. On shaking off the last drops and commencing his cotton wool routine, my father, thinking he was flanked by his two sons, turned to his left and emitted a reverberating growl. The very small man was frightened out of his wits, and regardless of the fact that he was in mid exercise, started away from the urinal in deshabille and rushed into a closet where he locked the door with a crash and could subsequently be heard panting.

After the morning growl my father disappeared to the dining room and then to his office, which reflected his own character in many remarkable ways. At waist height all around the room, on top of the wainscotting, there were inverted blades taken from old American saws. On these saw blades there hung perhaps some twenty pairs of almost identical stout brown shoes, the riser on the heel being gripped by the American serrated edge and each pair facing outwards as if on display. My father held that shoe polish was bad for shoes and gave each pair a generous application of Mars oil, which dripped off the toes of the shoes on to the boards beneath. The office reeked of Mars oil which he also applied to guns (of which there were several in an open rack), to his knee-high gaiters and to any other leather object within his reach.

In one corner of the office there was a leather-topped desk with a typewriter on a table opposite and a swivel chair between. The original wooden legs on the typewriter table had gone, because the table was either too high or too low, and had been replaced by metal legs turned in the workshop which were of the correct length but not fixed. Each leg was adjustable just in case, I supposed, anything were to happen to the level of the chair or the floor.

The office had originally been a smoking room of which the only remaining evidence was a smokers' cabinet and two huge smokers' chairs. My father preferred to ignore the smokers' cabinet and kept his large array of pipes in a special pipe rack that he had designed himself and which had been made in the workshop. The ends of the pipes' stems as they dangled from their well-turned holes, showing off the rings of dried white sputum that disfigured each mouthpiece, were level with my eyes.

There were no cigarettes kept in the smokers' cabinet. Instead my father kept boxes of Herbert Loves' Pure Virginia cigarettes in pale blue boxes of 100 in the bottom drawer of his desk. People said they were very choice cigarettes when new, but since my father seldom smoked a cigarette and had an unquenchable impulse to buy consumable goods in bulk, Herbert Loves' best might well be eighteen months old by the time they were offered to a guest. We always watched the victim as he lit up. Sometimes the Pure Virginia went off like a firework, sometimes a little trickle of dust dribbled out at the end as the guest leant forward to have his cigarette lit, at the third or fourth strike, by one of my father's Wax Vestas.

In the fireplace behind the two huge smokers' chairs (they faced the wrong way – *away* from the fire) my father kept his cartridges. Again his urge for bulk buying had ensured that there were enough cartridge boxes in the hearth to have supplied a syndicate shoot for a dozen seasons. They stood in a massive pile almost as high as the chair backs. One day when one of the chimneys went on fire (a common occurrence) pieces of ignited material came down the office chimney and set the cartridges alight. The result was a cannonade of explosions as the powder in each cartridge heated up to ignition point. Aggie Crosbie, brave soul, ran down with a bucket of water and put a stop to the conflagration. Actually there was no danger, but she did not know that and became the heroine of the hour. 'When I haird the bangin,' she would say, bursting with laughter and excitement, 'I jaist ran doon the stair and when I saw what it was I got the watter and when I was throwin it on the yins at the back the yins at the front was goin' off between my laigs!' Shrieks of laughter, huge bust wobbling, and both hands shot down to her crotch in an inverted attitude of prayer.

But this was not the end of the office. In pre-wireless days it was cluttered up with models from the workshop, usually built of Meccano screwed on to a wooden base. It was often hard to see what these models were for. There was one, for instance, driven by a small steam engine with a mass of pulleys and belts and also sprocket wheels and chains, which drove a small pump at any one of six or seven different speeds. The pump moved water out of a small glass jar into a tin cistern above the engine. From this cistern a small pipe led to the hole in the top of the boiler. When the engine had cooled down, after a burst of exercise, a tap on this pipe was opened and the boiler refilled. I thought that it might have been simpler just to pour in the water from a jug and said so, but no, my father was trying to prove something. He and the Matchetts spent many hours with their heads bent over this contraption which would disappear to the workshop and then come back to the office for further test and experiment. There were many such objects of experiment, and one – the LPI, or Loton Power Intensifier – broke through into the real world. This device was something to do with extracting greater mileage from motor fuel. The LPI, an ungainly object which fixed on to the carburettor, was taken up by Sir Oliver Lodge and marketed to car manufacturers, but it didn't catch on and all I remember of it is a box of twenty or thirty LPI's kept in the garage, no doubt for emergencies. Apart from this one glorious breakthrough the workshop was dedicated entirely to domestic experiment.

When the wireless arrived it became the centre of workshop and office life. In the office, as well as the coffinlike cabinet and the junction box, there was one huge horn suspended upon a bracket with the device 'Amplion' emblazoned upon it. There was also an amplifier of white crenellated paper, circular within a silver frame, which was thought to offer exceptionally good quality sound complementary to the Amplion. But my father was not satisfied and decided to devise his own improved style of horn. Unfortunately for him he had never studied the theory of sound as it is affected by the shape of a horn. Nor had he ever heard, I think, of the exponential curve nor of the logarithmic curve, nor did he apply to his horn experiments any deduction from observing the bell of a french horn or any other wind instrument. He plumped for a geometrical line from the sound source to the horn mouth. His horns were, in fact, pyramids made from plywood and glue.

The first horn was about four feet long, and when the great moment came and he and the Matchetts crowded round at the business end of it, they were disappointed to find that it did not amplify at all. This was thought to be because it was too small, so a monster pyramid was built; perhaps seven feet high and four feet wide at the mouth. It would only just go through the office door and it rested on the four arms of the smokers' chairs. Again there was no vestige of any amplification. It was then decided that this was because the angle was too wide. So the monster horn was cut down from four feet at the mouth to two. But once again when it was reverently laid on the smokers' chairs it failed to deliver, although some claimed it achieved something in the matter of the clarity of the sound.

At this point the horn experiments were discontinued and the team turned its attention to the directional effect of the radio signal upon the aerial. Clearly 90° from Daventry should give the best results . . . but no, the results from 90° were very poor indeed, in fact a parallel aerial gave better results. How could this be? So a veritable cat's cradle of aerials was slung from the oak tree on the lawn to the roof and from different points all over the roof.

Then my father had an inspiration. If the radio signal was fragmented by the hills and coming in from all angles why not a circular aerial? So a huge aluminium ball was acquired. It looked like a land-locked navigational buoy except that it was silver coloured and had wires coming from the bottom. When hoisted to the top of a mast above the nursery wing it shone splendidly in the sun. But when the signal from it was passed through to the coffin it was not as good as the signal from the parallel aerial, although some claimed that it improved the clarity of the sound.

At this point experiments on the aerial were discontinued and attention was directed to the valves, coils and rheostats within the coffin, all of which were beyond my comprehension – but I did observe that an immense number of new parts arrived each week in the workshop and an equal number of old parts were discarded. I do not know how these last experiments fared but at the very least I am sure that my father and his team managed to improve the clarity of the sound.

Experiments were not confined to models and to the wireless. We made our own electricity and a whole imposing stone building was dedicated to the huge horizontal petrol engine, to two generators (the second only a standby but just as big as the first) and a roomful of jumbo-sized accumulators to provide electricity for house at night when the trek-trek-tridala (the nursery version of the engine's rhythm) might keep early bedders awake. Here was a rich field for the amateur mechanic but the bold experimental team did not escape without casualties. Jack Matchett gave himself a nasty electric shock when pioneering some new device in the accumulator room and Father Matchett got an iron filing in his eye when turning some additional part for the engine. This thickened his eyelid and gave him a perpetual leer which was frightening to small children but actually quite endearing once one got used to it.

The main centre of engineering activity, however, was the garage. Each genus of car had its own succession. The De Dion Bouton was followed by the Charon and later by the Sezaire Berwick. These were stately landaulettes. The Star, a tourer which lasted for fourteen years, was followed by a succession of Talbots. The Star was my father's own car, his pet, his joy and his preoccupation. The Singers, first a two seater with a dickie, followed by a family tourer, were intended to be for my mother, but when she proved decisively that she could never learn to drive by running off the road several times and finally knocking down the dyke at Milton Farm, they became run-arounds for when my father had to go on bad roads or farm tracks that might have upset the delicate sensibilities of the Star. Every car, but especially the Star, was covered with all the gadgets then available to the motoring fraternity. Motoring in the 1920s was a sport and a hobby as well as a means of getting from place to place, and on the days when the motoring journals arrived through the post – the *Motor* and the *Autocar* – my father sat long over his breakfast, his two cups of tea (he always poured two cups at once so that they would be ready for drinking at the same time) going stone cold. The Star had a self-starter (very rare in those days), trafficators to obviate the need for sticking out the arm, a hand-operated windscreen wiper, a spare petrol tank on the running board, five or six successive horns including a Klaxon, a footwarmer under the floor at the back, a second windscreen for rear seat passengers, two suitcases custom-built to fit the curve of the car body above the luggage rack (which drove hotel porters wild because they would never stand upright) and numerous internal gadgets to improve the performance of the engine, including of course, an LPI.

On the matter of car engineering or anything else my father's relationship with the Matchetts was better than with any of the other outdoor staff. Father Matchett and he would sit for hours in the office, a drawing pad with a picture of the Prince of Wales on the front cover (of which my father must have bought a gross) lying between them, each one applying his pencil in turn like two schoolboys playing noughts and crosses. Father Matchett was a cautious man and was constantly tempering my father's bolder ideas with fail-safe devices 'to make assurance double sure'. When Jack Matchett attended these sessions he was not invited to sit down but stood between the two, watching and listening. He was, however, the most practical of the three and in later life ran a successful garage.

With the estate workers and the other outdoor staff my father's mode of communicating was jocular and hearty. 'Weel, Jock,' he would say, affecting a strong Doric accent, 'and hoo about a new pair of boots?' (One of Jock's boots had been mauled beyond repair by one of the farm dogs.) 'Why don't ye pinch a pair of Tom Quigley's?' (The owner of the dog.) 'I think a pair of Mrs Quigley's wad suit me better,' Jock would reply (Tom Quigley had very large feet), and this uneasy banter would continue as I stood transfixed with embarrassment, kicking stones or whittling a stick a few yards away. I knew that my father meant well but I also knew that Jock Wilson's wage was twenty-eight shillings a week, that a new pair of boots cost money and my father had at least twenty pairs of shoes hanging on the saw blades in the office. I knew this, Jock Wilson knew this, but my father didn't seem to see it at all. Also I had learnt Lallans Scots since I first could talk and had the intonation and vocabulary of a native. My father's music-hall Scots – his speaking voice was very English, almost Anglican – upset me aesthetically and socially.

The most awful occasions were when my father, usually with Sholto and myself, called in on the Quigley family at Craigielands hill farm of a winter's evening. As soon as he entered everyone would stand up. 'Hoo are you the nicht?' my father would enquire and the two girls Sissie and Bessie would immediately launch into peals of shrill laughter which continued as a giggling obligato throughout the visit and would rise to a climax when he made personal remarks about them – their rosy cheeks, their strong legs or whatever – and would sink to a pianissimo when he got round to the price of lambs or the cost of cattle cake and would only cease altogether if the conversation touched upon the matter of serious illness or death. My father stood with his back to the fire, supremely confident that everyone was having a whale of a time. We stood by the door in the shadows cast by the oil lamp and everyone, except my father, was heartily glad when the ordeal was over.

But encounters with Tom Quigley did not always pass off to my father's satisfaction. Unworldly beyond belief, I cannot think that my father was a top class farm manager. He left a great deal to Tom but did keep the farm accounts and once a month the two sat in agricultural conclave in the office, whilst my father's spaniel slept snugly in one of the smokers' chairs and Tom's sheepdogs sat outside shivering and whining for their master to come out. Sometimes I could hear from the billiard room next door Tom's voice raised in anger. The more he shouted the quieter my father became. I could not hear what they were saying, but if I drifted insouciantly into the office after Tom had stormed out I could see that my father was upset. He did not like a display of emotion and he did not like any of his fellow mortals to disagree with him except in a jolly argument about the bodily assumption or perhaps the crucifixion.

My father was very keen on field works, concentrating mainly on forestry and land drainage. Forestry took the form of cutting the dead lower branches from the trees in a spruce plantation. The trees were about twenty feet in height and my father got so keen on cutting off the branches that he had three little ladders made, one for himself, one for Sholto and one for me, which allowed us to go cutting on and on until we had removed much of the living wood right up to the crown. The second mistake he made was to sned clean the outside belt of trees which acted as a windbreak, with the result that in the first big gale after clearing was completed half of the trees in the plantation were blown down.

He then turned his attention to a small stream that cascaded down the steep wooded hill into the south park. For some reason I never discovered he decided to make a waterfall half way down the stream's course. This he did by cutting a level bed into the hillside for perhaps six or eight feet. The result was not spectacular, for the water only dribbled down the new vertical face and could not be seen from any path or vantage point. But now a sort of madness seized him and he dug deeper and deeper into the hillside, dislodging huge rocks and creating a vast pile of spoil which would have done credit to a small coal mine. When the frenzy was on him there was nothing for Sholto or me to do except wade about in our gumboots and wonder when the hell he would stop. His demoniacal digging was probably induced by rugby football starvation, I thought. The tools were kept in a little concrete bay outside the office and when we at last got back my father would clean his pick and his spade and go inside to make marks on a chart he kept on his desk.

Whereas my father's life centred around the office my mother was mostly to be found in her bed. This was a large ornate birchwood affair with a chintz canopy and curtains. It was tilted heavily towards the bedhead because my father had inserted two large wooden blocks under the footboard. This was thought to be good for the circulation during sleep. The bed was so huge that it blocked off a third of the window in the North Room, which was the centre of my parents' suite. Even on sunny days it was quite dark, so my mother, to meet the needs of her active bed-life, had an electric light on a flex hanging down inside the canopy behind her. This could be pinned into the position required by the nature of her activity; for reading in bed it would be on the far side, for letter writing and social activity it would be central, and when she had a headache it would be on the near side shrouded with a piece of black cloth. My parents were not early risers, my father's breakfast gong sounding at nine o'clock. My mother had breakfast in bed – weak china tea, two pieces of melba toast and sometimes half a grapefruit. My father's appearance in the nursery was the signal for us all to troop down and settle on her bed for prayers. Even toddlers came to prayers, though babes in arms remained in the Corner

Room next door. After prayers one or two children were sometimes allowed to remain whilst my mother opened her post, which was large. She would give a running commentary on each letter as she read it. 'T.O. has had migraine for ten days – we must get him to an osteopath,' or 'Aunt Phil is out of hospital at last.' News coming in seemed to be mainly about people's health, bulletins from other nurseries, letters of thanks and thanks for letters of thanks – for my mother was an amusing and challenging correspondent and seemed to generate a compulsive desire in any recipient of one of her letters to write back. Thus the corpus of her correspondence snowballed and in many cases was terminated only by death. The speed of strike, however, varied greatly. Any child absent from home would receive a letter each week without fail, her brothers perhaps once a month, and for a second cousin missionary in India twice a year would be enough. By half past ten the bed was littered with piles of letters, some to be answered today, some later, some to be passed to my father and some, a very few, to be thrown away. Now she began the task of writing back, sometimes still in bed where she would sit bolt upright with writing paper held on what she called a pasteboard with elastic bands at the top and bottom. She frequently ran out of writing paper and I still have many of her letters written on the wrapper for the *Times Literary Supplement*, on the inside of envelopes slit open for the purpose or even on the back of invitation cards, bills and scraps of cardboard. As she wrote, with her Swan fountain pen flowing fast and evenly across the page, her face reflected her feelings, sometimes for the recipient (a warm indulgent smile for her poor silly brother Neil, a frown for the Editor of the *Moffat News* who had reported the Women's Rural Institute outing inadequately) or sometimes the sentiment she was expressing on the page (eyebrows raised in amazement as she acknowledged Sheila's four goals scored at Lacrosse). For at heart my mother was amongst many other things a comic actress and a born mimic, with a percipient ear for intonation and accent and a precise sense of timing. When she entered into conversation with a friend or a local body (her word) she would unconsciously slip into the mode of speech of the other party, lapsing into broad Scots when talking to Maggie Hutchinson and into pinched ladylike English when to Cheltenham-Ladies-College-trained Aunt Jean. This was particularly true of her on the telephone. When she went down to the office to make her calls one of us would listen outside the door and come up before her to say, 'Mrs Hope Robertson, Dr Huskie and Aunti Vi.' My mother was always surprised that we seemed to know to whom she had spoken.

My mother did not always stay in bed to complete her daily correspondence. Sometimes she rose, dressed and continued on the writing table in the adjacent snuggery, which reflected her lifestyle as precisely as the office reflected that of my father. Dominating the room stood her beloved upright piano with the softest touch I ever encountered. In front were two piano stools, one for teacher and one for pupil, and on top, piled in the utmost confusion, was music of every description ranging from a piano score of *Lohengrin* to Billy Mayerl's 'Kitten on the Keys' (which no one played better than she) and including several of her own manuscripts in mid-composition and other manuscript exercises written out expressly for each child and labelled: 'Sholto: Tuesday' or 'Denis to practise all week'. But it would be an error to suggest that there was any system behind her teaching of music. Nothing could be further from the truth, in teaching as in all else she obeyed the impulse of the moment. On Monday she might be enthusiastic about the virtues of the Tonic Sol Fa system, only to discard it on Tuesday when it got too difficult for her to understand.

Elsewhere in the snuggery there would be a common jute sack half full of broken toys destined for the Fern Street settlement for destitute children in Liverpool. At the back of the writing table there would be a spirit lamp and small pan for making toffee. Books would be strewn everywhere, many of them with markers in with notes such as 'Women's Institute Thursday' or 'Loving kindness of God'. These were resources for incorporating into speeches and letters to the local papers. There was a large washbasket full of clothes for mending or pieces for making a patchwork skirt, but progress was slow in this department and serious work was sooner or later farmed out to Miss Anderson. Many garments served a year or two in the basket before they finally found their way upstairs to the nursery. Another large basket full of fir cones might be seen on the floor. My mother had a weakness for fir cones, sometimes painting them gold for the Brownies' party, sometimes sticking them in a winter flower arrangement, sometimes using them to light the fire, which was a mistake since their threshold of combustion was high. But she never gave up her belief in them. 'Those fir cones are damp,' she would say as the fire once again spluttered and went out. 'We must get Mrs Henderson to put them in the oven.' But it never worked.

In these two rooms, the bedroom and the snuggery, my mother spent the greatest part of her Craigielands life. When she was trying to master a set piece or working on a composition she would play in the snuggery for two or three hours without pause. She often lay in bed for several days on end when she was ill. Her illnesses were mysterious. Sometimes it was a headache which might carry her off in the middle of a meal, when she would go and lie white and as still as a mouse on the headache side of the bed with the light tamped down to a glimmer. At other times it was her back which prostrated her. This was treated by an Edinburgh osteopath, one Kelman McDonald (a German Scot), and usually entailed an overnight stay in the Cally for one treatment before and one after.

Although very young I was aware of some sexual chemistry taking place between Dr Dolly, as we called him, and my mother. There was never the slightest hint of anything improper, but I knew when I sat with her in the treatment room that she liked being massaged by another man and that he liked doing it. Dr Dolly often used to come down to Craigielands to fish for the day. I hated him and when it was suggested that he might do something beneficial to my back (with which there was nothing wrong) I objected violently, but was overruled.

If there was a public performance in prospect, a play in the village hall or a song recital at Craigielands, my mother would struggle bravely against ill health but at the last moment would usually succumb and the event would be called off. First night postponements became legendary.

When I was seven or eight my mother went into hospital for a hysterectomy. I asked her what was going to be done to her. She explained, using two pencils and a sheet of paper, that one leg was all right (she drove one pencil through the paper and held it still) but the other was wobbling about (she drove the other pencil through and wobbled it about until the hole was much too big for it), so they were going to sew her up so that the bad leg would have a right hole like the good one. This cock and bull story did not fool me for one instant. The ridiculous nature of the explanation, coupled with her obvious embarrassment, made me deduce that it must be something to do with her bowels, her urinary system or something else I didn't quite understand. 'Will it make you wee better?' I asked at a venture. She blushed scarlet, hugged me and said, 'You will understand it all when you are older.' This was a lesson to me. There were some things my mother and certainly my father could not speak about to me. Nor perhaps to each other.

When not lying in bed in a dim light my mother was always at the centre of Craigielands conversation. She was a racy raconteur and a good listener within the circle of the family and friends, but when formality broke in in the shape of a visiting bishop or one of Julia's business friends she lost her touch and became the conventional hostess talking about the weather and Lloyd George. She never lost her fear of 'society', born I suspect of the Loretto antagonism towards it. She herself had never been launched into society, much less 'come out'. After a happy childhood at home she had won all hearts at her boarding school, St Leonards, where she formed a special friendship with her headmistress, a Miss Grant. She possessed a remarkably true and pure high soprano voice and so was sent to Schwerin to train as an opera singer. She was auditioned by the great Blanche Marchesi who immediately offered to take her on as a pupil. After her first course of lessons, however, James Smith decided that an opera singer's life was not appropriate for a lady, especially a lady who was his daughter. I have seen Marchesi's letter pleading with him to change his mind, saying that my mother had a great singing career ahead of her. But it was not to be: she returned to Craigielands as the young lady of the house and there waited patiently for the return of my father from San Francisco. In this matter she got her way and the engagement which had been entered into between them in the oak tree above the Mill Dam in 1894 was finally announced to the world on the 20th of July 1906. They were married from Craigielands at Kirkpatrick Juxta Church, Beattock on the 2nd of April 1908. But she never sang in public.

Her first daughter was born when my father was a curate in Bishop Auckland and the second when he was a housemaster and chaplain at Loretto, where Sconnie was now Headmaster. But all was not sweetness and light between Sconnie and my father. I do not know the cause of the friction, nor whether it was the reason for my father's departure from Loretto in 1912 to become Gamma's factor at Craigielands. James Smith had died three years earlier, there were now no remaining resident members of the Craigielands set and Gamma must have longed for family company which Flora and the two baby girls would provide, also it would be helpful to have a man about the place to look after the estate. So for whatever reason the move was made and the troika that governed Craigielands was established and continued undisturbed for twenty years until Gamma died in 1932.

Although I do not remember it in my own case, I soon learnt that mother was a passionate baby-lover. Any baby would attract her like a magnet. She had that peculiarly ingratiating maternal smile which motherly women reserve for babies and animals. At the sight of an even quite elderly baby her normal form of diction, which was clear and strong, changed into mashed-up farmyard noises. She would often cry a little if the baby were really fetching. Her own babies were of course the best of all babies and she breast-fed them, pampered them, played with them and showed them off with pride at bedroom levées to visiting friends and family. She did, however, employ a stout Scots body, Nurse Black, to do the sanitary work and night duty.

As the babies grew into toddlers, my mother relinquished them to the nursery. But she remained in charge of their welfare and early education. As a modern woman she latched on to new educational theories and the one which she launched on our nursery was the Montessori Method. We had Montessori tables, child-size Montessori chairs, Montessori shapes which you had to fit into holes of the same shape, a Montessori sand table and Montessori braille letters stuck onto white cards. Once when Uncle Artie (Julia) came into the nursery and saw the braille he told my mother she must have ordered the wrong set and these were for blind children. She was furious and rushed downstairs to find the Montessori handbook, but couldn't find it and wrote to Madam Montessori herself and showed Uncle Artie her reply. The braille letters were not for blind children, they were to ingrain on the child's mind the shape of the letters by touch as well as by sight. It seemed to me that Uncle Artie knew this all along.

As a teacher my mother was bright and encouraging for the first five or ten minutes, but she was no stayer. If we got bored we could easily divert her attention from teaching to some other subject – say the names of birds – which would necessitate a visit to the window, and from that one thing would follow another and the lesson would be forgotten. Then she herself often got bored, or perplexed by the lesson she was giving and we would all give up and go and make toffee in the snuggery.

As a music teacher she was at her worst. She attempted to follow so many systems that one never got a fair crack at any one of them. After learning the names of the notes, five-finger exercises and pieces from the Anna Magdalena notebooks I learnt no more from her. My abiding regret is that she failed to teach me to sight-read. The reason for our break up was that she always got cross when one played wrong notes, once or twice lunged at me in desperation, striking the offending hand with a ruler. Wrong notes were too much for her musical sensibilities to withstand.

Her own musical persona was curious. As a singer she had a flute-like high soprano which might have been mistaken for a boy's treble but for its essential femininity, but she had a difficult transition to her chest voice which was pleasant but lacked resonance. Therefore she preferred songs to be pitched in the middle of the treble clef and above up to B flat and C. It was around the E above middle C that she met her Waterloo and she wrote everything for her own voice above this. I have recordings of my mother's voice made when she was over seventy and the intonation and pitch are still perfect, but the voice is very small. I suspect it always was a voice for the salon rather than the opera house. Her repertoire was not wide – Schubert, Schumann, Brahms, (no Hugo Wolff), Scots ballads, English traditional songs arranged by herself and arias from Wagner. I never heard her sing any bel canto, nor Mozart nor any song in any language other than English or German.

Her main preoccupation with music was, however, as a composer. Her taste was for light music and music for and about children. I would place her genre and style as somewhere between Roger Quilter and Percy Grainger in his popular mode. She was completely innocent of any theoretical knowledge but had an acute ear for form as well as harmony. Thus the first strain of her short songs would always end in the dominant, although she didn't know what the word dominant meant, and would return to the tonic often through the relative minor.

She composed at the keyboard and as the days passed one could hear a work progressing from an opening snatch of melody to a complete song. Knowing nothing of harmony, she found the chords she wanted by trial and error through her fingers. Her music was, of course, entirely diatonic, but she had a penchant for piquancy and colour which she picked out of the air from listening to Wagner and later to Delius. One of the faults was to introduce too much mickey-mousing. If a bell was mentioned in the text one was sure to hear it toll in the bass; if there was a lion there was likely to be a roar, and splintering icicles would cascade down the piano in glittering arpeggios. Sometimes it seemed as if one were on a musical ride from one sound effect to the next. As a pianist she had a beautiful touch and a full and resourceful command of the piano for music in her own style. But she never tackled any big stuff and by the age of twelve I could struggle through certain Beethoven sonatas better than she could.

Once she had finished a song she had a problem – she couldn't write it down. In the days before any form of home recording there was only one thing for it – to get a professional to do it for her. So it came about that Dougie Wilcox, the Musical Director of the Kings Theatre in Edinburgh, would travel down by train with a little black bag full of manuscript paper. Day after day he and my mother would sit side by side on the bench music seat by the Steinway and he would transcribe her music note by note to paper as she played it. No composer could have had a more meticulous or devoted amanuensis and Dougie's piano scores, which I have before me as I write, are objects of loving craftsmanship.

On his visits to Craigielands Dougie wore his theatre uniform: striped pants, black jacket, starched collars and cravat, with a carnation in his buttonhole, and it was a little incongruous to see this diminutive black figure taking his mid-day exercise, two hundred yards up and down the north drive and then two hundred yards up and down the south drive, in a world where everywhere else there were dogs, tweeds and Loretto dress.

The final moment of triumph came when we went to the Kings for the pantomime. Dougie would enter the pit below our box, smirk up at my mother in a meaningful way, tap the rostrum twice and sweep into an orchestral pot-pourri of my mother's songs.

My mother never published any of her work except privately, when she and Sconnie together created a song cycle, *Nursery Idylls*, which in some ways anticipated Hilaire Belloc's *Cautionary Tales* of a generation later. Some of them verged on the grand guignol:

Why here's a lark, cried playful Pat
Let's sprinkle salt in Father's hat,
Imagine poor papa's despair
To feel it smarting in his hair
But Patrick turned as white as milk
When Pa took up the hat of silk
He did not speak about the fault
But silently removed the salt
And with deaf ears for Patrick's cries
He tucked it in behind his eyes.

A climax was reached in 'Arrogance':

> Dick cried when he had done his play
> 'The maids are paid to clear away'
> He rang the bell with noisy glee
> 'Now Susan, tidy up,' said he.
> He did not know papa was standing
> Near the door upon the landing
> And in his hand he held a hammer
> As he came in to stop the clamour
> 'Put all your play-things in a pile,'
> He said, and wore a ghastly smile
> Down came the hammer, Blow on blow
> And Dick's complexion turned to snow
> For Father warming to his work
> Soon turned on Richard, like a Turk
> And Dick was smashed among his toys
> And that's what comes to naughty boys.

Only the milder *Idylls* appear in the printed edition. I have an idea the more brutal items would scarcely have passed muster with Gamma.

My mother's most prized opus, however, was a setting of A. A. Milne's poems *When We Were Very Young*. This was a real success. We all knew it for we had mimed to them in front of our invited audience in the Hall on two successive nights. She was persuaded to write to Milne to ask for the right to publish. He replied that he had just accorded that right to one Fraser Kennedy. This was gloomy news. When heard (on 2 LO), Kennedy's settings were pronounced to be much inferior to hers – and indeed, in respect of her two best numbers at least, this was so.

Both my parents were good listeners to music. They sat quite still in front of the radio or gramophone and did not talk even when the record was changed. As soon as the piece was over there would be an ecstatic outburst from my mother, such as 'Absolutely glorious', or 'Wonderful, wonderful', and my father would say something like 'old Beethoven knew what he was doing', or 'extraordinary that some people don't like Wagner.' It was clear that they were truly moved. Sometimes my mother would wipe away a tear or my father would let his pipe go out, a sign of deep emotion.

This kind of musical appreciation was passed on to Sheila, Michael and especially to Sholto. I have sometimes thought that the instinctive listener gets as much fulfilment from music as do those whose musical sense is more analytical. To me it is incomprehensible that a person with a true appreciation of music can listen to a Haydn symphony without knowing when the development section ends and the recapitulation begins, but they can and do, and when it is over they will use, as my parents did, some wholly non-musical descriptive adjective which gives a bluff and general impression of what the music meant to them. For these listeners, all music is a tone poem and it is tempting to think that this romantic approach can bring pleasure unalloyed, whereas analysis means the aggravation of toil and struggle. But in my heart I know that understanding deepens appreciation and knowledge can only heighten enjoyment, although it might also lead to the rejection of a great deal of quite personable music that lies in the second division.

At Craigielands, in music as in everything else, there was a right and a wrong. Beethoven was right. Chopin was wrong (sentimental and melancholy). Brahms was right (a thinker), Liszt was wrong (never gets down to it properly). The idea of black and white was applied to the arts without inhibition and this as much as anything else caused me to question the Craigielands creed. My mother's first judgment of people, as well as of plays, books or music, was to decide whether they were good or bad. 'But is he a good man?' she would ask in perplexity when someone had been describing the nature of Ramsay McDonald, then a rising star in politics. Asquith was good, Lloyd George was bad – really very bad. Baldwin was good but a Conservative. Hamlet was an enigma, he seemed to be good and bad at the same time. The Greek myths were very puzzling because they didn't seem to distinguish between good and bad at all: all the Gods behaved frightfully badly but they were Gods and so surely meant to be good. The Bible was much safer ground: here it was always possible to distinguish the good from the bad – except, possibly, in King Solomon and Pontius Pilate. With such pellucid simplicity did my mother view the world. But she could be dashing and 'modern' too, because she thought that woman, but only within carefully judged limits, should be emancipated. She rode a bicycle in knickerbockers, walked with the guns on a shoot in a jersey which showed off her figure, smoked in an amateurish but showy way, holding the cigarette high, taking an occasional little puff and blowing the smoke out almost before it had gone on. In her costume she was up with the fashion – or rather with some fashion – wearing William Morris dresses, draped wraps and enormous necklaces of large amber beads which dangled down below her navel. When going to Edinburgh she would wear a cloche hat and a well cut tweed costume, smart court shoes, off white silk stockings and black kid gloves. Her evening dress was almost indistinguishable from her afternoon dress, though it moved perhaps a little nearer to Pre-Raphaelite than to William Morris.

After her bed, which always remained the chief site for her morning levées, my mother was happiest at the dining table. Here, second down on the left from the head of the table, she orchestrated the conversation with wit and authority so long as it remained light, bright and amusing, only withdrawing into the background when it turned to matters such as the nature of the trinity or the transubstantiation of the flesh. But she would offer a view as to the character of the various disciples or on any of the more colourful old testament personalities. At table the theatrical streak in her nature led her to acquire a number of properties to work for her during a meal. The first of these was a raw egg, which before the meal began she broke into a wine glass and swallowed in one gulp to the astonishment and admiration of all new guests. Next, as the pudding receded, she started work with a battery of glass retorts and spirit lamps to make the coffee. This ritual had to be carried out meticulously: the coffee was ground and placed in the upper part of the Cona machine, the spirit lamp was applied to the lower, the glass tube of the upper inserted into the lower, then there was a pause until the water in the lower came to the boil and was forced by steam pressure into the upper where it activated the coffee like lava in the crater of a volcano. After a carefully judged period of bubbling and steaming, the spirit lamp was taken away and the dark brown stream of coffee was allowed to run down the tube into the lower retort, which now became a serving vessel. Under special circumstances – and only my mother knew what these were – the whole routine would be repeated and the coffee would be sent up a second time. Occasionally a pinch of salt was added. It is a mark of my mother's originality and fertility of invention that although she habitually gave a running commentary for the benefit of strangers throughout the whole of this operation she never seemed to repeat herself and one was just as eager for her act to begin on the hundredth occasion as one had been on the first.

Gamma sat at the foot of the table and the direction of the conversation fell to her when weightier matters came under discussion. She sat upright, her head cocked a little to the right when listening, and moving forward a few degrees when she began to speak. Rarely, when making an important point, she would place both hands on the table and lean right back. Like my mother she could be quick and witty in her repartee, but unlike my mother she always retained a sense of underlying gravitas. Even with children, even when taking Mr Dunderhead through his amazing adventures, the stern moralist was never far beneath the surface.

At lessons she was unsmiling and determined. Whether it was a matter of learning French irregular verbs or of placing the crown of each king of England in the right one of the little squares which denoted the decades through the centuries, her pupils were under relentless pressure until they got it right. Her punishments were by far the most effective. To be beaten by my father was something to boast about. One could show the marks and cheekily imitate his sudden flurry as he went into action. My mother's efforts with a ruler on the palm of the hand were simply pathetic. But Gamma would fix you with a steely eye and say, 'Denis, you will sit for twenty minutes.' As soon as it was convenient the victim was placed on a chair in the middle of the writing room, back to the window, and had to sit there alone for ten, twenty, or in extreme cases, thirty minutes.

This punishment was especially effective for me, for I could never bear to sit still at all. She enforced it by appearing unexpectedly from time to time, silhouetted in the doorway, and if one had transgressed by moving the chair even an inch, or by flashing across the room to kick the dog, the sentence was extended.

Quite different was the punishment devised for my sister Kaff. She was condemned to run round the house for ten or twenty minutes so that all the household could see her shame. She used to weep loudly as she ran and she put a pebble on the front steps to keep count of each circuit. When a decent number had accumulated I used to sweep two or three back onto the gravel so that poor Kaff had to keep running almost indefinitely. Sholto thought poorly of me for doing this, but I thought that Kaff really quite enjoyed her martyrdom, probably because this kind of punishment held no terrors for me. Had my grandmother made me run round and round the house I would have gloried in it, making faces at the housemaids through the windows, imitating the way Jim Rheilly ran, pretending to have pain in the stomach and wearing a different hat on each circuit.

I do not think that I ever loved Gamma. In the early years I respected her and feared her and sometimes found her a very interesting companion. But when my parents were away from home I found her regime repressive. Once when she had been in sole charge for what seemed a very long time I wrote a little note to my friend Barbara Craig, imploring her to get her mother to come across and take us all out on a picnic. The actual text I do not recall but I do remember that the word Dull was printed diagonally across each corner of the notepaper. I sealed the letter and got Aggie Crosbie to address it and was about to pop it into the postbox in the library when Gamma came in and said she must see it. It must be opened. She must know what I was saying in any letter that went out from the house when she was in charge. I was seized with panic. I clutched the letter against my chest, rushed past Gamma, ran upstairs and threw the letter on to the nursery fire. Gamma followed, but by the time she arrived the paper was all black and the writing quite illegible. I glared defiantly at Gamma, who gazed back at me with the look of a hanging judge. I knew that she knew that there had been something terrible about her in the letter, but I didn't mind. She had no right to go poking into my letters. We must have glared on for a full minute before she turned on her heel and walked slowly back to her haunts downstairs.

I was trembling all over. When she was out of earshot I shouted HELL twice – which was the worst word I knew – and ran downstairs, out of the front door into the dark and on down the north drive until I could run no further. The letter was never mentioned again. There was no punishment, but in a way we both knew that it was a declaration of war.

The relationships between the three top people in my life were constant. Gamma and my mother were not the same kind of people so there could be no intimacy between them. Their relationship was based on family affection rather than any other mutual interests, nevertheless Gamma's face softened and relaxed more than at any other time when she and my mother sat alone over the drawing room fire after tea and talked about family affairs, children, grandchildren, times present and times past. Gamma would also discharge her maternal role by keeping my mother on the right road if she were inclined to let a boy have a bicycle a bit too soon or a girl go to a party without an appropriate attendant. There was little they could actually do together since Gamma had no love of music, and my mother was not inclined towards discussing religious or political matters, nor was she interested in literature once it entered the heavyside layer. Here Gamma found her intellectual companion in her sons Sconnie and T.O., with whom she conducted a regular correspondence.

My father, too, was a non-starter on such serious topics. His contribution would usually take the form of some unusual theory concerning Christ or the apostles, such as the notion that at first Christ did not know he was divine. Indeed he did not know it until he asked the disciples, at quite a late stage in his career and after numerous miracles, 'And who do you say I am?', and they replied

My father at twenty, a Pal, and still a schoolboy.
He left Loretto at the age of twenty and one month.

My mother in the Singer coupé, before she met her Waterloo
in an encounter with a stone dyke.

Craigielands as the architect designed it (above) and after my grandfather had added a floor to meet the needs of a nursery. The two top floor windows nearest the camera are those of the dark room and the den, My bedroom is on the far left and the ledge of the perilous climb is beneath it.

A house party on the steps to the gravel. The late Mr Smith, capped, in front of the central pillar. Gamma third in front of the demon cyclist.

Gamma reflective: 'I wonder whether this boy is telling the truth?'

The Palship, dressed to kill, with the Child (my mother) in attendance. From the apex: BS, Grand Punt Master; the Child; Neil Smith, Luggage Master; Adam Forman, Chief Engineer; Edvard Melville (no portfolio), and Adam Lindsay (Beelzie), Chief Cook.

T.O. Smith, my godfather and a recluse, in the garden with Service, alderman of Eastbourne, lifelong servant and friend and the companion of the late Mr Smith at his death.

One of the Palship in minor trouble.

WACS (Women's Auxiliary Corps) pushing a trolley of sphagnum moss on the wooden railway devised by my father. His finest hour.

Top left. Nan and myself, my mother and Sholto.
Above. My mother as I first remember her, wearing a William Morris garment.
Left. Myself at three, equestrian.

Gamma engulfed in grandchildren. Back row: Sheila; myself, Michael and a cousin (the two babies); Sholto; John Smith, motorist. Front row: Kaff; two cousins and Roslin Smith (also a cousin but soon to become, with John, quasi sister and brother).

Craigielands steps: from the top, Michael, cousin, gollywog cousin, myself, Sholto, unhappy cousin, Kaff, unknown girl, Sheila.

Craigielands archers: Mr Sholto left, Master Denis right, Michael and Wee Pat centre, with Marnie – wig, smell and all – and her and Nan's sister Mrs Dunn.

'The Son of God.' From then on he knew he was Jesus Christ, but not before. Gamma would have none of this sort of nonsense but although she did not respect his intellect she did regard him as a good man and a satisfactory son-in-law. This did not eliminate a degree of friction between my father on the one side and my mother and Gamma on the other, which occasionally (and to my great delight) blew up into a mini row. Gamma was an afficionado of the Clyde estuary, and in particular of the Isle of Arran where she had spent holidays and had once taken my mother as a young girl. My father was an east coast man – he had stayed at Eyemouth as a boy with Forman aunts, and Loretto was in the Firth of Forth, so St Abbs Head, the Bass Rock and the Kingdom of Fife were almost holy places to him. As the East versus the West argument raged, my father sometimes ill-advisedly let drop some derogatory remark about Arran.

'Arran,' said my mother – 'you've never been there.' 'Of course I have,' he replied. 'You've never been up Goat Fell then,' said she. 'Yes I have,' he asserted, 'I've been up it several times.' 'Adam,' said Gamma, 'now you are talking like Denis.' She meant he was telling lies. I was so pleased to be quoted in this context, at least I had made my mark as a colourful raconteur.

But such little spats were rare indeed and my father and my mother appeared to be, and were, a devoted couple. Sometimes after lunch my father would say to my mother, 'What about a slank?' A slank was purported to be a rest, perhaps a snooze in the double bed in the north room. But as time went on I came to believe that a slank meant more than this. For one thing, when slanking my father and mother bolted the door, which was uncommon. For another, one could hear noises within the room during a slank, no more than vague movements but certainly not the noise of two people resting. When the door was finally opened and my father took in a tray of china tea and bread and butter, both parents were a little red in the face and looked enormously pleased with themselves and each other. I am now sure that my surmise was correct and that an unclouded sexual relationship, sometimes consummated during slanks, was the basis of their devotion to each other and of my mother's tolerance of my father's more tiresome domestic habits. They were perhaps two of the very few people who not only never have any sexual encounters outside their marriage but never even think of it as a possibility.

It is true that my father enjoyed manhandling small girls whom he would seize in a friendly bear-like grip and beat playfully across their bottoms. Whilst doing this he would usually cry out, 'Oh, you rabbit, what have you been doing, you rabbit?' Also at the theatre or in the Cally he would get very friendly with the programme girls or the waitresses, and their encounter might end in a playful cuff or quasi embrace. This was embarrassing, not for him, for he had not the least idea that his antics had anything to do with sex, but for my mother and myself, both of whom knew that they had. But such minor irregularities made no dent upon the abiding affection between my parents, which may well have been the root cause of the happy and confident nature of the majority of their children.

To me, during the first fifteen years of my life, the Trinity which ruled my destiny were three in one, a solid block of authority, and although, as with a more famous trinity, each had separate characteristics, together they reflected as nearly as three people can a single set of values. As time went on I found I did not like some of these very much, particularly the values taken from the Old Testament. God the Father had several disagreeable characteristics. He was vindictive, bloodthirsty and often mean-minded. He was also dictatorial. I revolted against the story of the Ten Commandments. Who did God think he was anyway? And Moses was a creep. If I had been alive then I would have broken every one on the first day. Jesus Christ, always the Kind Man to us, was a decent enough fellow, indeed he was wonderful in his way, but a bit wet and with no sense of humour. Not one single joke in the whole of the New Testament. As for the Holy Ghost, no one seemed to have the slightest idea of what it was. In pictures it was fire dancing on people's shoulders. But why? Really the case for the Holy Ghost had to be more convincing before one could begin to take it seriously. And it was not only the nature of God that I found distasteful. By the age of nine or ten I reacted against the smugness of pure faith. I did not like to be told that things were so, full stop. Why were they so? I wanted further and better particulars and was fobbed off with still more talk about faith. I didn't want faith. I wanted evidence.

I remember one day discussing the matter of obedience with my mother when I had flagrantly disobeyed one of the many Craigielands rules such as not getting up before seven o'clock, not reading a novel unless it was approved by one of the Trinity and not making off-key jokes about holy matters. Why should I be obedient, I asked? 'Because Dad, Gamma and I want everyone to be happy and live together the right way,' she said. 'Suppose I don't think it *is* the right way,' I said. 'Why should I believe the same thing as you?' 'Because we are three wise people who are much older than you and who know what's right and what's wrong,' she replied, 'and because we love you we want to make you understand it too.' I found this thoroughly unsatisfactory and divine discontent began to rise ever higher within me. I did not yet dream of challenging belief itself – but within this holy and loving family I had struck an obstacle, a submerged rock, and it was to change the course of my life. Over the next five years I started to steer an independent course as a private person whilst still appearing to be the familiar cheerful show-off extrovert. Which for the greater part of the time I was.

7

Getting Worse and Worse

The stirrings of dissent grew stronger as I moved up the Craigielands ladder and spent more time in the presence of the Trinity. Status in the household could best be measured by where one ate. At first it was all nursery; then, when reasonably continent and mobile at perhaps the age of three or four, one had one's first introduction to adult eating and adult society on Sundays, and more particularly at Sunday tea. This was an all-age mixed menu affair, loathed by visiting uncles because of its early hour, confused eating and the likelihood of a child being sick on the table.

There was no service at Sunday tea. It was felt that to let the maids off for Sunday tea was a nod in the direction of Sunday observance and the sort of behaviour expected of a holy employer (Yet the poor things had only just finished washing up Sunday lunch, which often went on until half-past three). After lunch my father led the Sunday walk, corralling as many of the lunch guests as possible, for since Gamma and my mother never came on Sunday walks he was in sole command. We started up Craigielands Hill, a climb so steep that the last hundred feet was scaled by means of a rough staircase made of pine logs. Once we reached the farm plateau at the top we did Six Breaths. For Six Breaths everyone stopped and bent over with their hands dangling down in front like lunatic apes, then gradually as they inhaled noisily through their noses they moved upright into a posture like the mascots on the cars of the day, chests pushed out, arms straight behind, as if attempting to fly, and head flung back. My father thought that Six Breaths were good for you and you should do them every day.

One day when doing Six Breaths I farted. 'Who did that?' said my father sharply. He was breathing in another direction. 'I did,' I said. 'Someone did it at last Sunday tea too,' said my father. 'Was it you Denis?' 'Yes,' I said. My father stopped on about the fourth breath and said, 'It is a very rude thing to do. Don't do it again.' This was the first news I had heard of farting being socially unacceptable and I brooded over it. Rude? What did that mean?

After Six Breaths the walk moved off over comparatively flat ground in the direction of my father's choosing. As soon as panting subsided, conversation began. This was often a matter of picking over the main luncheon topics – the nature of sin, the existence of a personal devil, or did dogs go to heaven. As the grown ups became engrossed in their discussion they tended to stop and face up to each other. Sometimes voices were raised. If this went on for any length of time the walk could disintegrate. Even when in motion it was an untidy caravan with the more energetic dogs and children in front and slower children and lazier dogs behind. I have seen a Craigieland walk cover as much as a quarter of a mile. But when it came to a standstill people got bored with the grown up argument and went off to do their own thing, such as visiting a known dead weasel, going up to the farm to feed the hens or, if feeling really bold, slipping off home to play in an empty nursery.

On returning from the walk the grown ups had china tea in the drawing room and almost before the last cup was downed the gong went at six-thirty sharp for Sunday tea. The children would rush in first and sit down where they wanted to sit, followed by Gamma who would put them in the places where she wanted them to sit. Tea itself was a mass of varied and mostly indigestible foods. There were toasted buns sodden with butter in a silver dish with hot water underneath which spilled on the tablecloth if you moved the dish too fast. There was a square box padded with scarlet flannel holding a huge pile of boiled eggs; there was potted head, a ghastly dish of pork in jelly made in a truly Scottish attempt to waste no part of a dead pig; there was potted rabbit with a yellow crust of butter on the top and underneath a grey mixture like wet cement; there was ham, cold game in season, usually pretty far gone, and platefuls of Scottish teabreads, scones, shortbread and cakes. Some adults who had barely digested their lunch picked dutifully at a little ham and toyed with a treacle scone. Others ate as if they had seen no food for days. Gamma was one of these, for she was a great eater and this was her favourite meal. She always ended up with a large helping of trifle which was liberally laced with sherry. As president of the Scottish branch of the Women's Temperance Association Gamma opposed alcohol in all its forms and did her best to impose a teetotal regime on the household. She had no idea there was sherry in the trifle but she liked the taste and the trifle would often reappear on Monday and for all I knew Tuesday too. One day Gamma sent for Dr Huskie because she had come out in spots. Dr Huskie informed her that she was suffering from a mild form of alcoholic poisoning. This was something of a shock for Gamma and there was no more trifle at Sunday tea.

After Sunday tea the children performed. It might be six verses of John Gillpin, it might be a short song custom-composed for an eight year old by my mother, or it might be a two-handed sketch adapted from J. J. Bells' Glaswegian comedies – *The Nickums* or *Wee McGrecgor*, again adapted and produced by my mother. I enjoyed performing if I had a good text but was sometimes embarrassed by the material. I refused absolutely to sing 'Mighty Like a Rose', and was punished for it.

For the adults to listen to the children was a complete role reversal. For the rest of the week the children listened to the adults. As one crept up the Craigielands eating ladder – lunch downstairs – schoolroom tea – breakfast in the dining room – and finally, after a number of special occasions, dinner in the dining room every night – the functions of eating food and listening to adult conversation became inseparable.

Children did not join in adult conversation. It was like a mediaeval university in Arab lands where the wise men disputed and discussed whilst the young persons sat at their feet to listen and learn. When the conversation was practical – was the old boat so unsafe that we should buy a new one? – would a diet of tomatoes cure a dog with a spinal ailment? – were the rabbit catchers taking some of the crates, destined for Leeds, off the train at Lockerbie and selling them locally? – all of this was good stuff. But it did not last long. At the drop of a hat you were into the true meaning of the parable of the loaves and fishes, from thence to the place of miracles in Christian belief and onwards and upwards until the grease congealed on the plate and Aggie Crosbie tapped her foot in an agony of impatience to get the table cleared. One could try to switch off into one's own fantasies but it was no good. Although the topics were heavy, the reactions of the speakers to each other were compulsive. I suffered silently during these debates. They induced a mood of sullen boredom.

(I think it only right to state here that the Craigielands experience of boredom had a lasting effect on my life. The horror of bores haunts me still and my threshold of boredom is low. I have been told that I have an unusual ability to identify a bore, even at a great distance. At Cambridge I wrote a short and cogent paper on the elements of boredom. I also arranged a bores match between Pembroke and Trinity Hall at which each side had coached their three leading bores to become even more boring than they were naturally. Of my two men one could whistle a chord and the other was passionate about the Assyrian tribes. The match was started by gunfire and refereed by umpires from neutral colleges. Pembroke won, but I failed in my attempts to persuade the appropriate committee to award a blue, or at least a half-blue, for participation in an Oxford versus Cambridge bores match. All of this stemmed from the supreme boredom I suffered at the Craigielands' dining table.)

At the same time, perhaps in self-defence, I developed a strand of mild cynicism. In a family where everyone was desperately keen to believe the best of anyone, I was alone in preferring to believe the worst. Time after time I stood by and saw my father conned by beggars, tinkers, salesmen or – nearer home – by Mr Bulman the schoolteacher and Mr Beattie in the Moffat garage. As I listened to the flattery, the creepy humiliation and the slick talk my stomach used to turn over. 'Ah well,' my father would say as he got into the car, having given away a couple of acres or parted with five pounds, 'he's a very decent chap really.' 'You fool,' I would think. 'Conned again.' But I was also embarrassed for him and bore the shame he should have felt but didn't.

The discomfort I felt during the dining-room discussions was also due partly to the impenetrable layers of self satisfaction with which every moral issue was despatched. Later I came to question the issues themselves, but in the early days it was a revulsion against the smugness of grown-up conversation that caused me to defect from the pack and start out as a loner. My early success as a bad boy had not been much more than a means of catching public attention. But now frustration with the heavyside layer of Christian goodness began to add reality to being bad. It was no longer entirely a theatrical gesture. I began to feel a compulsion to be as bad as a protest against the inspissated goodness that surrounded me.

One day when I had been driven half crazy by listening to an attempt to reconcile the God of Wrath in the Old Testament with the God of Love in the New I decided I would not only be bad, I would be as bad as possible. I would run away, break every rule I could and stay away until they were really frightened. By the law of diminishing returns if I broke twenty rules they would not punish me twenty times as much as for breaking one. So after tea, as soon as it was dark, I crept out of the back door and lit a carbide bicycle lamp (not allowed) and went down the south drive (out of bounds), leaving open a number of field gates on the way (punishable). I then returned by the Lake, threw the carbide lamp into it, unmoored the boat and passed on to the railway station (absolutely out of bounds). Here I took a chocolate bar out of a machine and ate it (grubbing), came back by the sawmill and turned the water over the water wheel. I opened the kennel doors to let the shooting dogs out but this was a failure. They just sat still and growled at me. On the way back past the laundry I threw a stone at a window and broke a pane of glass. By now I had run out of ideas and to my surprise I had been out for less than an hour. So I bedded down under a chestnut tree and covered myself with leaves. It was very cold and damp. Soon I could hear voices and see lamps like glow-worms in the park. I stuck it out a while longer, but when Jessie Croall, one of the good undernurses, came within yards of me, I surrendered. The final triumph, when hauled up before my father and mother was in recounting all the dreadful things I had done and seeing the looks of puzzled surprise on their faces. I was given the maximum punishment, six strokes on the buttocks with a cane, but went to bed proud and happy. Indeed as time went on this day passed into nursery mythology and I have not the slightest doubt that I improved the story considerably each time I told it.

My inner discontent did not inhibit me from entering heart and soul into the social life of the grown-ups. The most regular visitors were the uncles, amongst whom some were better liked than others, but any uncle was better than none because they leavened the lump of the Trinity and brought fresh attitudes, fresh ideas and fresh conversation to the dining room.

The loudest of the uncles was Uncle Neil (a relic of the Palship) who was now vicar of a London parish and full of cheerful Christian belief. He had a booming pulpit voice and constantly told rather simple jokes, reaching an ear-splitting crescendo as he approached the punch line. In telling jokes he was something of a recidivist and his family had been forced to devise a method of controlling him. As soon as he started on a joke all those who had heard it before put a fork across the top of their glass. If all glasses were covered, he had to stop. His eldest daughter Rosemary monitored this procedure. I always put a fork up whether or not I had heard the joke before because I thought the jokes were so terrible I did not want to hear them at all. One day I committed a *bêtise*. He was telling a joke about something that had happened to him in the park that very morning. I put my fork up and everyone went silent and looked at me. It was a moment of shame.

Another way of stopping him was to shout out the punch line long before he got to it. Each time, for instance, he began on a story about Biblical titles similar to those of the English aristocracy, Rosemary would cue us to yell back, 'Barren Fig Tree, Lord How Long, Count Not the Cost Thereof'. Uncle Neil was never abashed by such contretemps; he just went on to tell us another joke and/ or perhaps inform us how that morning he had saved a baby's life by the laying on of hands. ('Dr Huskei called just after he'd left,' my mother would say to me behind her hand.)

His wife Aunt May was a short emphatic woman with a voice like Dame Clara Butt and a figure not dissimilar, including an enormous Gibson Girl bust. She addressed Neil, whose head was some two feet above hers, as Giant. 'Giant saw Christ on the lawn this morning,' she would announce. 'On the lawn,' she would add as the company looked down at the tablecloth uneasily. 'Jesus. Just right out there on the lawn,' she would bawl out again. 'Jesus Christ, didn't you Giant?' Giant would bow his head forward with a look of ineffable holiness and nod silently twice. It was almost more than I could stand. If Christ had been messing around on our lawn I would have known about it. I was up before Giant. There would have been marks in the dew.

Apart from her being a tremendous back-up for God in Giant's life, there were only two things known about Aunt May: she saw every musical that went on in London (her favourite was *Over She Goes*), and she thought Swanage, where she took Giant and the family for their summer holiday, the prettiest place in England. It had been 'kissed by God'.

Quite unlike Neil was Arthur – the uncle who had acquired the mysterious nick-name of Julia when at Loretto. My father and mother called him Julia, Gamma called him Arthur and we children called him Uncle Artie. Uncle Artie was rich, sophisticated, racy and – like all Smiths – he was about six foot four in height. He had a long, yellowish, intelligent face, a yellow toothbrush moustache and a fringe of yellow hair round his shining bald head. He smoked cigarettes in a long yellow amber holder, dressed impeccably in grey flannel trousers and a quiet matching tweed jacket and waistcoat. In hot weather he wore a Panama hat, in winter a light grey homberg. In each trouser pocket he had a cache of loose change which he jingled when talking. Uncle Artie did the crossword in the library every morning after breakfast. He did not fish or shoot but went for a walk round the lodges each day before lunch if it were fine. If wet, he did not go out at all.

When at Craigielands Uncle Artie took the head of the table, my father being demoted to a position two down on the right hand side. We all recognised that Uncle Artie was a regular fellow. He ran the conversation with a continuous flow of slightly acid comment on the affairs of the household and the big world outside, then – slipping into a double act with my mother – would argue about the qualities of P. G. Wodehouse or Leslie Henson, or he would jolly Gamma into a lighter mood. Never once did he tell a set-piece joke, nor was God ever mentioned.

Uncle Artie had no great regard for my father and used to keep him firmly in his place, which was some distance beneath Uncle Artie. One day at lunch my father had a serious proposition to put. The Dog Trial men had decided they needed a new cup for hired shepherds living within twenty-five miles. My father had agreed to put it to Gamma and Uncle Artie that it should be called the Craigielands Cup and be paid for by them. My father started making the proposal in his meeting voice, but got no distance before Uncle Artie went after him. A cup? Why a cup? No one knew what to do with a cup. Why not something useful like a teapot? The Craigielands Teapot. My father struggled on, explaining that all Dog Trials gave cups; and on being quizzed again by Uncle Artie about the nature of the cup he told him that it would have a lid with a silver statuette of a dog on top. 'A dog?' said Uncle Artie. 'Why not a sheep? A sheep has far fewer features than a dog – much cheaper.' Still my father fought on, but it was hopeless. It ended in Uncle Artie saying he would give a cup for the best sheep in the Dog Trials – the sheep had a much worse time than the dogs and no one ever gave them a thought. After lunch in a corner of the hall I heard my mother say to my father, 'Julia didn't seem to want to pay for that Dog Trial thing, did he?' My father replied, 'He was just ragging.'

Another interesting thing about Uncle Artie was the visitors he brought with him. He had a raffish taste in friends. One was a lesbian (as I discovered much later) who ran a Daimler Hire service in Liverpool, had a voice like a man, sat with her legs apart and drank brandy; others were odd people he had picked up on cruises, for although the Chairman of Smith Edwards and of the Liverpool

Cotton Exchange, he did seem to cruise a great deal. Our favourite pair were the McLures, a lanky brother and sister in their forties, from the Glasgow shipping world. They had exquisitely refined Glaswegian accents which we loved to imitate and their greatest and best-loved line occurred when they were offered fruit. AIM NOT A VAIRY FROOTY PAIRSON they would say, and all around children would dive for cover as they exploded into laughter. The McLures must have wondered why, when they made it so absolutely clear that they were in no way fruity persons, they were so frequently offered fruit.

But easily the most dramatic thing about Uncle Artie was his marriage to Aunt Germaine. At the age of fifty-five he was staying at the Turnberry Hotel, no doubt to round off a Northern Capitals cruise with a week of golf. Each afternoon he sat close to the hotel trio as they played at tea time and one day he asked the leader if the young 'cellist would play a solo for him. He requested Saint Saens' 'Le Cygne', because he had learnt that she was French. Later he took the whole trio off to cream teas in Burns' cottage and a few days later proposed marriage to the 'cellist, then twenty-two years of age. She accepted him at once. When the bombshell dropped on Craigielands there was consternation. If she was French she was likely to be a Catholic. Yes she was. And if she was playing in a trio in a foreign country without a chaperone – well that sounded as if she might – well it did sound as though she might be *very* French.

Uncle Artie arrived on his own to quell the doubts. He sat two hours in the library with Gamma and when he came out he had a broad smile on his face and he strutted. Then he spent a much shorter time with my father and mother and they had champagne in toothmugs in the North Room because my mother was in bed. Marnie met Uncle Artie in the vestibule and with her unfailing instinct for a ham line threw her arms in the air, apron and all and with the gesture of a Druid priest said 'Mister Arthur, this-s-s' (when making a sententious speech Marnie would hiss on an S for a very long time) 'this is our Indian summer.'

Two weeks later Uncle Artie brought Aunt Germaine to face the

Craigielands ordeal. She won all hearts at once. Simple, sweet, intelligent and transparently good, she bowled Gamma over in a trice. I fell in love with her at first sight and she soon showed that she had a soft spot for me. A special relationship grew between us and she educated me in all manner of things that had never entered my life before. It was the first time I had encountered chic, and I liked it. Also, she played Debussy and Ravel on the Steinway and this opened up a whole new world.

The third son, Sconnie (again a never-explained Loretto nickname) we feared. He had been captain of the Scotland XV and was the Headmaster of Loretto. His way with boys of my age was bluff and abrupt. I remember a walk with him over the Red Brae with his son John and Sholto. As we walked he would bark out the terms of a competition which went on for most of the walk. 'Ballerina takes curtain call. Slips and falls.' Sholto would run ahead and go first, very self conscious. Next John, smiling and simpering too much, but getting the mime right: I would go last. 'One legged soldier, goes to salute the King. Trips over dog,' Uncle Sconnie would shout. So we all became one-legged soldiers in turn as Uncle Sconnie walked remorselessly on at the same pace. If you were overtaken in performance you just had to run forward again and start up from scratch.

Uncle Sconnie was an enthusiast for field sports and so was his wife Aunt Violet, who both fished and shot with him. She was a Russell from Essex and brought a whiff of English aristocracy into Craigielands life. She had high cheekbones, bright eyes, a mass of grey blue hair piled high on her head and a wild romantic temperament. I loved being with her and was content to ghillie for her on the lake – a thing I would not do for anyone else. Once, after fishing, we went up for tea and sat for half an hour listening to a visiting bishop holding forth about missionary work in Africa. As we left the room together she turned to me with a bright smile and said, 'What a ghastly man.' I squeezed her hand and she squeezed back and for a few moments we were intimate friends. Sconnie and Vi had another good quality; at table they talked about other things – birds, beasts, lichens, edible fungi, fishing – not about God.

Sconnie did talk about God, I knew (and preached sermons in Loretto chapel) but when he did so at Craigielands he had the decency to retire into the library and do it with Gamma in privacy.

Other guests flitted across the Craigielands scene, some of the regulars – like Gamma's sister Aunt Annie, who told us fantastic 'tales', very different from Gamma's 'stories' from real life or the short 'things', which were the briefest of documentary anecdotes; Cousin Lenore, a missionary from India; Temple Gardiner, a musical missionary from Africa; Bishop Dowell, an archi-episcopal bore from the see of Vancouver; Edinburgh cousins; distant Liverpool aunts; and one who was for many years the most regular of all visitors and my special companion.

The Reverend Karney, who worked with my father in the Missions to Seamen in San Francisco, rose to high office in the church and in the 1920s became Bishop of Johannesburg. His eldest son Peter was some six years older than I, and was sent to Rugby. Since he had no close relatives in Britain, he spent most of his holidays at Craigielands.

Peter Karney had curly black hair and a ready smile. My mother used to say he reminded her of a very handsome Galloway bullock. We became friends and – especially after Sholto went to school and began to stay with school friends in the holidays – spent a great deal of time together. Although Peter was much more knowing than I, I did not quiz him about sex, nor about public schools, nor about the ways of the big world – certainly not about religion, because if he had a drawback it was that he clearly intended to become a holy man. Indeed we didn't speak much to each other at all as we stalked rabbits with an airgun, tobogganed in the park, or climbed trees to search for a rare bird's nest. Our friendship was based on physical companionship and harmony of temperament. Peter was there, he was strong, he was breathing, he was kind, he was my friend. There was nothing sexual between us but a lot of what one might call dumb affection. Several times in later life, and particularly during the war, I have enjoyed this kind of friendship, usually with people with whom I had little in common. It only occurs when the two parties have to spend a great deal of time together alone. While it lasts it can be a most relaxed and rewarding relationship. Alas, without the stimulus of sex or the ties of family, property or business, it does not last long. All such friends disappeared quietly out of my life. But Peter and I still exchange a letter from time to time.

He said one thing which I will always remember. His mother, a really good woman, was giving him a talk about the facts of life and describing to him the relationship between urinary and sexual organs. 'I always think it such a pity,' she said, 'that He decided to put them so close together.'

There were some day visitors to Craigielands, but very few. To the south lay the county set with whom we mingled freely in later life but who were not yet deemed respectable enough to consort with Craigielands persons. They were fast, drank too much, were upper-class conservative and many did not go to church. From Moffat there were the McLarens and one or two elderly grace and favour visitors, and there was one family with whom we were on intimate terms.

Stanley Craig came of a Glasgow family that had made its pile in shipping, and he was a card, a comic, a friend. Elizabeth, his wife, came from Toronto and was a vigorous and sometimes hyper-active enthusiast for the project of the moment whatever it might be – transforming a farmhouse into a palace, bringing contemporary culture to the citizens of Edinburgh, setting up a foundation to study Canadian folk music, or making rugs in the Afghan manner. Then there were the girls, Deb, the same age as Sholto, Barbara for myself, Ruth for Michael and Judy for wee Pat. It was an exact match. The girls were tomboys, running wild as we did and operating with all the energy of their mother and the good humour of their father.

Stanley used to drive the smallest Austin Seven in Scotland. He was a huge man, six foot six and broad with it. He wore the loudest check tweeds I have ever seen and he would cram himself into this tiny car, plus the four senior children, which was tolerable on a fine day when the car was open but which inflicted serious hardship on one and all when the hood and the sidescreens were up. Stanley used to lead us in song, sometimes Harry Lauder, sometimes

Pagliacci and suddenly he would wave both arms in a huge theatrical gesture, whilst the driverless car swerved about the road, and call for silence. After an appropriate delay to build expectation he would give vent to the catchphrase for the day. One night, for instance when it was blowing half a gale and sleet was driving against the windscreen he pronounced:

IT'S A COORSE NICHT.

'Aye,' he went on in Harry Lauder style, 'I've seen some terrible weather in my time but I'm tellin ye that the nicht is' – and he paused for the chorus – 'is A COORSE NICHT' we all yelled back. Then he would perm the rhythm by going 'ITSA ITSA IT IT ITSA' and we would duly chorus: 'A COORSE NICHT.'

Then we might have a short recitative in the form of a weather forecast leading to an aria to the tune of 'La Donna e Mobile' but to the words 'Le Notte e scurillo.' This of course was all meat and drink to me, and I thought Stanley Craig to be the funniest and nicest man in the world. Once at a wet and windy covert shoot when he was missing a lot of pheasants I plucked his sleeve and whispered, 'It's a coorse nicht.' This cheered him up and he began to shoot much better.

But it was the Craig girls who made their mark on us. They were the only females of our own age with whom we were on easy terms. There was no romance, but from my frequent encounters with Barbara I learnt what it was like to be close to a woman's body. When we were pressed against each other in the airing cupboard playing sardines, or when she sat on my knee in the Austin Seven, I was aware of something peaceful and comforting. She never entered into my sexual fantasies but was always there in the heroic ones, as when I would rush out and with my bare hands save her from a pack of wolves, or when she was being tormented by big village boys I would lay them out one by one with a straight left and she would look into my eyes and say, 'Denis, you are wonderful'. Alas, nothing like this happened in real life since we were more likely to be slinging mud at each other, racing across the river, or else competing to catch the greatest number of black slugs.

Visitors and guests, unless they were men of the cloth, provided a degree of escape from the leaden cloud that hung over the Craigielands dining table. I was constantly on the lookout for some fellow spirit, for a sympathiser to whom I could unburden myself and tell about the mysterious sense of oppression from which I suffered. Alas, I found no confidant. Uncle Artie enjoyed putting my father down, it was true, but one could not talk intimately to an uncle. The Craigs laughed good naturedly at my father's wilder eccentricities, but they accepted the image of him as a kind and good man and would never have dreamt of criticising a grown-up person so well known and so well liked. Even Peter Karney let me down here, because with all my affection for him I knew his sense of values was dangerously close to those of the Trinity.

Another potential avenue of escape lay through the schoolroom, but this too turned out to be a dead end. After the Montessori period my mother gave up teaching her children. They then went on to sterner stuff, lessons with Gamma and less frequently, my father. But the moment came when it was thought proper for a tutor to be engaged for Sholto and myself. At that time my father was very thick with the village schoolmaster, one John Bulman, who had ingratiated himself to such an extent that in every organisation of which my father was President Mr Bulman became the Secretary, including the Beattock Show, the Dog Trials, the Curling Club, the Poor House Committee and several local charitable trusts. It was a relationship that was not to endure.

Mr Bulman became our tutor when Sholto was eleven and I was nine.

As soon as his school was dismissed he rode up on the south drive on his bicycle, and on Tuesdays, and Thursdays an hour earlier. Closely observed by Sholto and myself, he leant his bicycle against the great oak tree, walked over the lawn and entered the house through the door of my father's office and sat down between us at the schoolroom table in the billiard room. First he removed his bicycle clips and then began to sharpen every pencil within sight.

Mr Bulman was a small, ferret-faced Welshman with a furtive look and a twitch at one corner of his mouth. He had a small ginger moustache and the remnants of some golden ginger fuzz on his balding head, and when he was not smoking a Woodbine he sucked a pencil.

Sholto and I knew at once Mr Bulman was no good. He could teach the three R's up to elementary school standards but that was it. His main task was to prepare Sholto for the common entrance exam for Loretto and this was plainly beyond him. Nevertheless we spent many reasonably happy hours listening to Mr Bulman's reminiscences of World War One, in which he had evidently played a leading part. He enjoyed shocking us. He would tell us that he had gone to wake up his mate who lay doggedly still until Mr Bulman seized him by the hair and his head came away from his body and hung in Mr Bulman's hand. His neck had been severed by a piece of shrapnel. Did it bleed, we asked? Mr Bulman twitched nervously and gazed silently out of the window. Of course it did, he was saying. It might have been charitable to attribute Mr Bulman's character defects to shell shock. Less charitable to assume, as I did, that he had never been in the war at all and was nervous of being found out. He had a passion for pencils, keeping a row of them in a waistcoat pocket, ranging from HH to BB. He told us how pencils were made, how to maintain them and how to get good service and long life from them. He showed us some specimens he had kept for ten years because of their beauty or some uncommon characteristic such as a misprint in the writing on the side. He had a red HB on which the word Royal had been printed Rayol. This was much prized and he would only show it on special occasions. He made my father buy a pencil sharpener that screwed onto the table and was worked by turning a handle. Thus we were able to keep all our pencils in tip-top condition. To Mr Bulman a blunt pencil was pretty well a sin against the Holy Ghost.

After pencils Mr Bulman was keenest on tea. Aggie Crosbie would walk in at four-thirty with a dainty tray of bread and butter, scones and teabreads. As soon as she had laid it in front of him he put his hands together under the table and gazed earnestly at the spread before him. Perhaps he was considering in what order he wanted to work his way through it. Then after a long pause he would start talking again, pour his tea very slowly, and take the first item. He ate mincingly, like a cat, and masticated each mouthful until it seemed he would never swallow it. Teaching, such as it was, stopped during tea and we discussed general matters – the smell at Passchendaele, for instance, or taking boots off dead men's feet at Vimy Ridge. After tea, Mr Bulman dashed through my father's office to the adjacent smokers' lavatory and came back smelling, as I thought then, of disinfectant.

When lessons were over at five-thirty Mr Bulman usually moved into the office where my father was now typing and would sit and discuss one of the multiplicity of problems that faced them as responsible officers of so many important enterprises.

It was after Sholto had taken the common entrance for Loretto that the storm broke. A letter from the headmaster told my father that Sholto had failed in every subject except scripture and English. For Latin he had got no marks at all. He could not go to Loretto until he had taken the common entrance again and done better. There was a terrible row. Loretto had dared to turn down one of its own – Adam Forman's son! Loretto never used to bother about things like a boy not knowing any Latin. Something had gone wrong with Loretto. My father got into his car and motored up to see the headmaster. When he came back he told Sholto he could go to Loretto but it must be a term later and meanwhile he had to learn Latin and maths and other things too. My father would take over in maths and we would have a new tutor very soon.

Then the post mortem began. Sholto's exercise books were scrutinised. It was clear that not much Latin had been done and what had been done was disgraceful. There was one simple exercise from Hillard and Botting for which Mr Bulman had awarded ten out of ten. Not one answer was correct. Further probing disclosed a wide range of enormities. The Trinity were incensed and had an indignation meeting. My father saw Mr Bulman and confronted him. At first he denied everything and then he wept.

And so Mr Bulman fell from grace, first as tutor and little by little, as the universal Secretary. For two or three years there had been small sums of prize money – five shillings here and two shillings there – going a-missing. Suspicions were aroused, and when Mr Bulman became a close friend of the Treasurer of the Beattock Show Society and a bill for £19.11.00. owing to William Clader of Leith (Marquees, Windows, Blinds, Tents, Flags, Tarpaulins, Sails, Lorry Covers, Rick Cloths) went unpaid, Mr Calder wrote to my father saying: 'We have written to Mr John Bulman several times recently regarding our account for £19.11.00. for Marquees hired. We should not have sent you this personal letter but for the fact that Mr Bulman has not even had the courtesy lately to reply. Four months ago he wrote saying a cheque would soon be forthcoming.' They went on to threaten a writ.

To this my father replied: 'I cannot get much satisfaction from the Treasurer owing to holidays etc but to ease your mind I enclose herewith my cheque for £19.11/- for which I will be glad if you will send me a receipt so that I can recover from the Treasurer later on. I imagine it is owing to slackness that the account has not been paid so I will be obliged if you will say nothing more about it to either Mr Bulman or the Treasurer so that they may imagine it is still unpaid. They want waking up.'

Whether or not the Treasurer or Mr Bulman were successfully woken up and whether my father ever recovered his £19.11.00. is not known. I think it unlikely and I also wonder whether there was a public confrontation between the President and the delinquent Treasurer and Secretary. My father would not want the General Committee, which included several of our own estate workers, to know that he personally had bailed out Mr Bulman. But worse was to come.

It was revealed that Bulman drank whisky, sometimes to excess. Now that he had fallen from grace all sorts of stories about him came out of odd corners, some of them five or six years old. A brawl with a neighbouring farmer, ejection from the Black Bull for riotous behaviour, found legless in the school playground at midnight, a drunken spree one night after the Dog Trials during which a tent fell in on him. Some of the stories went too far, like stealing the schoolchildren's pocket money and beating his wife, but it was agreed by one and all that Mr Bulman was a very bad man indeed. Such was the first moral guardian selected for Sholto and myself by the Trinity. And from now on I was able to distinguish the respective smells of Johnny Walker and disinfectant.

Mr Bulman was replaced immediately by Mr Dunn, selected by Uncle Artie from the outgoing classical students of Liverpool University. He was the opposite of Mr Bulman, a profound scholar, a model of probity and one of the most stunningly dull men I have ever met. He had a handsome swarthy face, two suits, one navy blue and one brown, and he lodged in Moffat in a bed-sitter where he read Plato every night. It was not thought proper for a tutor, a single man, to sleep in the same house as my sisters.

So now the bicycle arrived at the oak tree at nine-thirty and stayed there until five-thirty. The lugubrious Dunn would stride across the lawn, a Liddell and Scott lexicon under his arm, his pockets bulging with Virgil and Livy, and with his short filthy black pipe clenched between his teeth, giving off poisonous clouds of Diggers Gold Flake. He would start right in almost before he had sat down. Hillard and Botting, soon for Sholto to be triumphantly replaced by North and Hillard, Kennedy's Shorter Latin Primer and the huge Lewis and Short dictionary all had to be at the ready.

I believe that with Sholto Mr Dunn had some success, for if I remember correctly when next he took the common entrance (only for practice, because he was going to Loretto anyway) he got forty out of a hundred. With me Mr Dunn was a total flop, and I with him. I did not see why I should put myself out to oblige so unprepossessing an individual, so even when I knew the right answer (which was not often) I gave the wrong one.

MENSA
MENSAT
MENSAY
MENSING

I would go, driving Mr Dunn into a frenzy of rage and frustration.

'Denis you are IMPOSSIBLE,' he would shout, and would sometimes slip out of the office door and pace about on the flagstones until he had his hatred for me under control. When he came back he would puff out his Diggers Gold Leaf until the fog was so thick you could hardly see your hand in front of your face.

Mr Dunn stayed on in spite of me because he thought Sholto was a game little trier, he liked the food, he admired the Trinity, he fell in love with Sheila and he needed the money. It was worth putting up with me for such considerations. He hoped to introduce discipline and to give me a hard time, but as it turned out I gave him a much harder time than he gave me. Although he probably believed in God, his true religions were the Greeks and cricket. I therefore read enough about Greece to enable me to make derogatory remarks about those Greek things he held most dear. 'What a pity about these vases,' I would say, turning the pages of an illustrated Greek history. 'The horses are so badly drawn.' Or 'I don't believe the Greek tragedies were written by the Greeks at all. Some clever dick Roman saw money in it.' Such casual remarks made him apoplectic. He would yell at me, banging the Liddell and Scott with his fist. 'Don't you realise that Greek civilisation has made us what we are?'

Cricket was even easier. One only had to suggest that county cricket should be replaced by county rounders – a much better game – to have him pacing the flags for five full minutes. Once when he was in his fist-shaking and shouting mode because I said I thought Jack Hobbs was a kind of bird, Gamma appeared in the doorway. He shouted on for a moment or two until he spotted her, then sprang to his feet in confusion, dropping his pipe on the parquet floor with a clatter. 'I was just trying to drive some sense into Denis' head,' he said. Gamma looked at him evenly, turned on her heel and left without a word. It was not long after that Mr Dunn left.

Mr Dunn amazed me because he thought I was stupid. He also amazed me by being such an easy touch. You could get a rise out of him every time. The solemn, pompous, Greek-loving fool. I remember our parting exchange. As he shook hands on the Craigielands front steps he said in his frightful jolly uncle manner, 'And I hope that in the fullness of time you will come to appreciate the beauties of cricket.' 'I think I am too old for it,' I said. 'I think cricket is for younger boys.' He stormed off.

And so it was that I learned nothing from either of my first two tutors. One was a dunce and a petty crook, the other a pompous fool and although they did divert my attention from the pressures of the Trinity to some degree, it was not to much advantage.

It was about this time that a profound change came over my life. Sholto went to Loretto. John and Roslin Smith joined the family. Their father Sconnie, the Headmaster of Loretto, had died of a heart attack in 1926, and, five years later, their mother, Auntie Vi, had been killed in a car crash. My parents took them in as members of the family on equal terms with the rest of us. During the holidays John Smith, nearer to me in age than Sholto, became a close companion in fishing expeditions and in clowning about during the long hours of holiday life in a country house. During the term time I entered a period of comparative isolation. With the Trinity I was reasonably polite but always looking for an escape. My mother and I could still have fun together but the other two were beginning to get on my nerves. Sheila was a young lady at a posh finishing school in Lausanne, Kaff and Roslin were schoolgirls at Wycombe Abbey and St Leonards respectively, Sholto and John were at Loretto, Michael and Patrick were so far away down the Craigielands ladder that I saw little of them. Everyone came home for the holidays.

I had a special bond with my mother (which was shortly to be seriously threatened) and with Sheila too, who was so good, so dutiful that she found in my outrageous behaviour something of an escape from the prison of her own puritanism. One day she was called out of the room by my father just as she was about to eat a chocolate. 'See the dog doesn't get it, Den,' she said, laying it on a low table.

As soon as she was out of sight I ate the chocolate and when she came back I said, 'Terribly sorry. Rab got it when I wasn't looking.' She gave me an uncertain look which I returned with a gaze of pure innocence. On that occasion she was not sure, but as similar experiences multiplied she rumbled me and although one part of her condemned such gross dishonesty, at the same time she admired and enjoyed the effrontery of it. She would look at me laughing, and say, 'Denis, that is a terrible thing to do and you know it; you are getting worse and worse and you will come to a bad end.'

But Sholto had been my real running mate, my constant companion, almost – because I was as big as he – my twin. In those later Craigielands years when we were parted I was, to begin with, like an animal that had lost its fellow. Because he immediately adopted the persona of schoolboy we rapidly drew apart. He became more censorious (and goodness knows he had plenty of grounds). I became impatient of his precious schoolboy world, his new schoolboy vocabulary, his keenness on the right things, and his transparent honesty. I was then opposed to the right things, thoroughly mendacious and already tended to be agin' the government, whatever the government might be. We therefore went through the process of an emotional divorce and have never really seen eye to eye on fundamentals since, although this has not impaired a lasting brotherly friendship.

One incident from a much earlier time illustrates the difference between us. It was chocolates again. Two chocolates had been left on the lid of the piano in the drawing room. My parents came into the room and saw that the chocolates had disappeared. Only Sholto and I had been in the room and there were no dogs present. My parents confronted us: who had eaten the chocolates? We both denied it strenuously. As the pressure mounted Sholto began to cry, still protesting innocence. My mother looked at my father and said, 'I think that the one who cries is the guilty one,' and Sholto was punished. It was I, of course, who had eaten the chocolates. I had little difficulty in suppressing any feelings of shame or guilt. It was foolish of Sholto to have cried.

For the rest it is a mistake to believe that a big family engenders close relationships between siblings. It doesn't. There is a pack ethos, common modes of behaviour, common jokes, a private language and also strong ties of affection. But family affection, however strong, is a different thing from intimacy.

So it was that the year came to be divided between the holidays when the house was full of young people and noise and laughter, and the term time when I lived alone with the Trinity. Through solitude and solitary pursuits I found out who I was and became a private person. My private persona was undetected within the family group. To them I was the same dashing show-off, but during these two years of comparative isolation I formed a new relationship with a different class of person that became for me an alternative society.

8

The Likes of Us

Craigielands Farm, sitting high above the big house, high above the woods, so high that if offered a panoramic view of half the hills in Dumfriesshire, was my special place. The farmyard itself was like a thousand other lowland farmyards, a group of single-storey slate and whitewash stonebuilt cattle sheds, store rooms, lofts and loose boxes with room for up to sixty or seventy animals 'in the house'. The corn was threshed by horsepower, three great Clydesdales walking round in a circular housing, their hames fixed to three inverted U's as commonly seen on a Russian troika which were fixed to the central vertical shaft. This was geared at a ratio of 4:1 through two bevel wheels, the second on an axle that ran through into the next building and drove the threshing machine itself. This was early industrial machinery of grandeur and power.

Only the bothy on top of the stables, and the farmhouse itself, broke the low skyline of the buildings. Within the farmyard there was always life: men and horses going to drink at the sandstone trough, the pig's dinner cooking in an open-air boiler, the pig himself, poor innocent, standing vertically to look over his door, his snout between his trotters, and everywhere hens and more hens and, herding the hens incessantly and pointlessly, old Pat, a grey-nosed sheepdog long retired from active service. It was to the farm that I ran every morning in summer before breakfast, at seven o'clock (any earlier start had been forbidden) and found out what was going to happen that day and where. Tom Quigley would tell me if he were there, if not his son Jim would be watering the horses before they were yoked at seven thirty. Tom and Jim were my friends but just a little inclined to be my guardians too. They were responsible not only for my safety but for my character, and they wanted to make a man of me and in particular they wanted to make a farmer of me.

Jim was tall and lantern-jawed. He was the head horsekeeper and when he laughed he wrinkled his nose like a horse sneezing and showed a flashing array of red gums with short brown teeth set into them. He would let me ride his horses when unyoked, but was much stricter than the other men in matters of safety. He would allow me to drive a cart, standing on the cart floor like a professional, and he would let me plough if I didn't make a mess of it, but he would never allow me to drive any other piece of farm machinery. Jim and I talked only about farming. I questioned him endlessly. Why not sow the corn earlier? What did a liverfluke do to a sheep? Did horses have any feeling in their hooves? He would answer each question fully and carefully, even difficult ones like how did he train the horses to piss when he gave the signal? (a low fluctuating whistle like the call of a mezzo-soprano curlew) and what was sheep's afterbirth for? Sometimes he would walk in silence behind the plough for three minutes before answering, but I knew he would in the end.

Ploughing was the loneliest job of all. From November to January three quarters of an acre a day was good going in the days of a single-furrow horse plough. So it took some thirty days to turn Knockhill, a field of twenty acres. You could plough in frost until it got three inches into the ground, but it slowed you up. You could plough in lying snow until it was three inches deep.

Not all the men were so friendly. Two of them, Bob Wilson and Jimmie Moffat, both as I thought very old (perhaps they were in their fifties) were no more than tolerant of me and also gruff. They always thought I was going to get in the way, which I never did. When they were geligniting sections of the trunk of an oak tree, they made a hole with a huge two handled auger, dropped in the gelignite and tamped it down with earth and sawdust. As one crouched over the fuse he would shout to the other, 'Hev ye gottim?' to which the other would reply, 'Aye I've gottim,' at which the fuse man would ignite it and walk casually back to where we stood some fifty yards away. I found this insulting. Got him, indeed. I knew just how far away and where to stand when a shot was fired. I did not care too much for Bob Wilson and Jimmie Moffat and used to imitate Bob's habit of tripping over his own feet, which always got a laugh, also Jimmie Moffat's habit of wiping his nose on his sleeve, then wiping his sleeve on his arse, then rubbing his arse against a tree.

Jock Wilson, Bob's son, was a different matter. He was young and dark-haired with a bright inquisitive eye. He had worked as a porter at the station but had been laid off for being cheeky to the stationmaster. He and I would chat in a very relaxed fashion. He called my father 'Forman' which impressed me greatly. He was also irreverent about him which impressed me even more. 'Have ye seen Forman's new motor?' he would say to one of the other men. 'He disna ken whit to dae wi it. Up and doon the Glasga road jast playin' hissel.' The other men would look at the ground when he spoke like this, and once when Tom Quigley overheard him he told him to keep his mouth shut and get his feet moving. But I did not dislike it.

When the men worked alone, even when it was cutting hay, lambing, or sowing corn with the fiddle, it could get boring. But collective work never failed to please, whether it was haymaking, tattie lifting or logging with teams of two horses dragging tree boles on a chain to the brink of an almost vertical drop and then galloping down with the trees at their heels until they reached the level where the log sled stood below. At haymaking the best moment was when delicious treacle scones were brought out by Bessie and Sisse Quigley and eaten in the matchless aroma of fresh hay. I never knew whether I should take a treacle scone or not. The girls laughed at me and said go on, take one, you're a worker. But I was shy and refused. So Jock often took an extra one to slip me later on.

Of all the collective occasions, harvesting and sheep shearing were the best. At a sheep shearing men came from the farms all around, making up with our own workforce a team of between twelve and fifteen. Each man sat on a triangular trestle and a boy would collar a ewe and haul her across to him, exposing her underparts in a most indelicate way. Then the shears would snip and snip until the ewe, shining white in her nakedness, was branded with hot tar on an iron which marked her with the letter S for Smith and she was released to join her mates. Then the clags and any other dirt were clipped from her fleece, it was wrapped in a bundle and chucked into a huge sack hanging from what looked like a set of extra-stout goal posts standing some eight feet above the ground. Inside the sack a farm boy sweated and tramped, half suffocated by the oily smell of freshly cut fleece. When the sack was full he jumped out and lay on the ground while the sack was sewn up and a new one mounted. Once a boy called Bonzo, fresh from the Glasgow slums, lay on the grass and refused to get into the next sack, saying he was dying. But he wasn't, for after Tom Quigley had taken him behind a shed for a short talk he jumped in again and was quite well when work finished some four hours later.

The shearers sweated phenomenally as they worked. It was my job to keep the fire going under the hot tar, and occasionally to brand an exhausted or otherwise immobile sheep, and I had plenty of time to study the workers' methods, demeanour and clothing. This last never varied. Next to the skin they had John Ells, the cuff of the legs visible between their socks and their trousers, the sleeves of the top half rolled up with their shirt sleeves. Then there was a thick woollen shirt and tweed trousers, with hill boots, the sole rising sharply at the toe, then a tweed waistcoat and on top of that either a blue or a brown one-piece overall, full-trousered and with braces from the back to hold up the chest piece in front. It was just after midsummer and I wore only two garments, a cotton shirt and my old Oliphant tartan kilt. As I watched them sweat and sweat I wondered how long it would take the principle of Lorettonian dress to penetrate as far as Craigielands Hill Farm. (It took about fifty years. In about 1975 I saw Tom Quigley's grandson working a tractor in a sports shirt and shorts.)

Sheep shearing was competitive. Each man kept his score either by cutting nicks on his trestle or by making marks with the flat wood pencils they used to carry in their waistcoat pockets. Nothing was ever said about these scores until the end of the day when Tom

Quigley, who seemed to have second sight, would walk over and seize the winner in a warm handshake, at the same time announcing his score. 'Tommy Bell, fifty-three sheep sheared,' and there would be a chorus of 'Well done Tom,' or 'So it's Tommy again.' Throughout the whole day there was no drink but tea or water from the pump and no food but two generous servings of pan scones, soda scones and treacle scones, some filled with cheese and some with jam.

Harvesting was a longer and more dramatic event. One day in August two men went out to the first field to be cut (we grew nothing but oats) with scythes over their shoulders and whetstones sticking up from their back hip pockets. As soon as the dew would let them they started to 'open up', moving their scythes and feet in exact synchronised rhythm. They cut outwards, towards the edge of the field, the windrow of the left-hand mower lying on the grass by the dyke. A third man or a boy would arrive an hour or so later and bind the cut corn into sheaves, knotting a twist of straw to hold it in the middle. In about four hours the mowers would complete the circle of a twelve acre field, whereupon they would give their scythes the full treatment: not just the short thirty or so strokes which was enough to keep them going whilst they were mowing, but a long and careful honing of the whole blade with perhaps some adjustment of angle or balance. A scythe blade was very personal to a man, a great scythe was treated like a Stradivarius and only loaned, if at all, to other respected virtuosi. So began the second round and when completed there lay an open road some ten or twelve feet wide, ready for the binder.

In those days the binder was the king of all farm machinery. It had only just taken over from the reaper which did no more than simply cut the corn. The binder cut it and delivered it back on the field in neatly tied sheaves. For some days now Jim Quigley had been oiling our binder, cleaning it, repairing torn canvases and checking his tools and spares. Jim would never take his binder to the corn if the ground were too soft (for the whole apparatus was driven by one massive central wheel which must grip the surface and neither sink in nor skid), nor if the dew were still on the base of the stems, for this would wet the canvases and make them heavy and prone to tear. On a good day, at around twelve noon, the glorious moment would come when the binder rattled and crashed its way down the farm road to the chosen field and the sweet music of the harvest began. The three Clydesdales, Polly, Dick and Ned, were yoked side by side with a double and a single swingle-tree geared at two to one, which gave complete flexibility to the motive power of the horses like a universal joint on the transmission of a car. Jim sat on the elegantly moulded cast-iron seat, lord of the harvest. I walked by the sheaf ejector. If the corn were laid or tousled in any way it would not eject cleanly, and without human help a binder could have six or seven tangled sheaves trailing behind it. I watched the binder twine and when it got low raced over to the reserve stock and brought back two new six-pound balls for Jim to put into the string canister. I also killed the rabbits and hares which had clapped down below the binder knives and were often horribly mutilated. I remember one big hare with all four legs neatly cut off, screaming like a baby.

If the corn was badly laid it had to be porked, or raised up with a pole to allow the binder knives to get beneath it. There were already two men stooking the sheaves and porking called for another two, sometimes three. As the little forest of uncut corn shrank, so did the animals, at least those who had not clapped down, congregate in the centre. At the right moment, and everyone knew when it came, porkers and stookers would congregate with sticks and stones ready for the slaughter. As each rabbit, or hare broke cover there would be a wild yell and it would be assaulted from all sides. If it escaped the first onslaught it could be run down, at least by Jock Wilson or by me, because the short newly cut stubble hurt its paws and reduced it to a sort of hop-hop gait, very unlike the fast flat run of a rabbit over grass.

Then the binder would move, even at seven o'clock at night, to the next field, for in Dumfriesshire dry cutting days in August were rare. Thus for perhaps three or four weeks, depending on the weather, the music of the binder could be heard and the area of uncut corn grew smaller and smaller. As I walked by the binder I calculated how much would be cut that day and the next and how long it would be before we finished. But calculations could go astray and one year when we had gales and storms in September we were still cutting the Mill Shed field on November 5th and then had to abandon it to the pheasants and wild duck.

Walking by the binder was sheer happiness. There was the rhythm of the great machine itself, the sight of the three Clydesdales sweating and straining in front and the companionship of Jim just up above my head. When it was time to piss, Jim dismounted, gave his horses his low warbling whistle and they stretched out their hind legs as pedigree dogs do at Crufts and obliged. Jim went discreetly to piss on one side of the horses, I pissed on the other. When it came to lunch time Mrs Quigley brought out a special piece for me because there was now no doubt I was a worker.

One day the binder juddered to a halt. Jim got down and went underneath, and when he came out his face was like death. The bracket that held the twine needle had sheared off. We might lose a day. Stookers, porkers and the Quigley girls all gathered round. Jim unbolted the two broken pieces and they were passed from hand to hand. There were gloomy forebodings as to how long it would take to get a replacement from Austin McAslan in Glasgow. 'Shall I take it down to the smiddy and see if Jim Porteous can sort it?' I said. They thought it unlikely that Jim could sort it but it might be worth a try.

I raced across the field to my bike, half a broken bracket in each hand, jumped into the saddle and flew down the steep and bumpy farm road to the smithy in Beattock village below. Jim Porteous, the acknowledged king of the village, was busy shoeing a huge horse when I arrived. 'Jim, Jim, you must stop,' I said. 'The twine needle bracket on the binder has sheared off and we're losing cutting time.' 'Losing cuttin' time?' said Jim. 'That winna do, young man. Let's see it.' He handled the broken bracket as a cowboy handles a gun in a Western, twirling it in his fingers, fitting it together, tapping it on the anvil. No, he couldn't mend it. It would have no strength. But he could make a new one. How long would that take? As long as it would take a pig to get to Lockerbie, said Jim.

So a piece of metal was selected and thrust into the furnace, made shining and white hot by the work of the boy at the bellows and soon the metal was white hot too. Then began the clanging and beating and the bending until a perfect replica began to take shape. Finally Jim made four holes through the glowing metal with a hard punch and cast it into the water butt, where it sizzled and sent up a cloud of steam. All this time, as was his wont, he kept up a running commentary. 'So what will they pay ye for this, young man?' – 'Tell Jim Quigley next time he should run down the hill hissel. It would take some o' fat off his arse.' – 'My cuddy could get further and run faster than Jimmy's fancy bike' (Jim had just bought a Raleigh motor bike), and much more of the same.

Then he wiped his hands on his leather apron pitted with spark holes, lifted the bracket out of the butt with a pair of tongs, handed it over to me, and with a skiff on the head said, 'Here ye are, young man. Tell ye father he can pay for it with a big troot.' (Jim meant a day's fishing on Craigielands lake.) He then returned to the horse, which had been very patient.

As I rode up the brae with all the strength at my command I thought Jim Porteous was probably the most impressive person I had ever met. My return with a serviceable bracket after an absence of only two hours was greeted with incredulity. It was a moment of great glory, but suddenly I remembered I should be at lessons with Gamma. When I panted out my story to her she just said: 'You did something very useful and very good. You will do an extra hour tomorrow.'

The corn stood in stooks for four weeks, perhaps six, even eight weeks in bad weather. If the crop was light the stook would be made up of eight sheaves, if heavy only six, to expose more of the wet bottoms to the air. From time to time the sheaves would be turned in the stook to let them ripen better and to give some air to their damp bottoms. Sooner or later the day would arrive when the corn was ripe enough and dry enough to lead, or cart, off the field. In Moffat weather it was always the aim to lead a whole field in one day and since work could not start until the dew had lifted, this meant a mighty collective effort. All hands were summoned, Davy

Johnstone and Sam Boa, normally estate workers, Jim Sloan the carpenter's son, even Andre Grieve the keeper and a very superior person. There were six carts and only five horses, so old Simon, a grey gelding from the adjoining Broomlands farm, was pressed into service.

The carts were all fitted with frames which jutted out almost to the horses' neck in front and equally far all round. They were adjusted to lie above gate-post height and provided a platform upon which the towering square edifice of sheaves could be built. The well of the cart looked the size of a matchbox in the middle of the spreading timbers.

The skilled work lay in building the load on the cart in the field and building the ricks in the stackyard. Jim Quigley and two others worked on the carts, Tom and one other laid the sheaves on top of the growing stack. One man, Jimmie Moffat, who was a nonentity for the rest of the year, came into his own at leading time. He was the quickest and most dexterous rick builder in the parish and had once given a demonstration at the Eaglesfield show. The other men forked sheaves up to the builders. The carts were led by boys and by Sissie and Bessie. It was the job that called for least skill and least strength, but I gloried in it. Tom and Jim kept an eye on the work flow and if a queue developed or if there was a pair of idle hands anywhere they would shout in their rich, slightly strangulated Lallans voices, 'Up one row, Jimmie,' or 'Haund that cairt at the yett, Jock.' We didn't even stop for tea and a piece. Mrs Quigley roamed the field with a basket of scones and flasks of tea and dispensed them to any workers who had a slack moment. I stood close to Prince all day, which was nice since he was 'my' horse but not so nice because he had a running abcess on his cheek which discharged pus copiously, smelt horrible and attracted a swarm of flies. Every hour or two I wiped it clean with a knot of hay and the flies would follow the hay. But soon they were back again.

At the start, usually about midday, there was much joking and shouting from the men, and the girls especially attracted a lot of badinage. But as the hours passed the field quietened and by six o'clock there was absolute silence except for the creak of the carts and the snottering of the horses as the corn dust got into their nostrils. As it grew dark Mrs Quigley would bring out the storm lanterns, one for each cart, and a Tilly lamp at the stackyard gates. Now it was becoming a desperate struggle against time. Tom and Jim, aware of the required rate of stooks per hour, would keep looking anxiously into the gloaming to see what was left and would then pull out their turnip watches. We always finished. The latest I remember was ten thirty. As the last carts reached the stackyard the now redundant field workers dribbled up the the stackyard gate where, set out under the Tilly lamp, were scones of all sorts and again flasks of tea. There was little conversation, but each of the carts on this final run was given a greeting and when the very last cart went through the stackyard gate this was recognised by one and all in low-key Lallans style. No one shouted 'Three Cheers for Tom Quigley', there were no flagons of beer and no harvest home song as described in some of the English farming books which I had read. Instead the climax of the day was marked by exclamations which ranged from 'So that's it' to the simple 'Aye' or the universally expressive 'Uha'. The group then silently put their mugs back in Mrs Quigley's basket, wished each other goodnight and disappeared down the hill into the dark. I was an hour late for bed that night and was unable to make my father and mother understand why it would have been impossible to get home any sooner.

Away from the farm I had two special friends in Davy Sloan the carpenter and Andrew Grieve the gamekeeper. Davy was a man of nearly sixty with a hunched back and a drip at the end of his nose. His special qualities were his willingness to let one try almost anything with any of his tools and his scepticism about my father's theories in relation to constructing rabbit hutches, gates, trap doors or whatever was the job of the moment.

'You see, Davy,' my father would say, making a few quick strokes on a pad with his pencil, 'you do it this way, you put the cross member here, not there.' Davy would look at the sketch in silent misery. You know best, Mr Forman,' he would say. 'You know best.' 'What's more,' my father would add with a sudden inspiration, 'you could attach a wire to the underside, run it through a staple and make a fail safe device.' Again Davy would gaze glumly at the paper. 'You know best,' he would say again, and wearily return to his bench. He never contradicted my father and never told him how it should be done. It was not his style. He went away and made the thing, whatever it was, in the correct manner in the hope that my father would have forgotten all his theories by the time it was finished. But sometimes he was forced to make it the wrong way because my father insisted, and when the whole thing collapsed or broke or didn't work he did not appear to get any satisfaction from the debacle. It was often quite clear that my father didn't know best, but proving this only seemed to make Davy sadder.

When we were alone Davy and I sang together. Our repertoire was the complete works of Frank Crumit, a popular light baritone, all of whose records Davy owned and played on his secondhand HMV portable. Our favourite was Abdul Abulbul Amir and another a song which included the memorable lines:

Silly as it seems
The lady of my dreams
Taught me how to play the second fiddle.

Davy sang in a soft counter-tenor and I joined in with my treble. We changed the rhythm to suit the job. Thus each syllable of A-BUL-BUL-A-MIR would synchronise with hammer blows and when using the plane the stroke would start on the downbeat of each bar. We didn't talk much, but we had a close rapport.

Andrew Grieve was an entirely different matter. He was our guardian and outdoor tutor and used to take us for walks at times set by my father. He had been a despatch rider in World War I and after that a keeper in Glendaruel in the Highlands. He knew everything there was to know about wild animals, birds and shooting dogs, which he trained in large numbers. But more than that he knew about volcanoes, about what made the weather, and about natural forces, and was particularly keen on a region of the world which he called the Anatartic. He was a formidable man at any time and a terrible man when angry, but respected by all of us and regarded as the final adjudicator on any outdoor matter, such as was it a weasel or a stoat. He imparted wisdom as he walked, stopping only when the subject became so absorbing that it overcame movement.

Once when Sholto and I were on a long walk with Andrew we saw a kestrel fly off her nest in a tall Scots pine. We had no kestrel's eggs in our collection. Without saying a word Andrew stripped off his coat and waistcoat and putting a dog's chain round the trunk, started to climb up the clean bole of the Scots pine as boys climb up palm trees in the Pacific islands. Up and up he went, amazingly fast until he reached the first branch where the tree forked and he could use more conventional methods. In minutes he was down again, and on lifting his cap took four freshly laid kestrel eggs out of his hair.

One morning I was on the back road near the ash tip and I saw a strange black dog tied to a tree. I was going forward to inspect it when a gun went off. The dog collapsed in a heap with a little scream. I ran up to it and found it was dead, with blood pouring out of its ears and mouth. I was stunned with shock and was bending over the dog when I felt a hand on my shoulder and heard Andrew's voice saying, 'It had tae be pit doon.' He then put the dog in a sack and made me help him dig a hole to bury it. Digging the hole with Andrew talking to me all the time made me feel better.

Andrew and his stately Highland wife had two daughters, Kathy, our most popular undernurse, and Madge, a sweet, attractive girl who was a nurse at the local cottage hospital. One day after the last drive of a covert shoot Andrew was counting the game with guns and beaters all round him when a car drew up and Madge's young man, Ken, got out of it looking white and scared. I caught some of the words he said to Andrew '. . . motor bike . . . Madge . . . looks pretty bad.' Andrew finished counting the game and made up a brace for each gun, then got in the car and drove away. When he arrived at the cottage hospital Madge was dead. All Craigielands mourned for her. We children talked in whispers for a day and when Kathy came back to the nursery her eyes were red with crying.

There was one other and different relationship I had outside the house and that was with the boy. Farm Boys came and went and I can remember three: Ian, Alec and Bonzo. The boys came from Glasgow, recruited no doubt by some benevolent church agency, and when they arrived they were put into the Quigleys' tin bath together with a cupful of Jeyes Fluid. Mrs Quigley cut their hair and boiled their clothes. They were given the last boy's boots and a tarpaulin jacket. Then they went to live in the bothy next to the hayloft above the stables. They slept on a straw palliasse on top of an iron bedstead and there was a corner cupboard deep with grime, with a tin plate and mug in it and a knife, fork and spoon. Mrs Quigley gave them a plate of porridge in the morning, a 'piece' at midday and a plate of tatties for dinner at night, also bread and raspberry jam out of a tin, which they kept in their cupboard.

Bonzo was the boy I came to know best. He was about four years older than I and for many months remained in a state of shock. Although only sixty miles apart it is hard to imagine two cultures more disparate than those of the Gorbals and of Craigielands Hill Farm. I decided to take Bonzo under my wing.

At that time I was absorbed by farming and the affairs of the farm were my preoccupation. I knew the name of each field and would recite them as I ran up and down from the farm each day, always ending: TRINALLY KNOCK, PAPERKNOWES, CAULDHAME MARCH, DOGSBURN. I knew the crop rotation and how it would affect each field in the coming years. I knew how much cattle cake we had bought and what we had paid for it. I knew the identity of all the cattle and the outstanding personalities amongst the sheep (not all four hundred and twenty as did Tom Quigley). I knew the work schedule for the coming week and how it would be affected by weather, and I travelled by train to Lockerbie or Lanark with Tom Quigley and the lambs to flush the lambs around the sale ring. Each lamb had been prepared for the great day like a film star, hooves pared, face washed, dipped in a handsome yellow wash and given the final touch in the form of a scarlet streak, or keel mark, across its buttocks. It was nervous work in the ring. Eighteen shillings for the tops was all right, twenty shillings was good, sixteen shillings was disaster, and rather than let go at such a low price Tom would take them out of the ring. Although it took perhaps four minutes to sell each lot, when it came to our turn it seemed to take an hour. Tom shook his head angrily all the time as the bidding progressed until the auctioneer gave his second tap and looked at Tom as he said 'Going, Going,' and then Tom would nod if the price were right and in a trice the lambs were no longer the lambs of Craigielands but of some unknown butcher who would bundle them off to a slaughterhouse in Carlisle and kill them. It was a sad end, but if the price were good that was a consolation. The next day we scanned the local newspapers anxiously to compare the price of Craigielands tops, or seconds, or thirds, with the price made by surrounding farms. If we were low in the league table it was a disgrace, and if near the top next time we went to a sale everyone congratulated Tom Quigley and offered him a whisky. But he did not drink.

I persuaded Tom to let Bonzo come to a sale and he did well and enjoyed it. I spent hours with him in the bothy telling him about farming, wrote out the field names, made a chart of the rotation and gave him my father's *Farmer and Stockbreeder* each week after I had read it. It was some time before I realised that none of this coaching was of much assistance to Bonzo because he was unable to read. He was also frightened of horses and had a particularly horrible form of eczema between his legs and in his hair. Nevertheless, I struggled on and found him at the same time pathetic and bellicose.

When he got bored with my endless lecturing he would hit me and square up for a set to. This apparently was the customary form of communication between young males in the Gorbals. But I didn't want a set to, I wanted to make him as keen on farming as I was. I made little progress.

One day, when Bonzo was about to go back to Glasgow for his annual holiday, he told me that when he got home he was sure his mother would have sold or pawned all his things and he would have 'nae claes'. I thought about this and then rummaged through the huge store of Craigielands boys' garments and selected some tussore shirts and a singularly appalling patterned golf pullover, the gift of some outlying aunt. These I put in a fish bag and took them up to Bonzo in the bothy, bursting with dowager-like pride in my good act. As I laid my offering before Bonzo I expected gratitude, perhaps even tears. Bonzo fingered the garments in a disdainful way. 'I cudna put on thae things in Glesga,' he said at last. 'Thae things is nae for the likes of us.'

In a flash I was aware of the British class structure, a thing that had, except for one occasion, entirely escaped my notice up to that time. Of course Bonzo could not have worn those clothes in Glasgow. His mates would have laughed at him. They were clothes for young gentlemen, not for slum boys.

I now saw that there were many different worlds and that I could hardly communicate with his, which was the lowest of all. He was lower-class than the farm men, who themselves were lower-class than Mr Bulman, who was lower-class than us. Was there any class above us? Yes, the country set, the Hope Johnstones of Raehills, and probably a lot of the top people in London. I put the tussore shirts and the pullover back in the fish bag and walked thoughtfully home.

The episode of Bonzo and 'the likes of us' took me back to a scene on the broad gravel sweep in front of Craigielands House in 1926. Two horse lorries came up the drive and stopped without a by-your-leave opposite the front door. With them there were about twenty poorly dressed, wild-looking men and some of the men were blackened up as nigger minstrels. As the household collected on the steps the nigger minstrels gave a show and passed round the hat. They were miners from the Lanarkshire pits thirty miles away. They were on strike and they were hungry. Mrs Henderson made 'pieces' for them. But when my father arrived he walked up to them and in his schoolmasterly way began telling them that they were all wrong, they should not be on strike and they had been fooled by their leader Arthur Cook. At this the men became angry and shouted back at my father, so loud as to frighten me. Then they geed-up their horses, slapped the reins on their backs and drove off at a trot. Two of the miners threw down their 'pieces' on the gravel.

So now I could see that the miners and Bonzo were not the likes of us, and my interest in the indices that distinguish class from class quickened.

There were occasions in Craigielands life when the classes mingled, albeit like oil and vinegar. One of these was the covert shoot, which took place five or six times a year. The guns were either staying in the house or drove up by car. Sir David Drummond, a retired doctor and near neighbour, rode a pony at covert shoots because he had a bad heart, dismounting only when he reached his peg. There were friends of Julia from Liverpool, and Uncle Sconnie but no Aunt Vi, because shooting ladies, no matter how well they shot, did not take a gun at covert shoots. Stanley Craig would be there, and other neighbours. There were eight guns, including my father, who organised the guns. Andrew Grieve organised everything else – including, so far as he could, my father. The guns all wore tweed plus-fours, boots or sturdy shoes and leather gaiters. If it rained they wore tweed overcoats. On their heads they wore tweed hats or grouse helmets.

The next social class was the keepers. Some of them arrived by car with their guns. Others had walked perhaps five or six miles, and they made up the same number as the guns. They wore the plus-four suits that their guns had worn six or seven years before, cut about to fit them. They had hill boots and woollen stockings and flat caps, and if it rained they just got wet.

The third and lowest class on the shoot was the beaters, ranging from one or two estate hands, who could be spared, to railway porters and big schoolboys, selected for their strength and good manners by Mr Bulman. They wore their working clothes, the railway men with LMS on their lapels. At lunch time the guns sat down to three courses in the dining room. Whisky was available on request, but in my father's office and not in front of Gamma in the dining room unless Uncle Sconnie was staying, for he would have no nonsense and insisted on a decanter of whisky and a soda water syphon covered in wire netting being placed on the table right in front of him. Some of the guns, although no doubt longing for a dram, knew of Mrs Smith's views and refrained. Others as they helped themselves glanced furtively down to the end of the table to see if they were observed.

The keepers had their lunch in the game larder on the trestle table, and sat on forms. They had one hot dish – perhaps Scotch broth – sent in from the kitchen. For the rest they brought their own 'pieces'. Each keeper was given a small bottle of Holyrood Ale.

The beaters, about twenty in number, had their lunch in the boiler room in the stables. They got nothing but an urn of Camp coffee. There was a jug of milk and a sugar bowl by the coffee urn. On one shoot Andy Smith got in first and ate all the sugar in the sugar bowl before anyone had had any coffee.

When the shoot was over and the dead game was being carried into the game larder festooned over the backs of the beaters, the guns had china tea in the drawing room. Andrew Grieve paid the beaters (four shillings for a man, half a crown for a boy, one shilling for an estate worker), sorted out the presentation braces and sat down with the keepers to talk about the great hits – or more likely the glaring misses – of the day, while their dogs steamed and panted on the floor. When the guns had finished tea there was a short meeting of guns and keepers on the gravel when money changed hands. Tipping was then, as it is today, one of the main preoccupations of the guns. 'I say Johnny,' one would say to another, 'what's the tariff here?' 'Not quite sure, old boy,' the other would say. 'Haven't shot here for a year or two. Better ask Adam.' But when they did ask Adam they got little satisfaction. 'Entirely up to you,' he would say. 'Just give what you feel you want to give.' So guns kept asking other guns what the tariff was, but none was eager to commit. Of course I asked the keepers what they got and most of them were too canny to say, but Pansy McMillan from Auchencastle, who had a streak of malice in him, did tell me. He said most guns gave five shillings. Blair Bell from Liverpool gave ten. Stanley Craig slipped his keeper twenty Players as well as the tip. Sir David Drummond never gave more than half a crown. He also said Sir David had become so dangerous a shot that his keeper, Davie Campbell, opened his cartridges and took out the shot and replaced it with sawdust. I wasn't sure that I believed this. If Davie Campbell did do any such thing it was more likely out of spite for the half crown than in the interest of the safety of others.

If shooting was a class-ridden affair, curling was not. My grandfather had been an outstandingly keen curler and he had arranged things at Craigielands to give him the maximum amount of sport. Far down the south drive he had constructed an area of flat tarmac a little bigger than a tennis court. When frost was forecast two gardeners would water the tarmac at nightfall and return to do the same again at dawn. The sprinkling of water froze immediately even in a mild frost, and James Smith would not be slow to summon eight players to join him for a game. These would be 'friendlies' between members of the family and estate workers. Lunch was taken (a 'piece' and Camp coffee) at the little pavilion James had built by the rinkside to hold the stones for the tarmac game. As the day warmed up bits of tarmac stuck through the film of ice and scratched the stones' underside, so James provided at his own expense sixteen stones of varying weights and with varying degrees of keenness to meet the taste of each player.

Meanwhile, better ice was in the making on the Rink, a concrete tank about eight inches deep and wide enough to take two rinks. When this froze it offered real ice, albeit that the stones ran without the thrilling noise of curling on deep-water ice. Here everyone used his own stones, which were housed reasonably nearby in a stone store built on a wooded promontory on the lake.

If the frost held, Davy Sloan would go out on a board each morning and at several points on the lake drill a hole with a brace and bit, put in a wire with a stub at right angles at the end, and measure it against his watch chain. I never grasped how Davy's watch chain related to inches and fractions of inches, but he was never at fault. At three and a half inches of good black ice the great day had arrived, and curling proper could begin.

The Craigielands Curling Club was made up of some sixteen rinks, each of four players and each rink known by the name of its skip. 'Porteous' was Jim Porteous the blacksmith, his brother Wick, and two others. 'Kirkpatrick' was all one family who farmed Beattock House. The Craigielands first rink was Tom Quigley lead,

Davy Sloan second lead, Andrew Grieve back-hand and Adam Forman Skip. In the great frost of 1929, when I was twelve, I was promoted to lead in the Craigielands first rink, and Tom Quigley went to skip the second.

But rink play could not begin at once. Although the ground would already be too hard to work, some farmers were putting in a few days of threshing. Also at Craigielands we had to fill the ice house. This was an interesting operation. First Davy Sloan on his same board cut squares of ice about three feet square. These floated about in the water, to be hauled out by men with grappling hooks and thrown into carts waiting at the lakeside. When full the carts sprinted up a short hill and discharged the ice down a chute into a cavernous underground cellar where two men broke up the ice with sledgehammers. From above they looked like troglodytes and the noise they made was like that of the Niebelungen. All the game was hung from the roof of the icehouse. One year rats got in and stripped the flesh from every pheasant, leaving an array of hanging skeletons and a pile of feathers which disfigured the ice beneath until it melted in the late summer.

On the second day of curling on the lake the Points Medal was held. This was a contest of individual skill with rules and scorecards pre-printed by my father, which usually attracted about thirty or forty entrants. I entered every year and did my best when I could use my father's stones, a beautiful pair of forty pound Ailsa Craig granite with the rim on the keen side no bigger than a penny. They were the fastest stones in the club.

On the third day the rinks were filling up and we began the Colonels Cup. This was an intra-club inter-rink league contest which lasted between four and five days. Next we started playing other clubs in Annandale, Auldgirth, Lockerbie, Wamphray – about six in all. And if the frost still held, clubs from further afield came to Craigielands, among them Wanlochead, all sixty members travelling in a special train – and they beat us because, as we reflected, they claimed to be the highest village in Scotland and so had more practice than we did. And if the frost held yet further the Caledonian Curling Club took over and set up the great bonspiel on Connibshaw

Loch when two hundred rinks from the Lowlands took on two hundred from the Highlands. And finally, but only once in my time, came the International, England versus Scotland. (It had been played on Craigielands lake in 1902.)

The approach of curling caused me more excitement than anything else. As the frost grew I would run to look at the thermometer outside the library window every few hours, I would accompany Davy on his measuring trip and run back to the house to report the result; I would go to the curling house and make sure all the Craigielands stones were ready and polished; and then at last I would go with Andrew Grieve and Davy Sloan to score the rinks on the ice – only four or five to start with – carefully selecting the best ice whilst allowing room for another fifteen or twenty rinks. Then came the sweet music of the first stone on deep water, the gathering of curlers growing every day with an accompanying crescendo in the volume of sound, the yells and shouts of the 'roarin game' above the rich orchestration of half a dozen running stones – there was nothing like it in the world.

Curling offered more than a mere display of skill. It was an open air theatre for natural performers, especially for the skips. As the male community came together for its only truly communal event, men who had been living a lonely life on the farm, working in ones and in twos all year, came to life and played their part, often in the form of an assumed character part, in front of their fellows.

Jim Porteous always drew the biggest gallery. His line of patter was as good as a Scots music hall comedian and his local and personal references were greatly appreciated. 'No na,' he would shout at a poor stone gyrating down the edge of the rink, 'that yin's a Johnny Green' (a notorious drunk). Or again, as a bullet shot from the arm of his backhand, 'Steady Jimmy man, mind Mr Forman's motor car' (the Ford van was parked on the lakeside). For a stone badly off course he had a special phrase: 'Haud up haud up Jimmy (stop sweeping). That yin's awa doon Cuddy Lane.' Other less extrovert skips employed satire, abuse, exaggerated praise and four letter words to energise and motivate their players, amongst whom there were characters no less colourful than the skip. Crack

Down Jack Latta was the strongest firer in the club. The number of stones he had broken was legendary and when firing on his backswing the stone went up in the air behind him until it was vertically above his head. Robbie of the Holmes traditionally fell over a lot, tripping over his besom. Jack Kirkpatrick got drunk and played all the better for it. Davie Burgess cheated by moving the stones on the head with his foot when he thought no one was looking – but once exposed he made this a feature of his game and would pretend to cheat to please the gallery.

On match days curling started by a shot from Andrew Grieve's gun at nine-thirty and finished when the stipulated number of heads were completed or when the light gave out. There was a half-hour break for lunch, provided by Mrs Smith and brought to the lakeside by Jim Rheilly in the T model Ford van. Lunch was Camp coffee and two hunks of bread with a slice of Lockerbie cheese stuck between them. There was a legend that once an urn of hotpot had been brought down and put on the ice. Before anyone could eat it, it melted the ice and sank into the lake. Although it was frequently recounted I never believed this story. I never saw any hotpot.

Sooner or later the sad day came when the thaw set in and there was water on the ice. If it were a slow thaw play was sometimes possible for another two or three days, but the heart had gone out of the curling, the numbers shrank, the roaring was subdued, and players wore galoshes and the stones no longer resounded as they did in clear air and on hard ice. It was a bitter time.

The social climate of curling was just the opposite of that of the shoot. The players outnumbered the gentlemen by a huge margin and even the poorest people, who were of the beater class at a shoot, would play in the same rink on equal terms with gamekeepers and farmers. Amongst the sixty-four players in our club there were only three gentlemen, my father and two others. My father as president of the club was a respected authority and the senior skip. He skipped our rink well enough but played safe and never showed the aggressive panache of Jim Porteous or the low cunning of Davie Burgess. My father was what Davy Sloan called a cold curler. Although he indulged in all his usual Scots badinage and called everyone by his Christian name, he was never fired, never carried away into that curling frenzy that marked out the true afficionados.

When the play ended there was quite a lot of whisky drunk out of flat halves and my father took the other two gentlemen up to the house to drink china tea and to check over the printed cards which had arrived from Moffat for the next day's game.

It was a pleasure for me to see the gentlemen so outnumbered and so unimportant. The two outside gentlemen were not even skips and none of them was a bella figura on the ice. Curling was the time when the alternative society, my society, came into its own and asserted itself. The usual authorities disappeared and the gentleman's writ no longer ran, nor did that of the farmer. It was the society of Burns' Jolly Beggars rather than the structured society of the Cottar's Saturday Night.

As time went on I found that I was happier in the company of the farm hands and estate workers than at the Craigielands dining table. They were not exactly my friends, and nor were they my tutors or guardians, nor yet my equals. But there was a relationship, perhaps because I understood their way of life and respected it, and they knew that I did. However tiresome I might be, I was not like other upper-class little boys. I liked their good sense, their directness, their back-door humour, I admired their strength and the way they stuck at it whatever the physical odds against them and whatever the weather. I liked their laconic mode of speech and their sharp turn of phrase. Indeed it became my own favourite tongue and even at table I would often slip from drawing-room English into broad Lallans. I was checked for this and didn't mind: it was more painful the other way round. Once, when we were sawing up an oak tree by the drive, a gentleman neighbour came past in a car and asked me where my father was. 'He's gone to Edinburgh to see the osteopath,' I replied and I could hear the echo of Jock Wilson imitating my English accent in a high falsetto. 'Ed-in-bro to see the osti-o-path'. I felt deeply ashamed for a long time after that, but could not work out why.

They liked my clowning, my mimicry, and my boldness and dash. Once, when we were loading hay high in the Mill Shed, Jock

Wilson showed me how to skin the cat. Skinning the cat was a gymnastic exercise which entailed seizing two parallel beams in the shed roof and turning a complete circle between them. I could just do this, but only just. Then Jock Wilson began to show off by swinging away from the piled hay along the beams and skinning the cat fifteen feet above the concrete floor. I followed him and although everyone shouted at me to go back I tried to skin the cat again just where he had done it. But my strength gave out and I fell to the ground on my head. I was a little stunned, but in the end none the worse. I will never forget the care and anxiety that I saw in the circle of faces above me. It was such a nice reaction as I came to that it crossed my mind that it might be worth doing again.

They were not the sort of people to express any sort of opinion about each other, and certainly not about me. One day I was sitting on a cart with Jimmie Moffat, one of the most cussed and cantankerous of men. It was drizzling with rain and we had a sack over our knees and underneath it my thigh touched his. Something came over me and I said to him, 'Jimmie, what do you think of me?' He thought for some time and then came up with the least compromising of all replies. 'Uha,' he said, and again, after a short silence, 'Uha.' So that was it.

At first consorting with the farm men provided me with no more than an escape from the regime of the Trinity. But as I grew older and saw more of them I came to think that perhaps I preferred the likes of them to the likes of us.

9

Disputatious Matters

Right up at the top of the house, next to the lavatory at the end of the passage, lay the darkroom. The darkroom had no window and quite a lot of water laid on, so it was the ideal place to keep fish. In glass accumulator tanks we kept trout fry, salmon parr and tadpoles, occasionally a goldfish. Our interest in fish was spasmodic and our specimens had a poor time, seldom lasting for more than a week or two, because they had either been used as live bait or fried over a spirit lamp, or because the water had not been changed. This last was the commonest cause of death and when it occurred the dead fish floated belly up on the surface until they decomposed and an emerald green weed crept across the surface of the tank. The resulting smell, of acid drops and rotten eggs, permeated the darkroom, and up to six months after a harvest of death it still hung about in the room itself and in the passage outside.

One day, when stocking the tank with a fresh intake of minnows, I went into the next room, the den. The den was often locked, but on that important day it was not. The room contained only two features, a fire escape in the shape of a canvas tube fixed to a huge metal prong which was on a hunge to enable it to hang out of the window (no doubt an invention of my father), and rough book-shelves from floor to ceiling filled with books from my father's earlier life as a divinity student. As my eye ranged along the massed ranks of holiness it fell on a twelve volume *Encyclopaedia of Ethics*. My hand fell on the volume P–Q and I opened it at the entry under Prostitution.

I stood still with my eyes popping out of my head, reading on and on (the entry must have covered twenty pages) until my foot went to sleep and I had to sit down on the pile of canvas. Good Lord! So did people really do things like that? How exciting – and in temples too, free of charge. Not many prostitutes around St Mary's United Free Church (Continuing) in Moffat. What an improvement it would be, though, if when we went to church in our Sunday best a lot of prostitutes rushed out of the vestry, nobbled my father and dragged him off to practise whatever they did in the Minister's room. That would be life. The Minister's Man would be in charge of them; the elders would have first pick. In Scotland they would be sure to charge for their services. The church would never be short of money. No more need for a collection for Missions to Seamen. The prostitutes would pay for that. No more sales of work and fetes, just keep the prostitutes working away like mad. And when the customers in Moffat were exhausted they could send a few prostitutes up and down the valleys in small buses to outlying parishioners. The Minister's Man could drive them and collect the fees.

Every item under Prostitution gave rise to sexual and social excitement. When I had read the whole entry I started again at the beginning and read it right through again. Then the gong went for lunch and I stumbled downstairs to lunch with the Trinity, throughout which my mind was in a turmoil of prostitution.

I had never heard the word uttered within Craigielands House, nor any other word that described a prostitute nor the act of prostitution. Nor had I ever heard any reference to the physical act of making love. So far as the Trinity was concerned, copulation did not exist. More devious forms of sexual fulfillment not only did not exist but could not exist. Even the simple bodily functions were denied any place in conversation except by means of the most elaborate circumlocution. In nursery talk 'wee' and 'big' were common parlance, but once in the schoolroom they disappeared altogether and the sexes divided in the words they used when they could not avoid referring to the need to relieve themselves in one way or the other.

For boys the term used came, as might be expected, from Loretto. There the classrooms stood on two sides of a court or yard. On a third side stood the battery of lavatories appropriate to growing boys – low urinals and water closets with doors low enough for a master to look over the top and see if anything inappropriate was going on. When a boy in class wished to go to the loo he would hold up his hand and say, 'Please sir, may I cross the yard?'

This phrase stuck with my father all his life. Before going out in the car he would say to us standing in the hall, 'Do you want to cross the yard?' Between us and the loo there was only about eight feet of carpeted corridor, which could not possibly be described as a yard, but when thoughts of urinating or defecating entered my father's mind a mirage of the yard outside the classrooms at Loretto seemed to float in front of his eyes and he would transmute the geography of the actual situation, be it a drawing room, hotel or theatre, into a pitch-pine classroom with gravel yards all around it and with municipal-like batteries of urinals and water closets on the other side. So crossing the yard became, like crossing the Styx, a symbolic expression of a universal experience.

Once we travelled from Fort William to Inverness in the old paddle steamer *Gondolier*. We had with us our old Welsh springer Rab, a noble dog and one with the manners of a duke. It was a long trip and as we entered the dark waters of Loch Ness Rab ran up and down the deck in discomfort, whining in short sobs and looking soulfully at his master. Was a ship indoors or outdoors? Was it possible to piss? He was such a polite dog that he did not wish to embarrass us by doing anything that was not comme il faut. My father observed his dilemma for some time and gazing across the water that stretched in all directions, he said, 'I think that Rab wants to cross the yard.' (Eventually Rab broke down and pissed into a teacup which careless passengers had left, half drunk, on the deck beneath a seat. This was an immensely gratifying finale to an episode which had been full of interest from the start.)

The subject of defecation was only mentioned in relation to two specific states of the bowels, constipation or diarrhoea. Even then no descriptive noun or verb was used. 'Have you been today?' was a common question. (Been where?) 'How long is it since you last went?' (Went? Went?) Conversely one would be asked, 'Was it very loose?' (It?) 'Do you have pains in your tummy?' (No, in the lower bowel, just adjacent to the anus.)

The girls had only one word for all eventualities and it was 'retire'. 'Kaff wants to retire,' Sheila would whisper to my mother at a party, and my mother would lead her off. Such was the importance surrounding the word that I was unaware that it had any other meaning. One day when three nannies were gossiping in the nursery they mentioned a fourth nanny who was going to retire in a year's time. I rushed over to Nan and whispered in her ear, 'How can she wait so long?' Nan would not tell the other nannies why she was laughing so much, and I loved her for it.

Actions spoke louder than words, and so actions were even more carefully concealed. I never once saw Gamma or my mother enter or exit from a lavatory. How they managed this I simply could not find out. Getting in was, of course, much easier than getting out. Until one had one's hand on the lavatory doorknob one could pretend to be going somewhere else. Once or twice I did see a female putative of entering a lavatory divert at the last moment to the adjacent bathroom. And once Gamma, caught by a male coming out from the loo on one side and myself peering through the hall door on the other, took a sudden interest in the housemaids' cupboard in no-man's-land between us. When my mother was patently aiming for the one on the stairs she would stop suddenly on hearing a flush to scrutinise the Landseer stags on the staircase. But I never witnessed an exit. Did they put an eye to the keyhole? An ear to the ground? Did Marnie tap out All Clear with her stick when a lady was waiting for release? It was one of life's central mysteries.

If they were evasive in referring to the natural functions, when it came to sex there was an absolute taboo. The accepted version was as follows; a man and a woman fell in love; they kissed each other; if they were 'the right ones' they got engaged and then married; they went on a honeymoon; they had babies; it was a family – that was the end of the matter. My mother once gave me a lecture on 'the right ones'. Some distant relatives of whom I knew little had split up. She thought I might find out. So she explained that sometimes people who got married were not 'the right ones' and so were not happy. Only 'the right ones' were really happy. It was terribly important to be 'the right ones'. 'I think you and Dad are the right ones,' I said, and when she enveloped me in a huge embrace I felt ashamed at being trapped into giving such a corny line.

Apart from the accepted version, sex was not referred to at all. Nor was it seen, even when a pair of copulating dogs got stuck under the Charon in Moffat and had to be poked out with a mop handle and then drenched with water. 'What are those dogs *doing*?' I asked my mother. 'Just fighting,' she said. Funny way to fight, I thought. I had a fair inkling of what was afoot, if only because the grown-ups were so embarrassed.

But then sex began to happen to me. I had a wet dream and woke up stunned by the wonder and beauty of what was happening to me. I knew it was elemental, a sort of earthquake in my life, but I had no idea whether it was just me or whether it happened to other boys too. And then one night, soaping myself in the bath, I felt the most extraordinary things beginning to happen and continued soaping until they did. At once I understood the Venusberg music in *Tannhäuser*: so that is what it was all about. I could induce it myself. How wonderful – but no, not so wonderful, because this must be Self-Abuse. O Lord, Self-Abuse was pretty much a sin against the Holy Ghost. Also my Oliphant cousins, who were at the Edinburgh Academy, had called it Flogging Off and said that first it made all your hair fall out and then you went mad.

I must have known less about sex than almost any other boy if nine or ten in Scotland. I had no school life and no street life. The Oliphant cousins came down only once or twice a year and although they did teach me some dirty words they preferred taunting me for my ignorance to enlightening it. I had seen dogs and bitches and tups and sheep, and had put two and two together. I had never seen a naked woman nor a picture of a naked woman which gave me any clue as to what she had where I had my sexual and urinary organs. She seemed to have nothing at all.

One Sunday I bicycled to Woodfoot Farm because I had heard people say there was to be a bulling after church and knew from their tone of voice there was something sexually exciting afoot. Sure enough, within a bull ring a huge Ayrshire bull was straining and struggling to inject his weapon into a Galloway cow. He succeeded and then with a few convulsive spasms seemed to have achieved something important and was pulled off by his handler. The cow, who had stood under him as quiet as a dormouse, was led out and another came in. The performance was repeated about ten times. It was fascinating and exciting and all the observers, about two dozen in all, were equally captivated by the scene. I heard one man with a bottle of whisky tell a story to another man in a very loud voice. It had to do with a bulling which had been watched by a boy and his girlfriend. When it was over he turned to her and said, 'Och, Jennie, I feel like doin' that myself,' to which she replied, 'If you feel like that, Jock, there's plenty more coos in the byre.' I reflected on that story. The joke was, of course, that Jock had wanted to do it to Jennie. How would he have done it? Would Jennie have knelt down on the floor on all fours and Jock got up behind her like the bull? I thought this must be it. Funny, I thought people did it in bed.

It was at least a year after my first sexual awakening that Sholto and I had our first sex talk. Sholto was two years older than I so I thought he must have started before me, but in true Craigielands tradition he and I had never talked to each other about sex.

Evidently my father and mother had decided to split the heavy burden of telling their sons about the facts of life; my mother would deal with the female side, my father with the male. 'Once a month you will notice that women are very tired,' my mother said. I hadn't noticed that. On what day of the month did women feel tired? The first Sunday in the month? And was it lunar or calendar? There was no time to ask questions because my mother, scarlet in the face and looking fixedly out of the window, was going on, 'It is called a period and it is really just laying an egg.' Laying an egg? Good gracious, this was something that had escaped my notice entirely. There must have been a whole heap of them if all the women laid their eggs on the same day. How could I have missed this interesting natural event? But my mother was going on. The eggs broke inside the woman's body and it came out as blood. Well now, that was pretty disgusting. I did not like to hear that part at all. But from what part of her body did the blood come out? Ears? Nose? From the depth of my mother's unease I knew it must come out from some orifice between the woman's legs, otherwise she would have named the part. Then she went on to say that if the woman had been with her husband the egg didn't break but stayed in her body and made a baby. Been with? In what way? It must relate to the cow and bull business, but how? I waited eagerly for more, but that was it so far as the physical went. We now had a little lecture about being nice to women when they had their periods but not too nice because that could embarrass them. There was a young man (not a Lorettonian) who used to rush about and fetch chairs and cushions if either she or Aunt Mabel said they felt tired or had a headache until they didn't know where to look.

Well, I thought, that was a pretty patchy job she did. I still didn't know if all the women in the house (in Scotland, in the world) had their periods on the same day or whether each one had a monthly tired day of her own. If the latter, and the periods were lunar and you divided the number of women by twenty-eight you would know the number of tired women you would have on your hands on any one day. If at Christmas we had as many as twenty-eight women in the house you would have one tired woman every day. If there were fifty-six women in the congregation in church on Sunday an average of two of them would be tired. But never so tired, so far as I could see, that they weren't able to stand up and sing the hymns. From then on I was deeply interested in the concept of tired women and would study women in shops and on trains to try and decide which one of them was tired.

My father put up an even more pathetic show. After Sunday night bible lessons in the Office he started in. 'When a boy grows into a man,' my father said, 'his voice breaks and certain other things happen.' My voice hadn't broken and I was to sing treble solos for another six years. Certain other things? What were they? 'Sometimes at night you will have sensations,' my father said. 'Wet dreams,' said Sholto unexpectedly. Now, how the hell did he know that? I didn't. Wet dreams indeed – well one couldn't but admit that it was a pretty fair description. 'Wet dreams,' said my father. 'Have either of you had wet dreams?' Both of us looked silently at the carpet. 'The thing to do after a wet dream,' said my father, 'is to get up, have a cold tub, eat your breakfast and think no more about it.' But I loved thinking about it. I thought about it almost all day. 'The point of wet dreams,' my father went on, blowing his nose almost continuously into his blue spotted handkerchief, 'is that when a man and a woman are married the man squirts his seed into the woman's body and makes a baby.' Seed? What was that about seed? I knew what turnip seed looked like and rape seed and cabbage seed. I'd seen nothing like that around in the bed after a wet dream. Perhaps I was deficient, I had no seed, only a liquid substance that could in no circumstances have been mistaken for seed. (This continued to puzzle me until I started to hunt about in the bible for further and better particulars and discovered the story of Onan.)

So that was it. Squirt was such a funny word. What exactly did happen? I still had no clue that squirting part. Which postures were adopted by the squirter and the squirtee? Nothing known. Good heavens, what strange things went on in the world.

I returned to the *Encyclopaedia of Ethics* daily and read the entries under Marriage, Puberty, Sexual Beliefs, Manhood, Menstruation. I read them again and again, and though none of them came up to the standard of Prostitution (which I now knew almost by heart) for sheer excitement, there was some good stuff under puberty, including the description of some very bizarre acts, some of which in certain African tribes, proved fatal to a boy's foreskin. There was also an account of how a young Aztec girl was initiated into sexuality by an encounter in her teens with twenty braves on one sight. I was getting the hang of things by now, but twenty braves in one night! Whew! Suppose that night was eight hours long. That was twenty-four minutes for each brave with no time off.

But as I searched the more remote worlds an interesting thing happened. I began to find within tribal societies unmistakable parallels with the Christian religion. Under Virgin, for instance, I learnt that virgin birth was quite a common phenomenon. Many good class tribes had it in their mythology and there were two reasons given: first that virgin birth was a way of the woman avoiding shame and the man not acknowledging parenthood, and secondly that to be the child of a virgin birth conferred a numinous quality upon the baby. All virgin births, so far as I could gather, produced male offspring. Then take the miracles. All tribal religions and many sophisticated ones like Hinduism abounded in miracles, much more imaginative and colourful than Jesus' miracles. I thought his best to be walking on the water and turning the water into wine. The cures could have been fudged, also the loaves and fishes. But they were nothing compared to what the Greeks could get up to. And come to think of it, the whole of Greek mythology was one long parade of miracles with practically no space between them. The God of the Old Testament may have parted the Red Sea to let the Israelites through but the Greek giants piled Pelion upon Ossa. Jesus never turned himself into a bull or a swan so that he could have it off with ladies to whom access was difficult. In fact he never seemed to have it off with anyone. Perhaps he was a fairy, whatever that was.

Next I turned to the word Messiah. They were two a penny. Not only in Palestine just before Jesus (when the actual word Messiah was used) but all over the world. A messiah was a god who came to deliver man from some evil. Some messiahs led their people in war, some came to make them holy, Prometheus came with the gift of fire to free men from cold, Jesus came to free them from sin and possibly from the Romans, though that was uncertain. You could go on and on. But perhaps the clincher was the resurrection. There were several deities who had died and come to life again, usually through the agency of another deity. Not that resurrection would be all that difficult. All you had to do was to kill a double and keep the real guy in hiding until it was time for the denouement. Or in the case of Jesus if the real guy was killed, which was probably the case, to get a double to do the subsequent appearances. They didn't last long, just walk-ons really, and that was probably why. Quite easy to fake the nail holes, and that stuff about the Holy Ghost flaming on people's shoulders was probably done by fireworks. The Chinese had made fireworks years before Christ.

On the lower shelf there lay a volume which had never been opened. By sheer luck I used it to crush a wasp and as I scraped the wasp off saw that it was called *The Golden Bough*. It turned out to be a goldmine. I sat on the floor and read and read until I got stiff (there were no chairs in the Den) and then I sat on the upstairs lavatory for so long that it took three days for the red circle on my backside to disappear.

Frazer laid matters out in such a way as to support my instinctive belief that divinity was bunk. He was a scholar, he had studied tribal societies. It was a moment of great excitement. Now everything became clear to me. The earliest people had seen their gods in natural phenomena they didn't understand. They didn't understand thunder so they made a god of thunder. They didn't understand why there were good seasons and bad seasons so they made a god of fertility. And then the Earth Mother appeared all over the world, the universal god controlling the mysterious process of conception in humans, animals and plants.

But much later, when people did understand about thunder, the thunder god's day was done. Then Donner, Thor and Jove all looked pretty silly, so men moved their god up a notch into an area they still didn't understand, like the creation, and worshipped the mastermind who devised the masterplan which was beyond their comprehension.

As we comprehended more and more, instead of the power of the gods diminishing as their numbers reduced, their power seemed to get greater. Here we were as Christians with only three – and there was of course this ridiculous business of three in one which attempted (unconvincingly) to con us into believing that the tribal god of the Hebrews was the same god as Jesus Christ. One single god, Golly! That was putting all your eggs in one basket. In the good old days if the god of rain let you down you could still have a go at the god of rivers.

Why was it that if people couldn't understand a part of the system of the universe they immediately thought that it must be devised by a god? Science had dispensed with the existence of scores of gods. The casualties had been enormous. Why could no one see that this was a continuing process and sooner or later, perhaps still quite a long time ahead, we would know how everything worked and all the world's remaining gods would be redundant?

There were other aspects of faith that nauseated me. Turning to god for comfort seemed a peely-wally thing to do. To pray for the things you wanted to happen and to think you had some chance of winning was just silly. Your claim was no different from that of the guy who didn't pray at all. So this rabbit gets caught in a snare and prays to get out and the other rabbit gets snared and doesn't pray: they will both finish up in Andrew Grieves' game bag and the rabbit that prayed will probably be the sadder rabbit of the two because he will feel that God let him down. Prayer must be hokum. Just look around you.

Another reason why people believed in religion was because they didn't want to die. Or at least they wanted life after death. That was why the resurrection was Jesus' most powerful act. It was a symbol of life after death and people were just crazy to be told they would not die. They argued like anything about who would go to heaven. In the Wee Free kirk only the Elect went to heaven and the congregation spent half their lives debating who was in the Elect and who was not. Their numbers were very small, just the elders and one or two exceptionally holy parishioners. There were no women in the Elect. Heaven was an all male affair for the Wee Frees. Everyone else went to hell. Then in the Catholic religion there was purgatory, a sort of railway waiting room where you might have to sit for centuries before your name was called and you went on in one direction or the other. And what about animals? My father was insistent that dogs could go to heaven but not to hell. The reason for this was that no dogs were evil, it was only men that made them so. All dogs were born good, in his philosophy, and everywhere they were in chains. When pressed my father would acknowledge that horses, too, could go to heaven, but as you descended the brute creation to the animals he disliked, he lost his nerve. No, rats could not go to heaven. Why not? Because they were vermin. I could see that my father's argument would not hold up: it was either all animals or none. A dog might be noble and a rat criminal in the eyes of man, but in the eyes of God they must have rated much the same. But there wasn't any God anyway, nor any heaven, and the animal argument just made the whole thing more ludicrous.

The Trinity were all convinced, of course, that there was life after death and that they would meet the dead members of the family in heaven when they themselves died. Not one of them appeared to have the slightest fear of making it to heavens, or if they did they kept it to themselves. My mother said things like 'When I see Sconnie again I shall tell him that . . .' But would Sconnie be the same person she knew at the time of his death? Apparently one did not get older in heaven, but here on earth my mother was getting older every year. Suppose she died at ninety and burst in on Sconnie in heaven who was still only fifty-five. Sconnie might not be all that pleased to have his kid sister around now that she was thirty-five years older than he was. It would change their relationship. After one Sunday lunch I posed the question in general terms to Mr Smith, the Minister of St Mary's. 'These are disputatious matters,' he said.

No, it must be recognised that life after death was wishful thinking and heaven was bunk. All the philosophising, all the theories of the many different religions, all the books written about heaven and hell failed to recognise one thing. The after-life was there because people wanted it to be there, not because it really existed. Foxes died, stoats died, badgers died and their bodies lay about until they dried up or another animal ate them. When they were dead they were dead and it must be the same for people.

But there was one thing about Jesus Christ that stopped me in my tracks. After you had swept away all the nonsense about divinity, there remained the Christian message. It was a good message, particularly after you had ploughed through that everlasting Old Testament with its list of tribal chieftans fighting and begetting and with its *galère* of very disagreeable characters led by the God of Wrath. There were some nice stories in the Old Testament, it was true, but no better than Wagner and certainly not as good as the Greeks. But there was no social or moral message I could find that had any relevance to me. Denis Forman of Craigielands Beattock NB. I did not covet my neighbour's ox, nor did I have the slightest inclination to fall down and worship a golden calf, nor to kill.

But the Sermon on the Mount came through loud and clear. It was a new voice with a new message and it had relevance to me and 'to the likes of us'. At the same time I heard another voice just as powerful, the voice of Plato conveyed through the Dialogues which my father read to us on a Sunday night. I liked the Phaedo best and was tremendously impressed by Socrates. What nobility, what hard good sense, what a good idea to penetrate to the heart of a subject by debate, and to reach a conclusion that some things were good and others bad not through faith but through logic. I put Socrates ahead of Christ because he had a more original mind and didn't use those frightful parables, but in one respect and one respect alone I put Christ first: his concept of Love Thy Neighbour was a winner. So long as one acknowledged that these were both philosophers and teachers, hacking out a way towards our present way of thought, that was fine. But I did not want to see Christ with a crown of thorns, nor hanging on a cross, nor with any of those ghastly expressions he had in illustrated biblical books ranging from saccharine sweetness when with children to the agony of Gethsemane, when he looked just like Stanley Craig doing his act of pretending an elephant was standing on his foot.

This was the view of Christianity I had reached by the time I went to Loretto. Until a few months before I left home I kept it entirely to myself. There was no one to share it with. Obviously the Trinity would have been shocked and would not have believed me. They would have thought I was trying it on as an act just to get a reaction. This would not have been an unreasonable response and it might have been true, but for once it wasn't. Anyway I shrank from the indecency of exposing my very private thoughts to the scorn and derision of three such bigoted persons. I felt a glow of happiness about my atheism, partly because I had got there myself, rather like Plato, and partly because of an unshakable conviction that I had reached the right conclusion. I couldn't talk to the servants' hall; the nursery staff was now reduced to one elderly nanny, Nurse Black, or Doggie, who had been in charge of all our sanitary requirements for the first few months of our lives, and was quietly holy; the farm men were out of the question, and so were Davy Sloan and Andrew Grieve.

I did, however, summon up my courage and try it out on Jack Hannah, the doleful Mr Dunn's successor as my tutor. Jack Hannah came from a distinguished Scottish family known to my parents and was just down from Edinburgh University. His hair stuck up at odd angles, he had a beak-like nose with a drip at the end, wild staring eyes and huge steel-rimmed glasses, and he wore threadbare knickerbockers. Jack Hannah's problem, I was soon to learn, was coordination. He had naturally spasmodic movements and a brilliant but uncoordinated mind, and if talking about the Armada whilst eating a scone he was quite likely to drop the scone in his tea or put it absent-mindedly into his pocket. His lack of dexterity came into its own when we had to use the simple tools of schoolroom geometry, little celluloid objects such as triangles, protectors, and compasses. Our compasses incorporated a pencil that had to be pushed through a hole in one of the legs of the compass and then screwed up tight. When the pencil got blunt Jack Hannah had to unscrew it, sharpen it and replace it. To observe him carrying out this simple operation was a great delight. He fumbled, continually missing the hole in the pencil sharpener, then would drop the screw of the compass on the floor and hunt for it on all fours under the table, bumping his head as he came up, and with any luck stick the sharp part of the compass into his hand and get blood everywhere. I used to blunt the pencils with malice aforethought in order to synchronise his compass act with the arrival of his tea tray, for the combination of buttering, eating, pouring and drinking, added to the strain placed on him by the compass act, made it certain that mayhem and disaster would follow. There were numerous other ways of getting a little harmless pleasure out of Jack Hannah, such as applying Secotine to the schoolroom windows and then turning up the central heating, or putting an intimate item of the girls' underwear into his briefcase when he went for a pee.

He took all this persecution in good part and had a burning desire to be my friend. 'Call me Jack,' he had said at our first meeting. I never called him Jack, I just avoided calling him anything. Nevertheless, I liked him, although he had a tendency to tell me more than I wanted to know about the composition of water or what electricity was because he had read science at Edinburgh and was right up to the minute with radium and aerodynamics.

One day I decided to test out this friendly soul with an exploratory dialogue on the subject of atheism. 'What about the divinity of Christ?' I asked him as he was trying to extract a paper clip from the inkwell. 'Divinity of Christ?' he said. 'Christ was divine because he was the son of God.' 'Yes,' I said, 'but how do you know that Christ was divine, how do you know he was a God?' Mr Hannah then took me through a pretty long lecture on the history of the gospels. They had been written in Greek, probably within a hundred years or so of Christ's death, lost, rediscovered hundreds of years later in the library at Alexandria, studied by scholars and later Latinized by the Roman Church and translated into the English of Shakespeare by three scholars appointed by King James the first of England. 'Yes,' I said, 'but how do you know that what the gospels say about Christ's divinity is true?' 'I think your question has validity, Denis,' said Jack Hannah. 'Some aspects of Christian divinity are outside the parameters of the Greek language and all we get is at best an approximation of the subtleties of Hebrew thought. Also,' he went on, warming to his work, 'when you reflect that every word loses its finer shades of meaning in translation and when you consider that the gospels have been translated at least twice, and finally into a form of English which is three hundred years remote from our present understanding of the language . . .' He went on for quite some time longer, and when finally I asked him, 'But do *you* believe in the divinity of Christ?' he answered by saying that it depended upon which reference to divinity was under consideration. Some texts and some references to divinity were corrupt, others he believed to be valid. I gave up, and got only small consolation from an accident at lunch when, whilst talking over his shoulder, he poured a ladleful of scalding soup onto his fly buttons instead of his plate.

The process of divesting myself of myth and superstition was therefore lonely, and at time I nearly lost heart. Suppose the Trinity were right? Was I just cutting myself off from their moral support system on a false premise? But then the wave of conviction would sweep over me and I would realise the truth – the Trinity had got stuck at a point in the evolution of society. They had passed the tribal stage but by no more than a short head. Because they had accepted all the superstitions taught them by their parents and teachers they had lost the power of original thought. What they needed was a good course in Plato. Socretes would have sorted them out.

I had half a dozen trees where I had fashioned seats and peep holes within the crown to be used in fine weather. I built a hut in the wood from 'slabs' (the unwanted outer slices of tree bark) and sat in it when it rained. There were two haysheds where I had comfortable retreats on the hay up near the rafters. My two main solitary enterprises were music and fishing, but it was in these smaller portions of solitude that my mind worked away at the two secret subjects of sex and atheism. The Den was where I found my source material for both, but soon I had exhausted both the *Encyclopaedia of Ethics* and *The Golden Bough* and only returned to them for purposes of reference.

Half a mile below Craigielands, in the Annan valley, lay Broomlands Farm, and close by, concealed from the world by high earth banks and a forest of broom, was Broomlands House. This had been built by my Uncle Bertram – B.S. – who gave up biz in Liverpool in 1908 on the grounds that he had tuberculosis and should lead an outdoor life. He was an interesting man who combined farming with the construction of a fleet of caravans built by his virtuoso carpenter Johnny Thompson, and the authorship of a dozen or so books of considerable charm. He was the curling and caravanning correspondent of the *Manchester Guardian* and his books included a collection of essays on Scottish rural life and two novels about his schooldays. He died in the year I was born, and his wife died when I was twelve. Broomlands House stood empty for a year and during that year I made it my base. The back door key hung behind a drain pipe by the garage and one could steal past the kitchen and dining room into the oak-panelled sitting room with its huge south-facing windows and cosy inglenook. In the corner stood the greatest feature of the house – the pianola, a sturdy 1890 Steck, with three long baskets full of pianola rolls beneath it, and above it bookshelves that held all B.S.' scores, notebooks and musical texts.

It was not only for music that I went to Broomlands. I had been sexually attracted to B.S.' widow, Aunt Freda, who was a petite woman with a compact and curvacious body, a beautiful speaking voice and a bright intelligent eye. As I roamed the empty Broomlands house, and especially in her bedroom, I summoned up all manner of sexual fantasies that involved not only her but every women that I fancied at that time, and they were numerous. I peopled the house with their figures and imagined them stripping their clothes off, beseeching me for sexual attention (for I was of course the only male present) and indulging in what would have been all manner of sexual orgies had I known what a sexual orgy was. I would wander from room to room in a state of supreme sexual excitement until the climax passed and I could turn my mind to music.

In the empty Broomlands House I was my own man, fancy free and liberated from the heavyside layer of Craigielands. But although privately I gloried in my liberation from religious superstition, sexual guilt was always present and oppressed me mercilessly. Even after I had ceased to believe that masturbation would make my hair fall out or that I would be taken away by men in white coats to the Crighton (the local lunatic asylum, as it was then still described), I was still desperately guilty when indulging in any form of sexual fantasy or pleasure. By taking my solitary road towards unbelief I had broken bands of steel that should have bound me firmly to God and the church for the rest of my life. But I was powerless to break away from the Craigielands sexual taboos. I tried to convince myself that sexual freedom could exist and could be respectable. It was no good. Sexual desire had to be intense before it overcame the moral inhibition that swelled up to fight it, and guilt and black despair followed every sexual experience, even the mildest of sexual fantasies.

There is nothing in my early Craigielands days that I regret so much as this burden that the Trinity imposed on all the young people who passed through their hands. Some – interestingly enough, the two Smith cousins – cast off their sexual inhibitions in a few years and openly slept around; some were continent, I guess, until they met 'the right ones' and got married. Sheila never got married because as soon as a young man made a pass at her, though he might have been a prince and a hero ten minutes before, she immediately saw him as a lecherous predatory male. I carried the bitter legacy with me until middle life, unable equally to see any rationality in this fear of sexual expression and to free myself from the sex taboos that I had sucked in with my mother's milk.

10

The Occupation of a Moron

I became acquainted with trout at an early age, perhaps when I was four or five years old. When walking round the lake one day in summer, my hand held in Bell's vice-like grip, I saw a trout in the clear lake water cruising lazily along beside us. He was only three yards away when he spotted us, and with a sudden flick of the tail he was off, leaving behind him a couple of whirlpools on the surface and a smudge of mud below. From then on I pestered the under-nurses to let me watch for trout and sometimes they allowed it, but not being able to realise the importance of the matter they would become impatient and hustle me away before there had ben a sighting. Also they had no notion of the need for concealment, and with their great white aprons and quick movements they acted as effective trout-scares.

As soon as I was allowed to go to the lake myself I spent many hours watching the trout. In places the lake was surrounded by flags growing three feet high, and I could creep through these until I had a perfect view of the water below. I soon learned always to have the sun behind me, to remain still when a fish came into view and to be patient, often waiting five or ten minutes for the next sighting, which for a small boy of my temperament was an eternity and a measure of the fascination the trout held for me.

My first impression was of the beauty of their form and the beauty of their movement. A trout sauntering along on a warm May morning, looking casually for a little nourishment, was one of the prettiest sights in the world. They were quite different from the stuffed trout in the glass cases in the hall which had lost all their charm. Then I began to study their movements, nearly all of which had to do with feeding. I began to recognise the difference between a rise for a live fly hovering above the surface and a rise to pick up a fly that had settled on the water. For the first the trout's upward acceleration would be greater, his head would break the surface and his effort might lead him into a sideslip which would show off his white and gold belly shining in the sunlight. If the fly were settled and the trout keen, then he would carry out the classic rise, a circular roll over, like a porpoise, with the fly inhaled at the apex. Again, if nymphing just below the surface the trout would rise on a trajectory that flattened out and which allowed him to see and eat his prey without breaking the surface, leaving only a set of rings in the shape of an oval.

But the trout were not boring old things going through the same routine over and over again. They were capricious and never did the same thing twice. On some days they would leap two and three feet out of the water, but I never witnessed these major acrobatics from my hides, partly because the trout did not indulge in any spectacular leaping when the sun was out (and that was the only time I could see them clearly under water) and partly because they needed deep water and a good run up for a high leap, so most of such activity was away from the bank. But sometimes they would stand on their heads and grub about on the bottom; sometimes two or more trout would become aggressive and chase each other, or a whole school of six or seven would float past; and once I saw an old cannibal rush in and disperse a shoal of trout fry.

At the age of seven I caught my first trout. On a warm day in July Sheila and some school friends were idly rowing the boat across to the big island. For months now I had been allotted an ancient greenheart rod, a rusty old brass reel with thick sticky line on the drum, and a length of gut with one fly attached to the end. I was sitting in the stern lazily trailing my one fly behind the boat as I had done dozens of times before. There was no real expectations of catching a fish, the act of fishing was an end in itself. One was not exactly playing at fishing, one was fishing properly like grown-ups, but one had not yet reached the time of life when fish were actually caught.

At first I thought I had snagged the bottom, a thing that had often happened before. But no, the line was alive and vibrant, the rod tip bent and moved up and down; there was something alive at the end of the line. I had a fish on. For the first moment I sat absolutely silent, overwhelmed by the solemnity of the occasion. I could feel my excitement rising inside my chest like sherbert and when it reached my neck I began to shout at the girls. 'Haul her intae the wind,' I yelled in broad Scots. 'Haul her away frae that weed.' The girls were hopeless. They splashed away with their oars in an uncoordinated fashion, quite unaware of the high importance of the moment. I was playing a fish, my first fish, and it was thrilling, like a sexual thrill, not concentrated between the legs but spread all over my body. This living thing was determined to get away from me and I was determined he should not. He played courageously round the stern of the boat; he leapt into the air and I instinctively dropped the rod point as I had seen others do. He bored a little towards some weed and terrified me. He came nearer and nearer and now could only manage a few convulsions and short runs. He turned belly up, but when he saw me he was off like an arrow and the game started again, though now he was tiring fast. At last he lay alongside, all his white showing, his mouth gaping and his strength gone. There was no landing net in the boat. I seized the bailer, a rounded basin-like object with a wooden handle, and gently edged it beneath him. But he slipped off and gave a frightening dart under the boat. I turned my rod upside down until the gut cleared the keel and hauled him back. Once again he lay with his mouth open, gasping and exhausted. In a frenzy of anxiety I put my thumb down, gripped his lower jaw between my finger and thumb and whisked him into the boat. I then killed him by banging his head against the thwart.

I sat down trembling all over and began to cry. The girls thought that this was because my thumb was bleeding where his teeth had cut into me; but it was nothing to do with that. It was because something momentous had happened. I had won the most exciting battle of my life and I had killed a beautiful trout, one of the trout I loved to watch from my secret lairs. It was the beginning of a conflict which has stayed with me all my life, but on that day there was no doubt that the battle with that trout proved that the hunter's instinct was stronger than the plain shame at killing a beautiful animal; during the next fifteen years of my life the killer instinct was to ride high.

When the fish was put on an ashet in the hall it looked quite small. It was, in fact, just under half a pound. It was a Ferio Loch Leven, a descendant of the stock put in the lake by my grandfather. It had red spots amongst the black and silver and from time to time, until I went to bed that night, I poured water over it to keep it wet, shiny and beautiful. Next morning I had it for breakfast and didn't like it much. I had gone off trout and from then on only ate them when at the point of starvation.

But my interest in trout was not confined to watching them and catching them. Every autumn at the first spate the burn that fed the lake turned the colour of kitchen tea, and then the stripping of the trout began.

The section of the burn where the trout spawned was perhaps six hundred years long. A team of four men arrived with sticks, a tin bath and glass jars, and began to build the first dam with mud and stones. Andrew Grieve was in charge and it was he who fitted the square-framed landing net into the centre of the dam. When the trap was sealed the tin bath was filled with water and placed close by. Two men went fifty yards or so upstream and probed under the banks so that the spawning trout ran downstream into the net. One man, a longstop, stood at the top of the boat and splashed his stick to discourage any trout that felt inclined to go the wrong way. When the beaters raised a trout they gave a yell. It darted down and into Andrew's net and quick as a flash he would whisk it out of the burn into the tin bath. Sometimes there were two trout in quick succession, sometimes three or four and then he had to wait until they were all in the net before he flicked them out.

At the end of the beat there might be twenty or thirty trout of between half a pound and a pound and a half lying doggo in the tin bath. Then the team gathered round to watch Andrew do the stripping. If a hen fish were ripe, almost half a pint of coral-coloured eggs would pour out of her as Andrew drew his first finger and thumb down her belly. If she were not so ripe he had to press harder and the eggs came slowly. This exhausted the fish and instead of placing her back in the stream, Andrew would put her back in the small tub where she would float belly up until she regained her strength and her poise. Andrew stripped the males of their milt into a jam jar and then poured it into a bigger retort. Both milt and eggs were scrutinised against the light in their individual jars before they were put into the general reservoir.

At the top of the spawning bed, where the stream disappeared into its tunnel under the sawmill, the spawn was put into three or four buckets and the milt poured over it. Then the whole gang walked the half mile to the hatchery on the Kellobank burn and gently poured this fertilised spawn on to racks of glass tubes which stood in tiers, with the water from the top level pouring down stage by stage to the bottom. The hatchery had been built by my grandfather and was kept spick and span like a hospital laboratory.

Each morning I would run down to the hatchery and pick out with a pigeon's tail feather the eggs which had gone rotten and white. It was my job, and although Andrew would look in daily I thought myself to be the hatchery man and took my responsibilities seriously. In the early spring the eggs began to grow a head and a tail, and in April they were tiny trout. Not the correct shape. it was true, for they tapered away from their head like tin tacks and had some abdominal swelling where the yolk sack had been, but nonetheless fish, real live fish. On a warm day in May some would be slipped into the hatchery pond, the scene of my early humiliation, and some into the lake itself. Both had their hazards. Herons would raid the pond and the old black cannibal trout would be lurking in wait for them in the lake.

It was a sad day for me when my hatchery duties were over, but it did mean that the fishing season had begun. Every morning before running up to the farm I looked out of the Green Room window to see how many fish were rising in the lake, where the breeze was coming from and what the fishing prospects might be. Sometimes they were so good that I would run down and cast a fly before breakfast. But fishing on the lake was more usually a daytime or evening occupation. I soon became expert, and then a little blasé, only going out when one could be sure to get three or four trout to the hour. But then a new excitement entered my life. I began to catch trout in the burns.

Burn fishing was different from loch fishing or river fishing. Elderly gentlemen could flog away on large stretches of water and there was not much skill in it. If you could throw a cast, if you kept your flies on the water, you would either catch fish or not, and this depended upon them as much as it depended upon you. But burn fishing was full of variety and demanded physical fitness, courage and great dexterity. There were many ways of fishing a burn, according to its character and to the conditions of water and weather.

A burn could range in size from a small river to a channel in peat moss with about as much water running down it as would go through a biggish bath tap, and in length from half a mile of good fishing water to six miles. Every burn had its own profile from its source to the point where it joined the river and roughly speaking there were three types of water – flats, where the fall was small and the water ran shallow over a stony bed; linns, which were a succession of waterfalls often heavily overgrown with rowans, alders, birch scrub and oak; and staircases, which were something between the two, deep short pools, with small waterfalls or a two-foot rapid falling between the two. Staircases offered the best and easiest fishing.

To fish a burn out, that is to catch about a half of the biggest fish available on any given day, you had to be an adaptable fisherman. In medium water with little wind the dry fly was the most fun. You had to stalk a pool, especially one with a long tail, in order to get your first cast over the best lie, nearly always near the head of the pool. If you just cast up the pool your line would fall on the water, scare the wretched pygmies in the tail of the pool and they would run up and give a general alarm. So you had to land your fly over the prime lie first, with the most gossamer of casts gently alighting behind it, and you had to cast from the side, often crouching, sometimes lying flat and whirling your line to keep your fly dry, avoiding the trees, bracken, sprett rushes and other herbacious matter. But if you overcame all these difficulties it was four to one on that when your fly floated above the lie there would be a glorious plop and the line would go tight. At that point in all forms of burn fishing you flicked the trout straight out of the water over your shoulder. There were far too many snags and hazards around for it to be safe to play him in the water. If the trout were hooked on the bony upper jaw it would often fly off the line and a great deal of time could be lost searching for it in the heather.

In medium to heavy water you could fish upstream with a wet fly cast and catch more trout more quickly. In low water, even if gin-clear, you could catch trout in the runs and rapids on a clear water worm. This, the most skilful of all forms of burn fishing, entailed stalking the fish by crawling up the river bed below and landing your worm, on a single pennel hook, on a stone just above the trout's lie and then gently easing it into the runnel above his nose.

After one very hard day of clear water worming, during which I had been in near freezing water for several hours, I got home to be greeted by a posh fisherman, an Edinburgh doctor, who had been lashing the lake all day to no effect. 'So what did you catch?' he asked jocularly. I pulled a dozen burn trout out of my bag and laid them on the ashet. 'And what did you get those on?' he asked. 'Worm,' I said. 'How unsporting,' he said. 'Too easy.' I saw his big car outside with big white tyres on it. I thought of driving a nail into each one. But he drove off before I could do anything so unsporting.

The two least enjoyable forms of fishing, but each with its own attractions, were heavy-water, or spate worm fishing, and dynamiting. When the burn ran up to spate level and the water turned cocoa-coloured, the trout left their usual lairs and congregated in backwaters and other sheltered spots until they could once again go about their normal business. If one hit the right spot one could stand on the bank all day and haul out half the trout in a quarter of a mile of river with a brandling worm. I kept my brandlings in moss to make them hard, and gave them red brick dust to make them colour up nicely.

Dynamiting was only to be used when all other methods were impossible. In the Garpol Glen, for instance, there was a linn pool with a twenty-foot sheer waterfall above and another of equal height below it. It was walled with rock and the rocks were covered with bushes which spread over the water, leaving only a mysterious black oval in the middle. This was the first pool I dynamited. I was determined to discover what the trout population of the pool might be, for it was waterfall-locked and had neither ingress nor egress for spawning fish.

There was a tin of carbide kept in the game larder to service the many bicycle lamps of the Craigielands household. The bicycle lamp I had thrown into the lake on my bad day had exploded a few minutes after it had struck the water. I made deductions from this and took an empty Stephens ink bottle and half filled it with lead shot so that it would sink. I took some carbide in a tin and wrapped it in one of my father's oilskin tobacco pouches. I went to the Garpol Glen, took off my kilt, left my fishing rod at the bottom of the waterfall and started to climb. When I got to the top I made a dam so that all the water would come through one narrow channel. Then I put as much carbide into the ink bottle as it would hold, let in some water, screwed on the top and lobbed it into the black waters of the pool. For an awful moment I thought the bottle had too much air and not enough lead in it, and would gently float down to the waterfall and explode just as it pass me. But no, it sank, and I crouched down behind a buttress of rock, sweating with terror and excitement. It took a long time, perhaps two minutes, but at last there was a muffled roar and waterspout some six feet high sprang into the air. I got out my landing net and held it in the escape channel. The result was disappointing. There were seven fish, two of them about three ounces, which was large for the Garpol, and they looked just like any other trout. I had read somewhere that an underwater shock stuns fish but does not kill them, so having bagged the larger fish I let the small ones remain in the net until they revived. But they didn't revive.

I used dynamite on only two other occasions, and never told anyone about it. The sheet terror of the operation I found attractive, but I stuck to my own fishing code which was never to use a coarser method of fishing when a finer method would kill fish, that is to say, dry fly and clear water worm went before wet fly, wet fly before spate worm and dynamite only when there was no other way of getting them out. I thought that was sporting and was worried when at Loretto I joined a dynamiting gang who would blow up a pool whether it was fishable or not.

Along with farming, burn fishing became my chosen pursuit, my preoccupation, my thing. On a free day I would be out early to gauge the exact direction of the wind (for this dictated which of the twenty or thirty burns at my disposal would be fishable that day). Then I would take half a loaf and perhaps a tin of sardines and set off. There were six or seven burns which could be reached within an hour on foot. I fished upstream at an average speed of half a mile an hour. If I caught four to the hour or more, I kept on. If less I tried other burns or packed it in. If I caught upwards of six an hour I went on and on. Turning the pages of my fishing log, which records the period just after Craigielands, it seems to me that anything around twenty trout was not disgraceful for a day in the burns, fifty was good and the great bags ran to sixty and seventy; the largest being an overnight fish up one burn and down another at dawn, with a miraculous change of wind to make both equally fishable, and a total score of eighty-seven.

Strange things happen to a lone fisherman. One dark and still day at the Earshaig Lakes, a slow deep peaty burn, a fish put his head out of the water and stared at me. He wouldn't go away. I thought of the poem about the man who wasn't there, and so I went back on the next day to see if he wasn't there again today. He wasn't and I never saw that black Earshaig trout head again. On another occasion on the lake I saw the triangle of a huge dorsal fin cutting through the water towards me. The shark (for it was he) sank below the surface just before he reached the boat. I told John Smith about this and he said it must have been a trout. Trout will do anything, he said, including playing at being sharks.

My worst experience was with the tramp. As soon as the weather warmed up all the old men and women who had spent the winter on the parish in the poorhouse took to the road. They streamed to the back door at Craigielands, sometimes eight or ten in a day, where they were given a cup of tea and a piece. 'It's the hot weather that brings them out,' Mrs Henderson would say, as she surveyed them from the kitchen window, just as if they were horseflies. There was one tramp who had eyes like frosted glass (but he could see perfectly well), a broken nose and jet black hair hanging down his back. I do not know what he was called but I thought of him as the Black Tramp. One day when I was fishing the Lochan Burn at the foot at Queensbury I turned to look downstream and saw the Black Tramp sitting on a rock about two hundred yards away. I thought nothing of it and fished on, but two hours later I saw a figure standing upstream by a cairn on the side of the burn. It was the Black Tramp again. I didn't like this. I walked a couple of miles across country and started to fish another burn, the Kinnel. After a while I looked back hoping not to see him, but I did. He was hunkered down smoking a pipe. This was too much and I turned and ran towards him in a sort of frenzy. I must have it out with this frightful man and tell him not to follow me all the time. As I came out of some dead ground I looked where he had been, but he had gone. I quartered the ground and shouted 'Hey!' but he was not to be seen. I went to Kinnelhead farm and asked them if they had seen him, but no, they had seen nothing. I went home puzzled. Two weeks later I went to fish the Auchencat burn some six or seven miles in the opposite direction. On the bridge where the Auchencat ran under the road was the Black Tramp. He sat there deadpan and motionless as we passed. I told Miss Jackson, who was driving me, that I had made a mistake. The wind was wrong for the Auchencat. Could she drive me back to the Moffat Water?

For weeks after that I feared the start of each burn fishing day. Would he be there? Well no, he was never there again, but it took some time for the shadow of fear he had laid upon me to disappear.

Miss Jackson was my first fan and an important person in my fishing life. Every morning when Jim Rheilly drove in to do the messages Miss Jackson's maroon Austin Seven was parked by the statue of the ram in Moffat High Street. It was a matter of minutes to locate Miss Jackson. This one did not so much by looking as by listening. If one stood at the bottom of Well Street one could usually hear Miss Jackson in street conversation with other shoppers. She was a huge woman of irregular shape with a large beaky nose and the air of an amiable vulture, and she did not so much chat as discourse. She had a chest voice like a foghorn and an unrelated high metallic laugh, and she ran all the flag days and charitable events in Moffat and therefore had need of frequent street encounters with her helpers, patrons and benefactors. I don't suppose a day went by but that Miss Jackson raised some money for something. She was particularly strong on the blind and the lifeboat men.

When I appeared on the scene she would bellow out, 'Here comes my fisherman,' and in a minute or two we would be bowling along in her Austin Seven to the foot of the Cloffin burn, the Fopperbeck, the Crofthead or the Lochan. This was a convenient way to reach The burns beyond walking distance and I also had the advantage of hearing all the up-to-the minute news of pretty well every charity in Scotland.

All of this was quite straightforward but what was less easy to understand was the way in which Miss Jackson knew where and when to pick me up at the end of the day. We never made a rendezvous, and often when she dropped me I would decide to move over to the next burn, or to fish up one and down another. Sometimes I got a lift from another person and sometimes I would walk five or six miles on my own. But as I set out on the road home, as likely as not the magenta Austin Seven would appear and Miss Jackson would throw open the door and shout, 'Behold your carriage.' I knew she must have been patrolling for me. But she would never drive me to Craigielands front door, always dropping me off at one of the lodges or at the Curlers Gate. I usually gave her some trout and once she kissed me in saying thank you. She knew she had gone too far there and went red in the face, blew her nose and began talking very loudly about the latest from St Dunstans. After all I must have been a good twelve years old.

Apart from Miss Jackson, burn fishing was a solitary pursuit until John Smith came on the scene. Here I met my match in fishing skills, and indeed as an all-rounder John was a better fisherman than I, having fished a greater variety of water, learnt to tie his own flies and generally to deploy a natural gift for throwing a fly and striking at exactly the right moment. We became fishing companions, rivals on the water but tireless buddies on the long journey to and from our chosen fishing field. In the morning we parted to fish our own burn or our own stretch of water and as the hours went by anticipation mounted. Will he have a better bag than I? By weight? By number? At the moment of reunion we never divulged our secret at once. 'Well, it was a pretty good water,' John would say. 'They were rising a bit short,' I would reply, 'but the big ones seemed to fasten all right.' We would carry on with teases and evasion and downright lies until at last the moment came to open up and throw our catch on to the grass to be counted, examined, weighed and wrapped in wet moss for the journey home. Although John was the better fisherman, I had the sturdier temperament and was a more practical man on the water. John would often start the day with some theory and waste time trying to prove it: that the barometer being low the trout must be nymphung, perhaps, or that the new fly he had invented was especially suitable for this particular burn. Meanwhile I was steadily pulling them out on an old Zulu and a flea-bitten Greenwell's Glory. On the way home John and I would spin out fishing fantasies by the dozen and I was happy in his companionship and was absolutely myself – that is, my fisherman's self. We never talked about matters outside fishing and the family until years later – our fishing partnership lasted for over a decade – when, as we used John's MG to plunder the Highland burns, he told me about his sexual experiences.

Occasionally when younger I had gone fishing with my father and Sholto on the big Annan; that is the river Annan after it has been joined by its two main tributaries, the Evan and the Moffat Water. I was bored by these trips. My father stood pretty well still for hours and Sholto and I ranged the long banks of gravel and stone, occasionally catching a salmon parr. We kept them, which was quite against all the rules of good sportsmanship, and indeed of the local angling association. One day the water bailiff rode up on his motorbike, and started to pass the time of day with my father. I stood behind him with a communal fishing bag over my shoulder. He asked my father what luck we were having. Not much, my father replied, just one or two small ones. I could not let this go by. We had at least a dozen in the bag. 'We've got more than that,' I said and turned out the contents of the bag on to the stones. There were about a dozen salmon parr and two small trout. There was an embarrassed silence until my father explained that the salmon parr were taking very greedily and many had got badly hooked and would only have died had we put them back in the river. The bailiff, who knew his place, gravely accepted this patently false explanation and rode off. As soon as he had disappeared Sholto and my father turned on me. Silly thing to do. Could have got us all into trouble. Lucky that the bailiff was a decent chap. Silly thing to do. Could not come fishing again if I was going to do things like that. I stood there absolutely outraged. I didn't know we were doing anything wrong in keeping salmon parr. My father had told a lie. I had acted in good faith. All right, if that was the way they behaved I would not go fishing on the Big Annan with them again. Of course I did, but at the first sight of the river my indignation boiled up again.

Sholto was not such a keen burn fisherman as I, and anyway my burn fishing mania reached its peak after he had gone to school. Nobody seemed to know or care that I spent whole days on my own. When I got home I would carefully wash the fish and lay them out on moss or grass on an ashet. Occasionally my mother or Sheila would look at them and say, 'What a lovely lot of trout.' Every other member of the household ignored my fishing, including the nursery and the servants' hall. In fact Mrs Henderson didn't like it at all because it upset her plans suddenly to get thirty or forty unsolicited trout which had to be cooked whilst they were still fresh. No one knew where I had been. It might have been ten miles away.

I might have broken a leg and died of exposure and starvation. And so I came to feel a sense of separation through my fishing, not exactly of martyrdom because I was not doing anything good, and not of rebellion because burn fishing was in no way subversive, but rather the independent pride of an explorer or a lonely scholar. In all the household I alone knew about burn fishing. Only I would dare to chuck a carbide bomb into a linn pool. I had a whole empire of knowledge and skills at my command which no one else (until John Smith arrived) knew anything about. This made me a secret specialist, who alone could judge my success or failure in the matter of burn fishing. Although probably I was the best burn fisher in Scotland, no one knew it. I got no appreciation, no praise. My isolation caused me some resentment, some moods of defiance, and at the same time some secret pleasure.

I have often wondered what influence the long solitary hours spent with a fishing rod in my hand had upon my development. They provided, I suppose, a fallow patch, just as stamp collecting or cricket scores do for urban boys. But they also taught me an indifference to physical hardship, whether it was in the form of standing up against driving rain or crawling down through freezing water, and they offered an opportunity to frighten myself not only by bombing but by attempting hazardous climbs up slippery waterfalls, wading into spate water up to the ultimate margin of safety – and there was the occasion of the adder.

The adder lay on a pebble bank, his head raised as if he were obliging a snake charmer, gazing intently at the water. I watched him for ten minutes and decided that, like me, he was fishing. He was very pretty yet sinister, and I decided to kill him. I crept downstream and selected a rock about the size of a loaf of bread and moved silently round behind him. It was a moment of great exhilaration. There he lay, motionless below me as I raised the rock above my head and held it poised to kill. It hit him about amidships, and all hell broke loose. He writhed and jumped like a dervish, seriously wounded but defiant. His dance of death took him almost into the burn, and fearful lest I lose him I cast my Stewart tackle over him and fixed a hook firmly into his tail. But he surmounted the bank and set off through the heather with me, rod point up, playing him like a fish. I found that if I elevated his tail he lost the power of locomotion, so I gradually dragged him backwards into the stones. What to do now? Could I get him into the stream and drown him? Could I stone him to death? What would happen if he bit me? I must be at least two miles from the nearest house. He gave up for a moment and appeared to flake out. Instantly I jammed a rock over his head to keep him immobile and got out my fishing knife. I sawed away at his neck until I had cut him in half. So that was it. He was dead. I could lie back on the bank and relax. It took me some time to stop trembling, collect my thoughts and sling his two separate parts over my shoulder. I set off home in triumph, with his blood dripping down my kilt. This time they would look at the ashet – and indeed they did, and the day of the adder passed into Craigielands mythology.

The death of the adder led directly to the arrival of the mongoose. I planned to have my adder stuffed and put him in the vestible cupboard and then forgot all about him. In due time the most appalling smell began to permeate the vestible and the hall. This was nothing new, for we often suffered in the same way from decomposing rats. Davy Sloan took up a number of boards but could find no rat. My father had been reading about the lifestyle of the mongoose in *Blackwoods* magazine and he ordered one from Edinburgh Zoo. Jim Rheilly brought it up from the station in a crate and the whole household gathered on the gravel to see it before it was slipped into a hole in the basement which would give it access to all the inner and secret parts of the house where the rats resided in their hundreds. We never saw the mongoose again and there was no visible reduction in the rat population. But the adder's smell, though growing weaker, lasted for at least a year, and even when the sticky mess was at last discovered and removed, the thought of the smell in that area was so powerful as to resurrect a belief that one could still smell the smell itself.

I did not have the same enthusiasm for shooting as for fishing. This was mainly because Sholto and I were so dragooned over the matter of gun safety that we got no fun out of it. For a year we had to carry a gun unloaded to make sure we handled it correctly when we climbed over dykes or opened gates. Then for a second year we carried two silver dummy cartridges in our guns and threw them up and clicked the trigger at any game that rose. Finally, we had a single cartridge in the right barrel, but we seldom hit anything. So much effort had gone into safety training and so little into teaching us actually to shoot that we became two of the safest shots in Scotland, and two of the worst.

But shooting was compulsory, like fieldwork, and I spent many hours trudging the moors behind the farm with my father, Sholto and Andrew Grieve. The sport was good and the game various and the bag would often include pheasant, duck, grouse, partridge, snipe, woodcock, blackgame, rabbit and hare, but I didn't care too much about that. Shooting was yet another time for solitary thought, for fantasies and for playing music in one's head, for I never became a real participant.

Mr Dunn did not think highly of field sports. Far behind the times in everything else he anticipated the anti-blood sport movement by decades. He concealed his dislike of shooting from the Trinity for fear, I suppose, of losing his job because the Trinity were in no way tender hearted when it came to the matter of killing game or vermin and indeed still allowed Andrew Grieve to use gin traps and snares to keep down the rabbits. Mr Dunn was therefore forced to express his dislike of killing animals in private. On the day of a covert shoot, during a particularly noisy battle, I remember him clenching his fists and pacing the schoolroom exclaiming, 'Disgraceful, disgusting.' (We watched him carefully at table, however, to see whether he would eat pheasant, and he did, and this we thought seriously undermined his moral position.) He used to quote Oscar Wilde's 'the unspeakable in pursuit of the uneatable' in respect of hunting, and also some professional animal lover he had encountered in Liverpool University who designated shooting as a sport for perverted sadists and fishing as the occupation of a moron. I didn't mind this. Mr Dunn was not going to get a rise out of me. I only asked him whether he had himself either shot or fished.

'Good God, no,' he said, brushing some sweat off his forehead. 'I try to lead my life on civilised principles.'

In retrospect I believe that aside from the lust for the sport itself, fishing provided a pause and a space for emotional and mental digestion. As I went out to fish and walked up the burn, the adrenalin was already beginning to rise, and this meant that there was no room for anything but an obsessive concentration on the fishing prospects. Then the act of taking fish was in itself sublime and absorbed all the faculties. But there were many many hours when the fish were not in the mood, and many more hours on the long walks home when I turned over in my mind the data gleaned from the *Encyclopaedia of Ethics*, and would test my hunches until they seemed to become certainties, or else lapse blissfully into a series of sexual fantasies that could last from the top of the Auchencat until I was picked up by Miss Jackson. The sight of Miss Jackson, alas, quickly extinguished any thoughts about sex.

11

God-forsaken Little Tunes

One Christmas Aunt Germaine gave me a record of the second movement of Beethoven's Seventh Symphony, played by Stokowski and the Philadelphia Symphony (HMV D1640 – I have it still). As a 'cellist she found the Philadelphia 'cello sound irresistible. But it was not only Stokowski and his 'cellos that made the record a sensation. It was the first electrical recording we had heard and so it brought the news to Craigielands that the gramophone had been transformed from a toy into a musical instrument. As we sat listening in the hall we were overwhelmed. My mother broke the rules by exclaiming whilst the record was still playing 'Absolutely extraordinary! The bass – quite amazing!'

The next day I played it again by myself in the library – and again, and again. Then I went to the keyboard and soon had the theme and the first two variations of the Allegretto under my fingers. Then I hunted out B.S.' score of the Seventh from Broomlands, also Groves' *Beethoven's Nine Symphonies*. This resulted in an overwhelming desire to possess the rest of the symphony, so I laid a plan. Taking advantage of my mother's passion for fir cones, I casually pointed out that the supply for lighting (or rather not lighting) the fire was running low. Would she pay me to collect some more? This was quite a common practice: the children were often paid pennies or threepences for some chore which was helpful to the household but not in the class of a compulsory duty. Yes, she said, she would pay me a penny a dozen. I immediately started figuring. The HMV twelve-inch blank label record in those days cost six shillings and sixpence. I wanted four to complete the set.

That was twenty-six shillings or 312 pennies. 312 pennies equalled three thousand seven hundred and forty-four fir cones.

I went to the Moss Room and picked up some empty sacks and then went down to the curlers' peninsula on the lake where there were two gigantic firs. Beneath them the fir cones lay thick on the ground. For three days I spent every spare minute under the giant firs. I counted the fir cones into the first sack, one thousand of them. I was wearing a loose grey sweater and by holding out the bottom seam in front of my stomach I could make a woolly hammock which would comfortably accommodate fifty small dry fir cones. Twenty loads filled a sack a little more than half full. I filled three more sacks to the same level without counting, but now the fir cones were from the second layer, damp, starting to decompose but still definitely identifiable as fir cones. I was satisfied there must have been four thousand fir cones at least in the four sacks. But then, like Robinson Crusoe and his boat, I was trapped. The sacks were too heavy to carry. I went up to the stables and harnessed Biddy to her little goat cart and took her down to the fircone site. With a great deal of shoving and pushing I got two sacks aboard. A second trip and all four sacks were standing by the front door steps.

I went into my mother, who was playing patience. 'I've got your fir cones,' I said. 'Oh good,' she replied, without looking up. 'Bring them in and put them in the basket.' 'It's not quite like that,' I said. 'You will have to come and see them.' 'All right,' she said, smiling sweetly, for she thought I had some surprise for her – had painted the fir cones silver or made them into a fir cone dog or something like that. 'I'll come as soon as I've finished this game.' I stood and watched her play. It was Mrs Milligan and she was not in the top class of patience players. I saw several opportunities slip by but did not want to protract things by opening up a discussion. At last she finished, turned to me brightly and took my hand. 'Where are they?' she said. 'By the front door,' I replied. When we got to the bottom of the steps she stopped. 'What is in those sacks?' she asked. 'Fir cones,' I replied. She was aghast. I opened the mouth of a sack to display the goods. 'All fir cones,' I said again. 'But that's far more than I want,' she said. 'However many are there?' 'Three thousand, seven hundred and forty-four,' I said. 'These ones are damp,' she said rather feebly, groping into another sack. 'They are fir cones,' I said, 'and at one penny a dozen you owe me twenty-six shillings.'

It took her some time to recover her composure. I knew she would pay, for she was the soul of honour, but I also knew she would have to report such a gigantic con to my father and Gamma, and she would also have to get the money out of my father, which might not be an easy task. But the next day he gave me the money himself and I ran down to Maggie Hutchinson's, bought a postal order and a few days later the magic box arrived, twelve inches square, packed with wood shavings which smelt delicious, and at the heart of the parcel four beautiful shiny black bakelite discs. I had the whole of Beethoven's Seventh.

From the age of three or four we had all become strummers. There wasn't a child who could not play a party piece in public or strum away happily in private. As I grew older I used to strum for an hour or more a day and began to struggle with the easier movements of the Beethoven's sonatas which I read with difficulty and played erratically and with a heavy touch. It was often a struggle to get to a piano. There were nine keyboard instruments available: the Steinway in the hall, a beautiful New York boudoir grand with a bass like a clap of thunder, which we were not allowed to play without permission. Then in the billiard room there were two seven-foot grands standing belly to belly and tuned together; a Hagspiel and a Collard and Collard. In my mother's snuggery there was her soft-toned upright, in the dining room a nasty little upright Allison, also a much worn anonymous harmonium, in the drawing room a Broadwood grand and a Hamilton harmonium, this last a mild little instrument with twelve stops, a swell and a coupler. And if one were really stuck one could run down to the Steck pianola at Broomlands, stiff and unsympathetic in touch but with a majestic concert hall ring to it. In the school holidays there were usually eight or so candidates seeking a piano at the most popular times, which were just after breakfast and between five and six o'clock at night. My mother and I were the two who went in for the piano marathons –

an hour or more at a stretch. Sheila came next with a limited repertoire of easy classics played in the best schoolgirl style. Then Kaff, a real musician, with my mother's touch but with little application. Next John Smith, an inveterate strummer, who aspired to a grand romantic sweep when inspired. Sholto's show piece was from a book of studies. It was called 'Stoccato The Demon', which we pronounced as 'Stock-a-toe'. 'Give us Stokatoe,' I would say when it was Sholto's turn to do his stuff and he would sit down and oblige in the most precise and stoccato fashion, his somewhat protuberant ears waggling to match the moments of high stress. Sholto could move his ears at will, a thing quite beyond my powers, for which I envied him. Nevertheless I always waited with pleasure for the two places in Stockatoe where there was an involutary ear-waggle. These were the high spots of his performance.

Every evening before dinner my father sat at the Steinway for ten or twenty minutes and played his evening voluntary. He had no repertoire of recognisable music. He played no tunes, but indulged in sequences of chords which ambled up and down the keyboard, occasionally moving to the relative minor but otherwise sticking firmly to the home key, which was always E flat. In later life, when I heard the organist in church filling in after a voluntary which had ended too soon, I heard echoes of my father at the Steinway. It was not so much music as a sort of harmonised in-filling. 'The great thing in music is melody,' he would say, and then he would embark on yet another sequence of chords as amorphous as usual and with no hint of any melodic line.

I did not learn much about music from playing the piano. I knew there was something intensely interesting and exciting lying behind the pages of Beethoven's sonatas, and here and there I could catch a glimpse of a glorious vision. I loved sonorities and would play the opening bars of Opus 31 No. 3 again and again. I could manage the first movement of the Opus 2 No. 1 in F minor, perhaps because it was the first in Volume One and I always started there, also the whole of the Pathétique and numerous other single movements. But I played badly, giving notes the wrong values, using wrong fingering and phrasing and thumping out the *forte* passages with a touch as heavy as that of Mark Hambourg. By this time my mother had given me up and I had no teacher.

But then at Broomlands there was the pianola and three baskets full of pianola rolls. Amongst them were some Beethoven sonatas and by listening to them I was able to correct and improve my own performance. By this means I reached a decent level of proficiency with one or two quite difficult movements, notably with the first movement of the Apassionata. For the rest the pianola led me into unknown territory. There was a great deal of Chopin, including the four ballades, but these upset me so much that I gave up playing them. Their melancholy penetrated my whole being and induced a deep sadness that quite undermined my cheerful view of the world. Chopin took you out of reality, but unlike the gas you got at the dentist, when you came to you were gloomy and unsettled, especially if it was raining outside and you were on your own for the rest of the afternoon. So I would run along to Broomlands farm and ask Lizzie Thompson if I could feed the hens, whose antics in fighting for the maize and corn helped me to drive Chopin out of my system and allowed me to regain my equanimity. But his preludes and studies were wholesome enough.

There was also a great deal of Grieg in the basket which seemed to be good plain stuff of which one tired very soon. The wonderful Brahms' waltzes were there, and also many works by Schumann and Schubert, but these I could not seem to bring to life from the printed roll.

I must be one of the first people to have been educated in music almost entirely by mechanical means, for far more important than the pianola was the gramophone. By the age of ten I had long outgrown the rickety machine in the nursery and anyway I had heard every nursery record a hundred times over. Next I turned my attention to the collection in the drawing room. This reflected my mother's interest in singers and all the great voices of the early twentieth century were stored in half a dozen Winall record cases on the floor under the piano. There were Caruso, De Reszke, Melba, Patti, Galli-Gurci, Calvé, and many others all on single-sided pink or white HMV twelve-inch discs weighing nearly a quarter of a pound each. There were also some more modern records. Plunkett Greene singing 'Erl König' and many jolly English songs: Agnes Nicholls singing Elgar's 'Starlight Express'; Elisabeth Schumann singing Zerlina's two arias from *Don Giovanni*; Maria Jeritza singing Bellini, and Chaliapin as Boris Godunov. I stood with my ear next to the mouth of the brass horn that fitted on to our tone arm, in a position not unlike that of the famous dog, and listened carefully to every record in the collection. Far away in the distance I heard the unforgettable sound of a studio orchestra acoustically recorded. Every instrument was there, but as I was later to discover, the sound of each one was transformed, the bassoons sounded like a beast in a bottle, the strings turned into mashed potatoes, the brass swathed in furs; the oboes shrieked like bats and only the flute kept true to its own musical persona. I now know that the sound of the acoustically recorded orchestra must be one of the most curious phenomena in the history of music. Even then it sounded so strange that in my mind's eye I saw them in a distant fairground, marching along as they played but sitting down sharply every time they came to a full close. When there was a repeat they were magically transported back to the starting post and did their march all over again. When the singer entered he or she stood on a podium beside a maypole and the orchestra marched round and round them until the piece was finished.

I did not care for all these early recordings and arranged them into three categories – Hum, Rum and Bum: Hum was were worth keeping. I was uncertain about some and they were the Rums, but the ones that did not please were Bum and destined to go.

At Pattersons in Dunfries you could get sixpence for an old record, no matter what it was, for this was the scrap value. A new HMV plum label ten-inch cost three shillings and sixpence, a twelve-inch four shillings and sixpence, and a twelve-inch black label six shillings and sixpence. Thus for seven, nine or thirteen old records you could buy a new one. I went to my mother with all the Carusos, fifteen priceless original discs, and asked her if I could sell them. She had never cared for Caruso much – indeed there was a story that on their honeymoon in the Italian lakes she had been kept awake by a gramophone on a boat below their window playing a powerful rendering of 'O Sole Mio' by Caruso and my father had thrown oranges at the boat until he scored a direct hit and Caruso was cut off in mid High C. I though this was rather an awful story but it did carry with it an implication of anti-Caruso bias and therefore there was a good chance of permission to sell. Sure enough my mother had no objection, and soon the fifteen old Carusos had been bartered for one new record of *Patience*, for I was then in my Gilbert and Sullivan phase. The next time I went to her and asked whether she wanted to keep Madam Calf. When this had been translated into Calvé she again gave her assent, and another dozen of rare collectors' items went on their way to destruction. So continued the rape of the prima donnas, as one by one they were sold off to pay for the nucleus of my own record collection which rose like a phoenix from the ashes of the recycled divas.

Once I had heard the first electrical recording I wanted a better gramophone. My father, never averse to mechanical improvement, humoured my by buying a Garrard motor to replace the old one and a variety of new soundboxes. The Garrard could play three sides of a twelve-inch seventy-eight without rewinding. The soundboxes all had triangular holes at the end of their stylus bars, for we used nothing but fibre needles which were correctly believed to prolong the life of a record but had to be clipped with a pair of special scissors after playing each side – indeed they often lost their point whilst playing loud passages. This dreaded event was greeted with cries of 'the needles' gone!' and the operator (usually me) had to get up, resharpen and restart.

But with all the assistance in the world our ancient machine was not keeping up with the times. Even the Craigs' Columbia cabinet console was better. The breakthrough came one day when my father was testing pianos in Pattersons, Edinburgh (he frequently tested pianos when at a loose end, although he seldom had any intention of buying one). I saw an exponential horn standing upright on the floor. It was about five feet high, made of papier-maché, and narrowed down to a tube of half an inch which with a right-angled twist held the socket to which the sound box was fixed. I pulled my father's sleeve. I knew it would be a pushover and it was. The next day the horn arrived at Beattock station in a crate, and an hour later Davy Sloan and I were at work.

Or rather Davy was at work and I was puzzling over a whole heap of diagrams my father had drawn to guide us in the construction of a new gramophone. The old Garrard motor was sited in a square of angle iron, strong enough for heavy industrial use, and from this base an angle iron projection three inches stuck out for three feet. At the end of the projection there was a vertical tube containing a ball-bearing mounting for the horn. The horn had a bracket fixed at the point of balance, which fitted into the tube. A small brass weight mounted on a rod below the horn could be moved back and forth to ensure that the weight of the needle (by now a thorn, not fibre) on the surface of the record was about two ounces, which was thought to be the optimum. The whole apparatus was anchored on the one ball-bearing mounting. A puff of wind or a slammed door could make the needle jump off, but on the whole it was a triumph. It worked, and sounded better than any other gramophone we had heard, and it was in fact a precursor of the EMG machine which was to dominate the quality gramophone market in the 1930s.

The arrival of the new gramophone had two effects: I became a record buff and I began seriously to study music. I carried with me the two major catalogues, HMV and Columbia, wherever I went. I subjected them to intensive study with the dedication that some boys will apply to cricket scores. I learnt the names and dates of composers, orchestras, singers and artists. This did not, however, help me with the pronounciation of the more obscure names and in conversation I often realised that there was something not quite right about the way I said Gounodd, Puckinny or Sconeberg. But I did learn to spell each one correctly, although some composers, like Tchaikovsky, have since strayed from the form then accepted. I eagerly waited for the monthly supplements announcing new arrivals and I came to hold in affection the records themselves. I would hold the dazzling bakelite up to the light and deduce from the pattern of the grooves how the music would correspond with what I could see with my eyes. I would study the label with a magnifying glass and puzzle over the many numbers, signs and symbols. With the help of a letter from a friendly sub-editor on *The Gramophone* I was eventually able to decode them and understand what they meant.

The arrival of the journal *The Gramophone*, then edited by Compton Mackenzie and Christopher Stone, was one of the events of the month. Tearing off its wrapper I would rush to the One on the Stairs and sit there devouring it until people began to rap on the door and tell me to come out. From *The Gramophone* I discovered the size of the world of music. There were vast continents upon which I had never set foot, dark areas of which I had never even heard, but then there were also occasional and precious beams of light illuminating that tiny spot of musical territory that I knew and loved.

I soon realised that there was more to music than just listening to it. It was all very well to let music roll over you like a river – that might be all right for Chopin and Grieg – but it was not satisfactory for all music. You had to understand Wagner, all those leitmotifs and things. If you didn't know the horn tune was Siegfried you missed the point. But there was something more subtle and more difficult to grasp going on in symphonies and sonatas and it was something to do with structure. I studied B.S.' scores of Beethoven symphonies heavily annotated in his own hand, and Groves' *Beethoven's Nine Symphonies*. I decided to 'analyse' the Fifth (Clemens Kraus and the Vienna Philharmonic), marking up the scores as I went. Using the word 'motif' instead of subject, I got some way towards discovering the golden symmetry of sonata form. I grasped the importance of the tonic-dominant polarisation but got lost in the development section, trying to make it conform to some hidden pattern that lay in the rest of the work, and it was not until I got to Loretto and had access to Stewart McPherson's constipated little book on musical form that I was able to take the great leap forward and really grasp the true shape and meaning of the main classical forms.

One night I had been analysing away for some hours and had stuffed my jersey into the glass lampshade above the library table, for my eyes were weak and the light had been glaring at me off the score. I went to sleep and woke up to find my mother standing beside me and the room full of smoke. The heat of the light bulb had made my jersey smoulder and when we took it out there were great brown holes in the arms. My mother did not scold me but gave me a hug and kiss on the side of my face, closed the scores and books on the table and said, 'You won't do that again. Now it's time for bed.' She came up ten minutes later and talked to me about B.S. and his great love of music until I was ready to go to sleep. When she kissed me goodnight we both cried a little. I didn't know why, for I was a great big boy of twelve and as tall as she was, and we were both happy. It was certainly the last time she ever saw me cry.

We did not always agree about music. She and my father held almost identical views which did not always coincide with mine and this was a theatre for discussion, for argument and even violent disagreement which could take place in the open. Although of central importance to all three of us, music was not an absolutely holy matter like believing in God, and one could more easily question the supremacy of Wagner than the divinity of Christ. My father and mother were Wagnerites, which meant they had been to Bayreuth (but I think only once) and expounded his cause as fervently as if it were a religious crusade. I was less enthusiastic and, always expecting *Meistersinger*, thought the other scraps and extracts of Wagner we had in our collection showed him to be both prolix and at times vulgar. At any such suggestion my parents would explode. Wagner had led music into a new world, he never wrote a bar too many, many people like me, poor things, could not respond to his force and power. And, most importantly, I was too young. After about ten minutes we generally gave up on Wagner, but then if the adrenalin of musical antipathy was running high we would turn to other well-trodden battlegrounds. For them most modern music was rubbish, not Elgar and Delius, who were still alive and were all right, but that Webern and the Shostakovich first symphony (which we heard on the radio) and that dreadful Gershwin, why that was almost as bad as jazz. Music must not be ugly, it must be beautiful. Jazz was a hideous noise and most modern music was pure cacophony. Just showing off, making a noise – not music, not music at all. But the greatest cause of dissension was Mozart. My knowledge of Mozart was confined to three works, the E flat symphony, the two-piano sonata K448 which I adored, although it made the pianola hubble and bubble with the density of its notes, and Zerlina's two arias from *Don Giovanni*. From these I knew he was a great composer, perhaps as great as Beethoven. But to my parents he was a dilettante who wrote pretty-pretty tunes and was not fit to be considered in the same breath as Brahms and Wagner. My mother used to tell a story about an Oliphant uncle who was music critic for the *Scotsman*, and a Wagnerite. When visiting Mozart's house in Salzburg he was reverently shown Mozart's piano by the guide. 'So that,' he said, 'is where he played his god-forsaken little tunes.' At this my father and mother would laugh their Wagnerite laugh, and rage and hatred would seethe within me.

Neither of my parents shared my analytical approach to music. My mother admired my dedication and knew that something good was going on, but was not quite sure what it was. My father was unaware that anything was going on at all, except that I was quite often in the library playing the gramophone. It was therefore a lonely road I walked, and it would have been even more lonely had it not been for the correspondence I had with my godfather and uncle, T.O. Smith, now living as a semi-invalid and recluse in Eastbourne. I had made contract with him during what must have been one of the most bizarre episodes of the whole of my childhood.

Since T.O. couldn't or wouldn't come to Craigielands to meet the family, Gamma decided that the family must go to Eastbourne to meet him. Accordingly, my father set to work to organise a trip. This great event began in one of the back sidings in Beattock station. One day two carriages appeared, a first-class sleeper and a saloon – that is a coach with a kitchen, a dining room, a large drawing room and the usual offices. For two days the Ford van ferried bed linen, cutlery and stores from the house to the station. On the day of departure the whole party assembled on the platform usually reserved for the Moffat train, to which the carriages had been moved. The party consisted of Gamma, my father and mother, six children, Marnie, one servant and Rab the spaniel. When the London train came in we got into our saloon which was shunted back and tacked on to the rear coach. I remember we had a cooked lunch shortly after departure and reached London just as it was getting dark. We were all bundled into bed and settled quietly in to a night of clanking, shunting and jerking until eventually we settled quietly in a siding.

The next morning after breakfast we were shunted right round London and finished up attached to the back of a train on the Southern Railway which proceeded at speed to Lewes. Here we were uncoupled and had lunch. For the final stage of the journey we had a tank engine to ourselves that proudly puffed the last few miles to Eastbourne. We were met by the stationmaster in a silk top hat and a delegation from the Town Council. This last would have been surprising had it not been that Hubert Service (the same Service who had nursed my grandfather James Smith in his mortal illness and who was still T.O.'s man) was now an Alderman. He could, in his quiet Service way, arrange anything, and he had arranged a nice reception for us. Two Daimlers were drawn up outside the station. We went on to a hotel in St Leonards; the servants, except the undernurse, went back to Beattock and the two coaches stood by in Eastbourne awaiting our return.

The hotel was a disaster. The management had gone bankrupt and the staff had left except for one or two venal survivors whom my father paid out of his pocket. Chief amongst them was a waiter, oily and ingratiating to a degree, who used to come up with two cold chickens and endless stories of how he had persuaded a chef to come in to cook for them, however hard it had been to get the gas connected etc etc. Our suites were rapidly turning into a slum, so Service booked us into another hotel in Hythe.

Meanwhile the visits to T.O. began. He saw Gamma most mornings, but the children were spread out in pairs – Sheila and Kaff on Wednesday, Sholto and myself on Thursday and the little ones on Friday. This was thought to be about as much as T.O.'s nervous system could stand. When Sholto and I arrived at Canford, a nondescript Victorian villa, we went into the waiting room and were warmly received by Mrs Service, Enid, an overwhelmingly amiable woman, and Miss Service, also Enid, about my age, with ringlets down to her waist and a front tooth missing. After half an hour of agonising embarrassment we were ushered into the drawing room where T.O. sat with my father.

T.O. was a large man, bullet-headed, with a bristling brown moustache, penetrating blue eyes and hair coming out of his ears. He was in tweeds cut in the style of the 1890s and looked ready for the grouse moor. Sholto and I were dressed in kilts and opened proceedings by dancing a highland fling, followed by a sword dance. T.O. thought Sholto danced better then I did. T.O. then fired a few questions at us and the event was over. As we left the room T.O. said, 'Which of you is my godson?' I showed. He said, 'Come and see me tomorrow.'

Now tomorrow had been laid aside as a rest day in case T.O. succumbed to the strain of the visits and was prostrated by a headache. So I travelled alone, and after the ordeal of the two Enids I was taken out to meet T.O. in the garden. T.O. sat in a deck chair wearing a tweed overcoat, with a grey trilby down over his eyes and with both hands on a walking stick held vertically between his legs. He scarcely moved as I was dumped on to the deck chair next to him. I spent some time trying to attain a dignified posture as I rolled about in its canvas belly.

'How many poems do you know by heart?' he asked. 'About twelve,' I replied. Panic seized me. Was he going to ask me to recite? 'Favourite?' he asked. 'Holy Willy's prayer,' I said. 'Holy Willy's prayer?' he said. 'Who on earth taught you that?' 'No one,' I said. 'It's a privately learnt poem.' 'Give Gavin Hamilton his deserts,' said Uncle T.O. 'He drinks and swears and plays at cairts,' said I. 'What else do you do up there in all that rain?' he asked. 'Play the piano and listen to music,' I said. I knew he was musical and had composed string quartets. 'What music?' he asked, and now we were off. He knew all the Bach and Beethoven I attempted to play, the bar numbers, the keys, the difficult passages and the interesting chords. We talked for perhaps three quarters of an hour. It was the longest session of the whole visit. And we discovered we were both fans of P. G. Wodehouse, although I had scarcely got beyond the school stories and Mr Mulliner. My parents thought P. G. Wodehouse was trash and forbade me to read him. Uncle T.O. thought he was a great stylist. This was immensely encouraging.

And so it came about that three years later, when I was twelve, I started to correspond with T.O. about the music I was studying and he would reply in my own currency. He explained about metronome marks and why Beethoven's were wrong, about the viola clef, and why the recapitulation stayed in the tonic, and he freely expressed views on music which were quite heretical. Above all he venerated Mozart. The fact that he was there in Eastbourne, friendly, scholarly and independent, was a great comfort to me. And after the visit he always sent me five shillings at Christmas and on my birthday.

Perhaps T.O.'s greatest contribution to my musical education was to reveal to me the proper attitude of a critic. Although we disagreed about some music in my family there was a central core which was beyond criticism. This included the *Messiah*, Brahms' symphonies and in the holy of holies Beethoven's nine symphonies, probably the peak of achievement in all music. In one of my letters to T.O. I asked him which of the nine symphonies he liked best and in what order he rated the others. His reply (which I quote from memory) was a shock:

Dear Denis,

My memories of the Beethoven symphonies are as follows:

1. Belongs to the world of Mozart and Haydn.
2. Boring introduction to first movement, second movement fine, Scherzo true Beethoven, don't recall last.
3. The first great symphony. Both funeral march and Scherzo too long. Other movements good.

4. Generally satisfactory, a good second movement.
5. A great success.
6. If you like this sort of thing supreme of its kind. Very Viennese.
7. Every movement a success. Joke at the end of the Scherzo doesn't come off.
8. In Beethoven's view the best, and I agree.
9. First movement dismal with patches of boredom, second movement a lot of padding, too long. The Adagio very fine, last movement clumsy and almost impossible to perform.

Yours ever,
T.O.

Padding! Clumsy! Fancy saying that about Beethoven. But now he had pointed it out I could see what he meant. So there was no such thing as a sublime masterpiece. All music was open to criticism, no holy places and no holds barred. This was a lesson that I have never forgotten and when in company with dedicated Mozartarians whose eyes grow misty with adoration for the master as they discuss this work or that, I find I still shock them, as T.O. once shocked me, by pointing out a weak linking passage or too great a reliance on formula. The reaction, as we used to say at school, is as if one had farted during the Oberammergau Passion Play.

Although I had Grove and the scores (and T.O.) I had access to no other books and strangely enough never thought of buying one. All my efforts went into completing my collection of the Beethoven symphonies. After the Seventh and the Fifth came the Eroica (Albert Coates and the Symphony Orchestra) then the Pastoral (Franz Schalk and the Vienna Philharmonic), the Eighth played by the same team, the Fourth with Casals and the Barcelona (a dreadful performance during which someone knocked over a music stand), the First which gave me the first chance to admire the wonderful ensemble of the New York Phil under Toscanini, the Second (Clemens Kraus again) and finally the Ninth with Albert Coates at his best.

As I went about my affairs, and especially when fishing, I would start playing a movement in my head and go right through it to the end. Sometimes I faltered, and I once took a score of the Fourth when relatively newly acquired up the Kinnel. But it got covered with trout scales from my hands and smelt disgustingly of fish, so I gave up. As a fish rose to my fly I would stop the orchestra playing and as soon as the fish was landed or the excitement was over I would tell the orchestra to go back to two bars before a letter B and start again. Which they did. By the time I went to Loretto, although I still had lapses and still made mistakes, I had by heart the outline of the scores of all the Beethoven symphonies I then possessed, and most of them I carry with me still.

My solitary pursuits did not seem to have any effect upon me because in public and in the family circle during the holidays I was still the same irrepressible extrovert, always playing for laughs, clowning, mimicking and collecting rather awful Scottish jokes from cheap joke books. John Smith and I specialised in these and some of the sillier one-liners passed into family currency.

'Will ye tak a drink or a meringue?' says the host at a party.'Na na, yer no wrang,' replies the guest. 'Ye're richt.' On entering a fishing pub years later John would turn to me and say, 'A meringue?' to which I would instantly reply, 'A large Strathisla.' This often puzzled the barman and was equalled in foolishness only by a story of which my brother Michael and I were both connoisseurs. It was about a big game hunter recounting his experiences in a London club. 'And then,' he would say, 'when I could see the whites of their eyes I raised my rifle and shot him fair and square in the Ewers.' 'What's Ewers?' some incautious club member would enquire. 'A large pink gin,' would reply the explorer. Michael and I were not so much intrigued by the idiocy of the story as by the intrinsic interest lying in the word Ewers, so as officers in the army, and even today as trustees of family trusts, we still sign our letters to each other Ewers, Michael (or Denis).

The rowdy and action-packed times of the school holidays contrasted sharply with the monastic life I lived during term time. I could not talk to anyone about the subjects that really excited me, sex, religion, fishing or musical analysis, and it was this isolation that forced me to become a very private person, living inside the extrovert and effervescent boy who appeared in public. Both personae were real, there was no shadow of play-acting in my public performance and no lack of sincerity in my private thoughts and beliefs. They were not being activated for public display, they were self-generated and self-driven, fed by internal stimuli, what I read about sex and religion and the music that I heard on the gramophone and read from the score. (Fishing was different: I was competing against natural forces and against the trout and I set my own targets and strove to achieve them, but even fishing was a private matter until John Smith came on the scene.)

The private person was often perplexed and often unhappy. The public person was all laughter and charm. As the two drew away from each other they formed a dichotomy which was to become permanent. Throughout the war – throughout my life – the worst news and best news, but particularly the worst, has been received with no visible reaction, always with good sense and good humour. Yet at the same time the private person might be in terror, struggling wildly to control the seething turmoil within. Similarly physical hurt and physical fear were never recognised in the outward behaviour. All was calm and stoical – and indeed the effect of them upon the private person was not so great, because the emotions were not so greatly affected.

The only sadness resulting from my years of isolation has been a lasting inability to communicate my most private thoughts to any other person, no matter how near or how dear. I imagine that this is true to some degree of many human beings, but from what others will keep telling me of their intimate affairs and the many astonishing confessions which are constantly being poured into my ear, I know that my plimsoll line of privacy stands far far higher than it does with the majority of mankind.

I have no doubt that this complete separation of the two people living inside one person is the result of those Craigielands years when the best way to get through life was to show a cheerful front at all times in the nursery, in the servants' hall, to the estate workers and above all to the Trinity, who if they had had an inkling of the wilder sexual fantasies that were racing through my mind would almost certainly have sent for Dr Huskie – who would, in turn, surely have prescribed a cold bath on the hour, every hour.

12

A Surprise for God

The dénouement came unexpectedly. As a closet atheist I was happy to keep my own counsel and even took pleasure in listening to some of my parents' more far-fetched excursions into Christian theology. I had no intention of challenging them. I was like a secret Bolshevik at the court of the Tsars, gloating over the knowledge that the whole structure on which their lives rested would soon be blown to smithereens. I don't quite know how I thought this would happen but I did have a fantasy in which Frazer and I sat on one side of the dining-room table and my parents on the other and as the discussion moved forward we gave as good as we got. In due course we moved on to the offensive and became inquisitors, searching and probing the grounds for their Christian belief and finding them wanting. The fantasy ended with my parents both apologising profusely and promising to repent and to do better in future.

The event itself could not have been more different. It was a wet Sunday in March 1932 and between the house and the lake the rain was whirling past in sheets. We had been to St Mary's church in Moffat and were sitting at lunch in the Craigielands dining room, my father, my mother, Uncle Beelzie, Sheila and myself. Gamma was ill in bed (she was to die within the year). I was gloomy because the early conversation had turned upon our father's plans to reform the economy of the farm. Uncle Mac, who had married a distant connection, had moved into Broomlands Farm. He had just returned from a lifetime of ranching in the Argentine and was about to turn Broomlands into a ranch. I thought Uncle Mac was a chancer, a phoney and a bit of a fool. Certainly he was broke and had to keep borrowing small sums of money from my father. I thought the idea of ranching, of abandoning our beautiful four-course rotation for an ocean of grass, was folly.

It was characteristic of both my parents to show a sublime belief in the virtues and success of any new enterprise, whether the arrival of a new undernurse or the construction of an underground flue for the central heating furnace. For the first week the new undernurse could do no wrong. 'Jennie!' my mother would exclaim. 'What a relief after Bell. She is so intelligent, reliable, clean, cheerful,' or whatever; and Jennie's virtues would be brought into the conversation at frequent intervals. Then suddenly Jennie would drop out of the conversation altogether and after a few days' silence my mother would say, 'I'm afraid Jennie has been a disappointment,' whereupon we would start speculating why Jennie, that one-time paragon, had come to disappoint, whether by lying or stealing money or being found in the bushes with a boy. Once shattered, my mother's belief in Jennie would turn into a strong aversion, and Jennie would disappear and never be mentioned again.

My father's confidence in a new idea persisted until – indeed often after – it was proved to be a flop. The central heating furnace, for instance, a huge cast-iron monster the size of a small bungalow, was fed by anthracite, and the fumes of smoke went up a large smokestack fixed on to the outside of the house. If it were to be taller than the house it would look unsightly and Gamma would not like it: If the same height, smoke came into the bedroom windows and dirtied the external paintwork. The furnace lay in the basement some fifteen feet below ground, so my father had the idea of building an outside flue which would run under the lawn and the back road and discharge the furnace smoke some seventy yards away in the wood. A great deal of digging and concreting was completed, the switch was made form the vertical to the horizontal flue – and alas, only a wisp of smoke came out of the chimney in the wood and the rest out of the manhole covers (of which there were several) until the furnace went out. From then on every remedy was tried. The manholes were sealed with heat-resistant cement. Parts of the flue were made deeper, other parts shallower. The chimney in the wood was made taller, then shorter. But my father never lost faith and in the end it worked, except that little jets of smoke still came up through the ground here and there like geysers, and there was a brown strip all the year round on the lawn and the bank up to the wood where no living thing could grow. Also the smoke still got into the bedroom windows because the chimney was now slightly lower than when clamped to the house and it was sited to the west from where the prevailing wind blew.

So now it was to be ranching, clearly a foolish idea because there would never be enough grass to see the stock through the winter. It was, I suppose, a combination of anger at the callous way that our farming methods were being slagged off, plus a great deal of recent exercise in the argumentative mode, that made this particular Sunday the day of reckoning.

The sermon that morning had sparked off the eternal debate about predestination and free will. I had heard it all before and I waited for my father to get to the bit where God, because he was God and could do anything, could offer a genuine option of free will whilst knowing all the time which option would be taken, therefore remaining the master planner predetermining away like anything. 'What would happen if I did something God didn't expect?' I asked. It was explained that this was impossible. God was omniscient and therefore knew what was in my mind. I couldn't surprise him. 'I've got a surprise for God,' I said. 'I don't believe in him. Why do you think that God knows everything? Is it because you want to believe he does?' The conversation was taking an unusual turn. I could see that no one liked it at all. When children asked questions about God it was usually to reach a better understanding of God's ways which were better understood by adults than by children. But this unmistakable aggression was alarming. Uncle Beelzie moved uneasily in his chair and made a number of throat clearing noises in rapid succession. Sheila looked miserably at the carpet – she could see a family row looming and there was nothing in the world she hated more than a family row.

'Why should I believe in God anyway?' I went on. 'There are lots of gods just as good as yours. He's just a leftover from what the tribes in Palestine used to believe. He's their tribal god and has got nothing to do with us at all. Why not Shiva? Why not Thor?' The words that had been dammed up for four years came out in an avalanche and as the adrenalin began to flow I pounded on. Faint cries came from both parents but I was unstoppable and only when I ran out of steam did I sink back into the golden plush of the Craigielands dining-room chair and wait for the counter-attack.

There was silence when I finished. I had expected an immediate onslaught from both parents but they were mentally winded, too shocked to respond. Nothing like this had ever happened at Craigielands before. They were encountering chaos and anarchy. Uncle Beelzie looked at his watch and said he had to get back to his lambing ewes. Aggie Crosbie looked round the door, realised something unusual was afoot and with her usual sense of occasion shut it with a bang. Sheila looked more miserable than ever.

Then the storm broke. My mother was white with anger. 'Denis,' she said, 'how can you say things like that? Jesus Christ is a divine God. We all know that. The other gods were not divine' – My father broke in, equally angry but more controlled. It was a matter of proven historical fact that Jesus had lived and his divinity was also a proven fact. He explained in his lifetime how it was that he was the same God as the God of Abraham. This was also a proven historical fact. Then they both started talking together.

The argument became uncouth. I was rude to my parents. They were superior and crushing. Their anger grew to the point when my father was shouting and my mother's visage had turned from white to red. When Aggie Crosbie looked in for the third time we moved, arguing all the way, into the echoing Palladian hall. We got no further. My mother stood on one side of the hall table, her hands pressed down on it. I faced her on the other, my father stood some yards away with his shoulders hunched. Sheila slipped into the library and stood listening. My mother leant forward over the hall table as she told me that all was decent, true and loving was due to Christ and his divinity, that I was not only wrong but wicked to say that he was just an ordinary man. Christ's word was the salvation of mankind. 'What about Plato?' I asked. Plato was a very good chap, said my father and God had helped him to become one of the best of philosophers, but the Greeks, although clever, had no god that was divine and that was why their religion, such as it was, could not endure. Our religion could never have lasted so long if it had been based on untruth. It was the only true religion, many of the others were decent enough religions but they were simply not true. Christianity had been proved to be true and that was why people believed in it. 'More people believe in Buddha or Mohammed than in Christ,' I said and then we got lost in a furious argument about the numerical count of each major religion in which ignorance in no way inhibited wild assertions on both sides. In calmer times we would have resorted to *Chambers Encyclopedia*, but we were too angry for facts. The climax came over the virgin birth. On the matter of Christ's divinity my mother, who simply couldn't grasp the depth of my scepticism said, 'But Denis, don't you see – Christ was divine because he was THE SON OF GOD, God was his father and he used Mary to send his son to us.' 'There are virgin births in dozens of religions,' I shouted back. 'Jesus was the son of Joseph just like any other baby, or he might have been the son of some other man that Mary had been going with.' There was silence for a moment. I noticed that there was a tear running down my mother's left cheek and that she was panting. I had never seen her like this before. 'Denis,' she said. 'Go to your room.'

'Go to your room' was a phrase I had not heard for several years. It was traditionally used as a preface to punishment. You waited in your room until a parent came up with a ruler, a slipper or in extreme cases a cane. Surely my father would not beat me for not believing in Christ? No, impossible. But what would happen? I went upstairs and lay down on my back on the bed. I was trembling and realised that I was in a state of panic. I knew that some family crisis had taken place. My father and mother would never feel the same towards me again. I would feel just the same towards them, but they wouldn't know that. The argument had changed nothing as far as I was concerned, but would they still be able to talk to me in a friendly way or would they treat me as a moral leper? With my mind in turmoil and the rain beating on the window of the Green Room, I lay in misery for a long time and then went to sleep. When

I woke up it was getting dark and Sheila was in the room with a mug of tea.

'Mumsie,' – our intimate word for my mother, pronounced Mumzie – 'Mumsie's gone to bed with a headache,' she said. 'She wants you to go down.' So I was not excommunicated. I would not have minded too much being dropped by my father, for he did not often speak to me, and when he did, it was mainly to issue instructions or to check me for doing something wrong, but my mother – I now realised that it was the thought of losing her that terrified me so. Now it was going to be all right I realised just how frightened I had been. She was the one person in the world who was close to me; we shared music, jokes, mimicking other people. I realised for the first time that I loved her, and loved her more than anyone else in the world.

Sheila just sat on the bed and said nothing for a very long time. Then she said, 'Mumsie's very upset.' 'I know,' I said. There was another long pause. 'I couldn't help it,' I said. 'I know,' said Sheila. 'I've often wanted to say it before,' I said, 'but I didn't.' 'I know,' said Sheila. It suddenly flashed across my mind that Sheila might share my doubts, or at least some shadow of them, but this was no time to explore matters of religion and belief. When I had finished the mug of tea Sheila leant forward and gave me a hug and a kiss, not a friendly family gesture but a passionate embrace as if she was my lover. We clung to each other for some moments, her hands on my shoulders, my arm round her back. We were both breathing heavily. I could feel her breasts against my chest and her heart beating. I feared I might cry, or she might, and so gently ended the embrace and got up to brush my hair. Sheila stood and watched me. That mug of tea, I thought, she must have got it from the servant's hall. They must be all agog. Aggie had heard the shouting and her reports would lose nothing in the telling. So with the matter of my mother off my mind I was already sketching out my act for the audience downstairs and as I caught myself at it I was disgusted at my callousness.

Sheila and I went downstairs together. She stood outside the North Room door. I opened it quietly and slipped in. My mother lay in bed in her headache position, her face looking very small and white. I went close to her and she took my arm and said, 'It will all come right when you grow older.' Optimist, I thought and gave her the statutory kiss which was no more than a peck. 'Go and see Dad,' she said, 'he's in his office.' So maybe there were going to be reprisals, if not punishment. I went into the office. My father was pretending to read the *Moffat News* but he had heard me coming and had prepared his act. 'Sit down Denis,' he said. 'Mumsie's very upset.' 'I know,' I said. 'I have just seen her.' 'I don't want you to behave like that again,' said he. 'You were very rude.' 'So were you,' I said. He could see things were not going according to the script. He had planned a dignified reprimand, not a resumption of our shouting match. 'I don't think we should discuss these things for a week or so,' he said. 'That will give you time to think about it.' Think about what? Did he really believe that within a week I would be converted? On the road to Moffat by a voice from the heavens? That I would abandon all the hard-won knowledge that I had gained from his books in the Den? But I realised that he was cornered and so was I. There was nothing we could do except shout at each other and I didn't mind that but it was true that it did upset my mother. I said nothing. He said nothing. The interview was over and I left the office and went straight out into the gloomy March evening and walked round the lodges.

We never spoke about it again. In a few week's time I went to Loretto and settled happily into a community whose habits were in many ways the same as those of Craigielands. I was rebellious over minor matters, such as refusing to acknowledge the more ridiculous public school mores (prefects could put their hands in their pockets with the jacket flap behind them, senior boys could undo the bottom button of their jackets, new boys must button up all over). Also I carried the HMV record catalogue in my right-hand jacket pocket and the Columbia catalogue in the left and for some reason the 'authorities' (as the prefects were called) decided that this was 'putting on side' and so I was beaten until I took them out and was thereafter forced to carry them inside my shirt. During my first term I was beaten more frequently than any other boy in the school, the climax being eight beatings in six days. This worried Sholto who was now in the middle school and was apprehensive lest I should disgrace him, but I was popular amongst my own year and I soon acquired a reputation as a bad boy who would stop at nothing. I gloried in this notoriety, for there was nothing I could do in sport or at work that would have put me in the public eye.

It turned out that my father and mother did feel differently towards me after the great religious row. My father had always regarded me as something of a nuisance, showing off, talking too much and also – as I see it in retrospect – as his rival in gaining the attention of female visitors. Now he felt I was a bad lot, an unbeliever, not through conviction but to gain notoriety. I was defiling the name of Jesus to attract attention to myself and although he was liberal in allowing that the best of the heathen might be admitted to heaven (Plato, Montezuma, Mohammed), there is no doubt that he did tend to equate atheism with immorality. I now became an immoral boy in his eyes. Three of his children were good – Sheila, Sholto and Michael – and Kaff was good at heart but impulsive and foolish. The youngest, Pat, he had not yet discovered to be almost as bad as me. Denis was the one he could not trust at all. He got around this by ignoring me almost entirely until suddenly, when I began to be something of a star on the rugby football field and in athletics, his attitude changed. There was good in me after all.

My mother was just sad that a son she loved very much had lost his way. It was almost unbearable for her to think about it. She did not, however, in any way blame herself or my father or Gamma for what happened, which she regraded as some natural disaster, like losing one's sight or going mad. She never talked to me on any subject approaching religion, philosophy or belief, even skirting round the matter of going to church or references to the deity. When the conversation bordered upon dangerous matters she looked down sideways with her head turned slightly away from me and she would go a little pink. But she made a determined effort to keep our relationship as friendly and as companionable as it had always been, although we both knew it was hard going.

It was not unit much later that I realised how traumatic had been the effect of the row upon her. We went to the theatre together in a family party to see a play in which there was a son whose worldly cynicism was pitted against the forces of enlightenment and good feeling embodied by his parents. In her hotel room after the show my mother turned to me and said, 'The play was really about us. Dad and I are the father and mother and you are the son.' I was dumbfounded, for I thought of myself as one of the most idealistic of men, striving selflessly for the good of mankind. But as I thought about it on the way home I saw that ever since the day of the row she, like my father – but in her case with real sorrow and compassion – had seen me as an immoral person who believed only in material things, and it seemed that this was imprinted on her mind and could probably never be effaced. (In the event it was, but not until I was seriously wounded at Cassino during World War Two, and came home to find that everything had been forgiven and I was the returned prodigal who could do no wrong).

The Sunday after the row my mother was in bed with backache. Sheila had gone away and my father and I were the only two remaining regular members of the usually much larger church party. When it came near to church time I did not change into the kilt, our Sunday uniform. Instead I stayed in the library in my old clothes playing the gramophone. When my father drove to the front door in the Talbot he didn't see me in the hall or vestibule. Hearing the gramophone he opened the library door and standing in the door frame slowly took in the scene. Satchmo was defiantly rasping out one of his scat vocals. It was a sound that my father particularly abhorred. Without a word he backed out of the library, closed the door and a moment later I saw the Talbot disappearing down the north drive. I was free, but at the price of serious displeasure.

In later years the arguments about religion and politics came into the open and one voice after another joined the chorus of opposition to my father. In their early days he was a great champion of Hitler and Mussolini (although once war broke out there was no more ardent Fascist-hater in Britain). Even my mother sided against him on this. Sholto dropped his belief in God in his mid teens; Sheila had always had her doubts. To Kaff I believe the matter was immaterial. Patrick was a sceptic from an early age. And so, with two or three school friends to swell the ranks, after-dinner discussions would develop into late night arguments, often heated, and lasting long into the small hours.

When I came back after my first term at Loretto, Craigielands had been sold. We had moved to the new house, Dumcrieff, which for all its classical beauty I could not love. With my box Brownie camera and many rolls of film I went over to Craigielands once or twice a week when the sun shone and documented all the places I loved best – the view of the house from my eyrie at the top of the beech tree, the trout hatchery, every aspect of the lake, the garage, the stables, the laundry, the farm. As I look at these faded little postage stamps of photographs today I see no people in any shot and no attempt to do more than to get into the tiny frame the outline of the objects which I had lived with and loved until my family had betrayed me.

Craigielands today is a scene of desolation. Some of the great park trees have been cut down to make room for time-share holiday lodges. There is a caravan park where the trout used to run up the burn to spawn. The lake is silted up and weed-covered, and in the remaining open water there is a flotilla of yellow plastic canoes. The house is uninhabited, its sole function being to provide for the sanitary and washing requirements of the holiday makers. The flagged basement is a store for fence wire, water pipes and the bric-à-brac associated with the maintenance of a holiday village, and in the Palladian hall, now a laundrette, where the stuffed otters and birds of prey used to stand, two rows of washing machines stare at each other with sad Cyclopean eyes.